# PRAISE FOR *SWEET EATS FOR ALL*

"As a dietitian who recommends a wholesome, health-promoting die ___ be remiss if I didn't promote occasional decadent deliciousness. From h ___ staples to cakes, cookies, ice cream, and more, *Sweet Eats for All* is swee ___ gluten-free heaven!"—Julieanna Hever, MS, RD, CPT, author of *The Complete* ___ *Guide to Plant-Based Nutrition* and *The Vegiterranean Diet*

"Allyson takes you from Almond Bon Bons to White Chocolate Peanut Butter Pretzel Tartlets and leaves nothing out in between. This is the new go-to allergy friendly cookbook for a sweet tooth. She brings cakes, cookies, pies, pastries, ice cream, puddings, candy and more back into your life. This book even has my new favorite dessert—Butternut Pots de Creme topped with smoked salt!"—Kathy Hester, author of *OATrageous Oatmeals and The Great Vegan Bean*

"Whether you're new to vegan and gluten-free baking or an old hand in the kitchen, *Sweet Eats for All* is an expansive, all-inclusive resource for every kind of treat you can think of. This is the book I wish I'd had when I first made the leap to vegan and gluten-free baking—and one that deserves a place on every vegan bookshelf."—Ricki Heller, rickiheller.com, bestselling author of *Naturally Sweet & Gluten-Free* and *Living Candida-Free*

"Allyson makes me want to get in the kitchen and whip up some sweet treats! She makes gluten-free desserts fun, accessible, and incredibly delicious!"—Kathy Patalsky, author and blogger, Happy.Healthy.Life (kblog.lunchboxlunch.com)

# PRAISE FOR *GREAT GLUTEN-FREE VEGAN EATS*

"Blogger Allyson Kramer does what many thought impossible: She makes tasty, delicious food that is gluten-free. Simply put, this book wooed a staff that, shall I say, hasn't always fully embraced foods made sans wheat protein. Kramer packs a winning one-two combo: She is a gluten-free flour expert, and she knows how to use them. You won't miss a thing."—Joseph Connelly, Publisher, *VegNews Magazine*

"Allyson Kramer's debut cookbook is the essential guide for deliciously creative, gluten-free, vegan eats! Filled with gorgeous photographs and mouthwatering recipes like Banana Berry Cobbler and Spinach Artichoke Dip, *Great Gluten-Free Vegan Eats* will inspire you to cook in a whole new way!"—Julie Hasson, author of *Vegan Diner*

"It takes a lot of talent to adhere to two dietary restrictions and still come out with tasty recipes the way Allyson Kramer has done in *Great Gluten-Free Vegan Eats*." —*Vegetarian Times*

"*Great Gluten-Free Vegan Eats* is a solid reflection of Allyson Kramer's style and a shining example of why her blog, Manifest Vegan, has become so popular. Allyson delights the senses with stunning visuals, flavorful ingredients, and simplistic recipes that will make you forget about eggs, dairy, and gluten altogether."—Alisa Fleming, author of *Go Dairy Free: The Guide and Cookbook*

"Being a gluten-free vegan just got a whole lot better, thanks to Allyson Kramer. In *Great Gluten-Free Vegan Eats*, Allyson dishes up a broad range of creative, tasty dishes. With beautiful photographs, this book will tempt eaters of all dietary persuasions."—Tamasin Noyes, author of *American Vegan Kitchen*

"Allyson's recipes are living proof that vegan as well as gluten-free food is delicious and fun! 'You can eat cake' . . . and then some!"—Carolyn Scott-Hamilton, author of *The Healthy Voyager's Global Kitchen*

# SWEET EATS
## for All

# ALSO BY ALLYSON KRAMER

*Great Gluten-Free Vegan Eats*
*Great Gluten-Free Vegan Eats from Around the World*

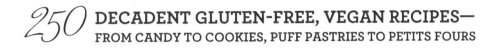

250 DECADENT GLUTEN-FREE, VEGAN RECIPES—
FROM CANDY TO COOKIES, PUFF PASTRIES TO PETITS FOURS

# SWEET EATS
## for All

# ALLYSON KRAMER

Da Capo
∞
LIFE
LONG

A Member of the Perseus Books Group

Designed by Trish Wilkinson and Tabitha Lahr
Set in 11 point Goudy Old Style

Library of Congress Cataloging-in-Publication Data

Kramer, Allyson.
    Sweet eats for all: 250 decadent gluten-free,
vegan recipes: from candy to cookies, puff pastries
to petits fours / Allyson Kramer. — First Da Capo
Press edition.
        pages   cm
    Includes bibliographical references and index.
    ISBN 978-0-7382-1730-7 (paperback)—ISBN
978-0-7382-1731-4 (e-book) 1. Gluten-free
diet—Recipes. 2. Vegan cooking. 3. Desserts.
4. Baking. I. Title.

RM237.86.K738 2014
641.5'638—dc23                          2014017396

First Da Capo Press edition 2014

Published by Da Capo Press
A Member of the Perseus Books Group
www.dacapopress.com

Note: The information in this book is true and
complete to the best of our knowledge. This book
is intended only as an informative guide for those
wishing to know more about health issues. In no
way is this book intended to replace, countermand,
or conflict with the advice given to you by your own
physician. The ultimate decision concerning care
should be made between you and your doctor. We
strongly recommend you follow his or her advice.
Information in this book is general and is offered
with no guarantees on the part of the authors or
Da Capo Press. The authors and publisher disclaim
all liability in connection with the use of this book.

Da Capo Press books are available at special
discounts for bulk purchases in the U.S. by
corporations, institutions, and other organizations.
For more information, please contact the Special
Markets Department at the Perseus Books Group,
2300 Chestnut Street, Suite 200, Philadelphia, PA,
19103, or call (800) 810-4145, ext. 5000, or e-mail
special.markets@perseusbooks.com.

10 9 8 7 6 5 4 3 2 1

This book is dedicated to my mother, Catherine Cain. Without her encouragement and shared kitchen wisdom, I would not be who I am today—or have the incessant sweet tooth that I do.

Thank you, Mommy, for your love and support throughout all my kooky cooking schemes, starting from when I was just a little girl flinging flour everywhere to when I first moved out on my own and called you constantly to ask for recipe advice, to my current pursuits in school and my career. I'm so lucky to have you as my mom.

# Contents

CHAPTER 3

# CAPTIVATING COOKIES AND BARS 83

## DROP COOKIES . . . . . . . . . . . . . . . . . . . . . . 84

## ROLLED AND SHAPED COOKIES . . . . . . . . . . . . . . . 107

## BARS . . . . . . . . . . . . . . . . . . . . . . . . . . 135

## CHAPTER 7

# CHOICE CHOCOLATES AND DANDY CANDIES

**231**

# INTRODUCTION

*I adore sweets.* Over the years, I've always proclaimed to have a sweet tooth, but I believe my penchant for sugar goes beyond that. Certainly I love the flavor of desserts, but I also enjoy their decadence and the reasons behind them—whether it be an unplanned stop into a candy shop for a bite of fudge, or the festive moment when the wedding cake is finally cut. For me, desserts symbolize the sweet side of life.

When I recall my childhood and the celebrations we had, what I remember most are the desserts that marked the various occasions: chocolate Devil's Food Cake on my birthday (page 38); fragrant Pumpkin Pies that filled the kitchen during Thanksgiving (page 152); boatloads of candy during Easter—including my favorite "cream eggs," for which I've created a recipe (page 257), Mexican Wedding Cookies (page 99) and chocolate fudge (page 263) during Christmastime, and so many more. I've been making my own desserts since I was a small child, and, over the years, I had

to adapt my dessert-making style to reflect my own dietary changes, first as a vegan, and then, in my late twenties, as a celiac.

To me, every good celebration requires an equally celebratory dessert. However, many people can't tolerate certain ingredients, and oftentimes those of us with food intolerances feel a little left out when it comes to capping off the party.

As hard as it is to swallow (pun intended), food intolerances—especially to wheat, dairy, and eggs—are becoming more and more common. Folks without food intolerances have thousands of comprehensive cookbooks for creating dessert at their fingertips. That's what this book is—only the recipes are suitable for those of us who have to eschew gluten, dairy, eggs, and/or other animal products. It's a book that celebrates dessert, whether you're eating it or creating it. This book is about luscious, sweet, sophisticated, gluten-free vegan treats—unapologetically.

# HOW TO USE THIS BOOK

*Before diving into* the recipes, I recommend that you peruse the contents of the front section, which includes a breakdown of ingredients used throughout the book as well as a list of tools and cookware that will make your dessert-making experience much more enjoyable. Get familiar with the flours; don't feel intimidated by them. Yes, there are a lot, but that's what makes this way of eating so much fun! It causes you to realize that there is not just one correct way to do things to achieve a stellar result. If you have doubts about baking with all these funny flours, try my Ultimate Fudgy Brownies (page 138) or Classic Chocolate Chip Cookies (page 85) and compare them to traditional goodies; I think you may come around.

Where appropriate, each recipe is also equipped with an icon designating whether it is also Soy-Free **S**, Nut-Free **N**, Corn-Free **C**, and/or Bean-Free **B** so you can decipher right away whether a recipe is suitable for people who may have additional common dietary concerns.

Each chapter addresses a broad category: Cakes, Cookies, Pies, and so on.

Within each chapter, you'll not only find the recipes for specific pies and cookies but also basic recipes for the category (such as piecrust, puff pastry, and so on). Oftentimes, I reference the basic recipes to use in various other sections of the book, usually listed as an ingredient, such as Quick and Easy Applesauce (page 229) or Strawberry Preserves (page 229). Feel free to substitute store-bought ingredients where these are called for to save time and personalize the flavor—just check labels to be sure they are gluten-free and free of animal products. Be sure to read labels of each ingredient you purchase—sometimes sneaky gluten can be lurking in the strangest places. So, for the health of you or others, become a vigilant label reader.

I truly hope you enjoy each of the recipes included in this book, and, above all, I hope this book both inspires old pros and helps to enlighten those who are new to gluten-free vegan dessert making. Whether you are creating sweets for yourself, or someone you know with a dietary restriction, everyone deserves to taste the sweeter side of life.

## Chapter 1

# STOCKING A SWEET PANTRY

*The ingredients I* list in this chapter are ones I use frequently throughout this book. For convenience sake (I'm a mother of two who works and goes to school full time, and most likely many of you are in a similar boat), I've mentioned my favorite brands of certain goodies, such as vegan cream cheese, margarine, etc., and recommend them (or equivalent brands, of course) as the recipes were all tested using the suggested store-bought versions rather than homemade. In this regard, I mean that I recommend using Earth Balance over homemade margarine not because I feel it superior, but because I lack the time to create my own homemade versions and have tested these recipes using store-bought ingredients. If you happen to have the ability and time to make your own artisan cheeses and nondairy butters, nut milks, and so forth, I applaud you and encourage it. I agree that almost everything is better homemade, but, for practicality, I've left out specific recipes for staple ingredients only because they can be purchased ready-made at most supermarkets across the United States and beyond. Check out the Recommendations section (page 303) for books and websites that include recipes and technique how-to's on making your own vegan staples.

Taste, texture, and tradition all come into play in the recipes I created for this book, and I chose the listed ingredients with care. Feel free to sub in or leave out ingredients to suit your needs as you wish, by either consulting the substitution suggestions underneath each listed ingredient or by following your own know-how. Just remember, changing the ingredients—even just a little bit—will change the end results. The recipes included in this book were tested exactly as they are written, and I can't, unfortunately, predict how they may react if ingredients are missing or changed.

# SUGARS AND SWEETENERS

Sweeteners are probably the most important aspect of dessert. While many people equate refined sugar as the sole proprietor of sweetness, the truth is, you can achieve an incredible level of sweet with a variety of different foods. While common white sugar does impart a reliable sweetness to cakes, cookies, and the like, there is so much more to explore.

**A Sweet Note:** While I have included a rather substantial chapter consisting only of refined sugar–free desserts, in most baked goods where I call for "sugar," you should have good results subbing 1 to 1 for coconut palm sugar, as I often use it interchangeably with evaporated cane juice or beet sugar.

## AGAVE

Agave comes from the same plant from which tequila is made. Agave plants are commonly thought to be cacti but are actually succulents. Agave nectar is sweeter than sugar and viscous, making it a good substitute for honey. Baking with agave can produce a darker result than sugar, oftentimes indicating a false doneness.

## BANANAS

Bananas can be used as a natural sweetener in a variety of foods, whether frozen, baked, or raw. When used in baking, they not only add a lot of sweet flavor but also act as a binder and an adequate replacement for oil in many recipes. They are a wonderful source of vitamin $B_6$, fiber, and potassium.

## BEET SUGAR

Common white sugar is oftentimes derived from beets rather than from cane sugar, which needs to be filtered with bone char to achieve its bright white coloring. White beets are used in the processing of beet sugar and the syrup is extracted from the bulb and then dehydrated and crystallized.

Check your favorite brand of white sugar to see if it is derived from beets if you are curious—the taste of beet sugar is virtually identical to that of filtered evaporated cane juice. When I call for "sugar" in the recipes, I am referring to white granulated beet sugar or organic cane sugar. Neither beet sugar nor organic cane sugar is processed with

bone char, so these are fine to use. Either can be used interchangeably.

## BROWN SUGAR (LIGHT AND DARK)

Primarily, brown sugar is produced by the addition of molasses to white sugar. Brown sugar can be reproduced at home by mixing molasses with white sugar: about 1 tablespoon molasses per 1 cup sugar. Hardened brown sugar can be resoftened easily by warming up the sugar; a shallow small pan set on low heat works well. Or even a short nuke in the microwave for about 15 seconds or so will do it. Use light or dark interchangeably depending on taste—in the recipes on the following pages, the variety of brown sugar I recommend is based purely on taste or color.

## COCONUT (PALM) SUGAR

Coconut sugar is made from harvesting sap from the blossoms of the coconut tree. The end result is a caramel brown sweetener (with a color that varies from light to dark brown as it's minimally processed) with a subtly sweet taste, similar to turbinado. Use 1:1 for turbinado, white sugar, or Sucanat when baking or sweetening foods. Oftentimes touted as less refined than turbinado, it is commonly used as a sugar alternative by those who follow a diet free of refined sugar since it is a lower glycemic option.

## CONFECTIONER'S SUGAR (POWDERED SUGAR)

This is a finely ground sugar that generally includes an anticaking agent, such as cornstarch or potato starch, added. This sugar is commonly used to make icings, glazes, and frostings and adds a subtle decorative quality to finished baked goods.

**Note for Corn Allergy:** Look for confectioner's sugar made without cornstarch, or make your own powdered sugar by whizzing sugar in a high speed blender along with a little potato starch, arrowroot starch, or tapioca flour. For each cup of sugar add 2 tablespoons starch.

## DATE SUGAR

This sugar is unlike other sugars in that it's simply made from pulverized whole dried dates, so it does not dissolve in hot liquids or while baking as do most crystallized sugars. Date sugar is best used to sweeten foods that are blended—such as smoothies, puddings, and batters—or as a sweet topping for hot and cold cereals.

## EVAPORATED CANE JUICE

Evaporated cane juice is less processed than white sugar but is still regarded as a refined sugar. Because some of the original molasses remains in the sugar after processing, it has a trace amount of minerals and a more caramel flavor than white sugar. You can use it 1:1 in place of granulated beet sugar in recipes.

## MAPLE SYRUP

Maple syrup is derived from the sap of the maple tree and has a distinct flavor that has won over the hearts of millions since its first cultivation. In cold climates, the starch from the tree is stored in the trunks and is eventually converted to sugar that rises in the sap in the spring. The solution is extracted then reduced, leaving the thick, gooey syrup we know as maple syrup. Canada produces over 80 percent of the world's maple syrup.

## MOLASSES

Molasses is a by-product of refined sugarcane (or also beet sugar, but the end result is different), which is removed during the process of refining the sugar. Blackstrap molasses is made from boiling down molasses syrup even further, until most of the sucrose is removed—yielding a much more bitter syrup with a higher nutritional profile. Seek out regular molasses—rather than blackstrap, unless specified—for baking, cooking, or candy making.

## TURBINADO SUGAR

Turbinado sugar (also known as "raw" sugar) is produced from the first pressing of juice of the sugar cane. It has a larger crystal than that of common granulated sugar and a caramel-like color. The flavor of turbinado is faintly molasses-like. Since the crystals are so large, turbinado makes a beautiful decorative sugar for sweets such as Palmiers (page 127) and also lends a nice crunch when sprinkled on cookies or pies before baking.

## STEVIA

Stevia, a tropical and subtropical plant related to the sunflower, produces leaves whose extracts are 300 times sweeter than common granulated sugar. It has been used for ages in Japan and is now growing in popularity across other parts of the world. Commercially, it can be found as a powder or a liquid, but oftentimes the powder has added fillers to enhance flavor, such as maltodextrin.

## SUCANAT

Sucanat is a brand name of a variety of whole sugar cane that has a much stronger molasses flavor and more pebbly appearance than that of turbinado or evaporated cane juice. It makes a great replacement for brown sugar in many baked goods.

# FLOURS AND STARCHES

Milling grains into flours has been an important part of human nutrition and culture since around 6000 BC. In fact, the desire to make more efficient mills is one of the driving forces behind much of our industrial progress as a civilization. We went from mortar and pestle to community mills to industrial mills to the home kitchen–size grain mills of today. The industrial-size mills, where most US flour is produced, make it possible for flours of many varieties to be readily available at our local supermarkets.

Although we have the ability to purchase prepackaged gluten-free flours, you can always grind them yourself, if you'd like. I recommend getting a high-quality grain mill, such as the NutriMill, if you are going to GYO (grind your own). The end result of fresh flours at a fraction of the price is certainly worth the extra effort if you do a lot of baking and recipe making.

The following pages outline my favorite types of gluten-free flours, how I like to use them, and whether they have a suitable substitute.

I added a few recommended substitutions for the flours, but these recommendations do not guarantee exact results as what I achieved with the flours listed in the ingredient lists of recipes. I wanted to include them simply to allow you to get familiar with the various textures of flours, the end results of each, how they blend with other flours, and what to expect from them. If you've worked with buckwheat flour, for instance, you'll know that it has a texture similar to coarser wheat flour, and there are a few other gluten-free flours with similar properties. That does not, however, mean that you can get identical results with another flour—the substitutions are simply based on texture, taste, and basic structure. I recommend getting familiar with the ingredients in the original recipe if at all possible before subbing, but the suggestions provided under each flour description should work just fine if you keep it to less than two small substitutes per recipe.

**Reminder:** Keep in mind when implementing the substitutes that the recipes in this book were developed using the flours called for in the ingredients list, and I chose to use them based on their unique properties with numerous test runs to achieve the specific mix. Substituting out one flour for another will alter the recipe, either slightly or drastically.

## ALMOND MEAL/FLOUR

Almond meal is made from finely ground blanched almonds; it adds a slight sweetness and a touch of moisture to baked goods. It also works beautifully in piecrusts and as a singular flour in many cookies and cakes. Many brands of almond meal use either "almond meal" or "almond flour" on their package labeling; sometimes the "flour" may be ground finer than the "meal." As far as the recipes in this book go, the two terms can be thought of interchangeably.

**Substitutions:** Finely ground pecans, macadamias, or brazil nuts. Any ground nut meal will work as a suitable replacement, but keep in mind the flavor profile will be different, as no other nut quite shares the almond's unique flavor, fat content, or texture.

## ARROWROOT STARCH

Similar to corn or potato starch, arrowroot starch derives from the arrowroot tubers. Also known as arrowroot flour, this silky starch makes a good secondary flour to use in conjunction with nut meals or drier flours such as buckwheat or sorghum. I like using arrowroot to lighten up otherwise heavy baked goods.

**Substitutions:** cornstarch, kudzu starch

## BESAN/CHICKPEA FLOUR

This flour is a favorite of mine for its versatility, buttery flavor when cooked, silky texture, and even its pale yellow color. I prefer to purchase my chickpea flour, or besan, from Indian markets and online, rather than relying on the major name brands of "chickpea flour" because a slightly different type of chickpea is used to make this flour, resulting in a more favorable taste and texture in baked goods. My favorite use for besan is as an egg replacer in various baked goods, dense cakes, and eggy-tasting goodies (like my Cherry Clafoutis on page 176).

If the batter or dough you are making calls for chickpea flour, though, don't taste it before baking. Trust me on this one, chickpea flour tastes bitter and harsh when eaten raw, but deliciously light when baked or toasted.

**Substitutions:** Because of its unique properties, it's difficult to suggest a good substitute, although fava bean flour and red lentil flour would probably work okay in many scenarios.

## BUCKWHEAT FLOUR

Buckwheat flour, despite its name, is not at all related to wheat and is therefore perfectly suitable for gluten-free folks. I like to use this flour as a main flour in many hearty baked goods. The texture of the final product is similar to whole wheat–based goodies with an earthier undertone.

**Substitutions:** superfine brown rice flour, teff flour, sorghum flour

## CERTIFIED GLUTEN-FREE OATS

Seek out certified gluten-free oats in grocery stores near other gluten-free flours and baking ingredients. Bob's Red Mill is one brand that is readily available in many grocery stores across the United States. When using oats to bake with in gluten-free recipes, be sure that they are certified gluten-free, which means that they have not come into contact with gluten from processing or cross-contamination. Many oats are processed in the same facilities as gluten-containing grains, such as barley and wheat, and therefore may contain traces of gluten. Be aware that some people with celiac disease cannot eat oats even if they are certified gluten-free. This is due to a response to avenin, a protein in oats that is quite similar to the gluten protein. So, if you have a friend who can't eat gluten, it's always nice to ask if certified gluten-free oats cause any problems as well, just to be on the safe side.

## COCONUT FLOUR

Coconut flour is made from ground dehydrated coconut meat and is especially high in fiber, but it is also a very thirsty flour that loves to soak up moisture. Best if used along with almond meal, tapioca flour, or sweet white rice flour.
**Substitutions:** almond meal

## CORNSTARCH

Cornstarch is made from the endosperm of the corn kernel and works well as a thickener of sauces and puddings as well as a secondary flour in a gluten-free baking mix.
**Substitutions:** potato starch, arrowroot starch

## HAZELNUT MEAL

Hazelnut meal is made from finely ground toasted hazelnuts and, like almond meal, lends a bit of moisture and a distinct flavor to desserts. I love using hazelnuts for piecrusts, and, combined with chocolate, they are truly irresistible. Also known as filberts and cobnuts, depending on the species of plant from which the nut originates. Make your own by pulsing hazelnuts in a food processor until finely crumbled.
**Substitutions:** almond meal, finely ground toasted pecans

## MILLET FLOUR

Millet, made from ground millet seeds, is a drier gluten-free flour and works well in conjunction with another main base flour and a starchier flour such as tapioca flour or sweet white rice flour to add a bit of moisture.
**Substitutions:** quinoa, brown rice flour, sorghum flour

## POTATO STARCH

Potato starch is made from the starch in potatoes and is bright white in color and light and silky in texture. Use as a secondary or third flour in baked goods and don't confuse it with potato flour! Potato flour is made from the entire potato, so the color is darker and the texture is denser. Potato starch consists of only the starch of the potato, making it a much lighter flour in both color and texture.

**Substitutions:** cornstarch, arrowroot starch

## RICE FLOUR

Rice flour comes in several varieties: brown rice flour, white rice flour, and superfine brown rice flour.

Brown rice flour is the most common of all these flours and is used extensively throughout this book as it has a mild flavor and lovely texture.

White rice flour is similar to brown rice flour but has a few less nutrients and is paler in color.

Superfine brown rice flour (I recommend Authentic Foods brand) is a wonderful, gluten-free flour that is made from brown rice flour that has been double milled, resulting in a silky smooth texture, which is perfect for baked goods, sauces, and all sorts of uses for gluten-free goodies. Regular grind brown rice flour can be used in place of superfine brown rice flour in certain recipes, but it's unsuitable for recipes that rely heavily on the flour being silky-smooth, such as in piecrusts or pastries.

**Substitutions:** sorghum flour, buckwheat flour, superfine sorghum flour

## SORGHUM

Sorghum is one of my go-to flours as it has a very pleasant texture and mild flavor, similar to that of wheat flour. Use as a main flour in baked goods as well as a thickening flour for sauces and batters. This is also a great choice for dusting lightly greased cake pans as the grain of this flour is relatively fine. Another option is superfine sorghum flour, which has a similar texture to superfine brown rice flour and is an even better choice than sorghum flour; it is much more elusive in stores but can easily be found online.

**Substitutions:** superfine sorghum flour, buckwheat flour, millet flour, superfine brown rice flour

## SWEET WHITE RICE FLOUR

Also known as mochiko, this is a good flour to use as a starch in many cookies, pastry crusts, and other desserts, as it comes from glutinous rice—which adds a sticky, or binding quality to the dough. This flour is also used alone to make the very famous dessert mochi, by adding water and steaming the dough.

**Substitutions:** If used in small amounts of a flour blend, then tapioca flour is a suitable substitute.

## TAPIOCA FLOUR

Tapioca flour is a useful flour when used in small amounts to add moisture and elasticity to baked goods. Although not very high in nutritional value, tapioca flour adds a great texture to gluten-free sweets. Also known as tapioca starch.

**Substitutions:** sweet white rice flour

### TEFF FLOUR

Teff flour has been used for centuries in Ethiopia as a staple cereal grain because of its versatility and fantastic nutritional properties. Teff is great as a main flour and works well with almond meal, especially in chocolate desserts, because it has a faint chocolate flavor. Be sure that you are using teff flour in recipes, rather than the whole grain, which is teeny tiny and can be hard to tell from the flour if you are unfamiliar with this ingredient.
**Substitutions:** buckwheat, sorghum

### A NOTE ABOUT GLUTEN-FREE FLOURS

When using flours in baking, be sure to measure correctly, or you could end up with surprising results, such as cookies spreading, or worse! I often use the scoop and sweep method (scoop measuring cup deep into the flour and then sweep off the excess with a knife), but I've also included a weight guide to help with various flours below; see page 302.

# FATS

### AVOCADOS

Avocados may not initially seem like a fat that you would use in desserts, but they are actually pretty perfect when you want to bake oil free—blending effortlessly into silky puddings and adding a good amount of moisture to many baked goods, especially chocolate ones (like my Choco-Cado Pudding, page 279). To use in other recipes, such as quick breads and muffins, sub up to half the amount of margarine or oil called for with pureed avocado.

### CACAO BUTTER

Cacao butter is the fat of the cacao pod left over after the chocolate has been extracted. Generally it is recombined with the chocolate liquor to get what we know as a chocolate bar, and it is also wonderful when used on its own, either in raw goodies or other uses. Cacao butter melts at a low temperature and should be liquefied before using. Since cacao butter is rather pricey and somewhat elusive outside natural foods stores, it's best to reserve it for special uses, or implement it only when you want a touch of white chocolate flavor.

## COCONUT CREAM

Coconut cream can be obtained by refrigerating a can of full-fat coconut milk for about 3 hours and scooping the solid cream from the top of the can—feel free to use the remaining milk for other uses, such as liquid in baked goods or smoothies. Works great where a high amount of fat is called for in a recipe and oftentimes can replace oil or melted margarine when used in quantities under 1/3 cup.

## COCONUT OIL

Coconut oil is available in two varieties, unrefined and refined, the latter having no detectable coconut flavor. Coconut oil is pretty amazing—it can make delicious raw desserts and also works great in baked goods, candies, and frostings. Unrefined has a higher smoke point (meaning, it "burns" at a higher temperature), so it's great for sautés and making crepes or pancakes. This fat is liquid at just above room temperature, so for using in frostings and baking, I recommend first chilling it in the refrigerator until solid, about 2 hours, and then removing it about 10 minutes before use for best consistency. Replaces margarine, butter, shortening, olive oil, and other oils 1:1.

## NONDAIRY MARGARINE

Nondairy margarine is available in an assortment of brands, and Earth Balance Buttery Spread is, in my opinion, the best one to seek, as it bakes and cooks exactly like dairy butter and is nonhydrogenated. For these recipes, if you are Soy-Free seek out soy-free margarine. In each recipe calling for nondairy margarine, I used Earth Balance Soy-Free to create them.

## NUT MEALS AND NUT BUTTERS

Nut meals and nut butters make a fantastic addition to baked goods and candies when a little fat is desired. Almond butter works beautifully on its own to create dozens of delectable desserts, or add some peanut or almond butter in your cakes or cookies to add a fun flavor and some good fats.

## OLIVE OIL

Olive oil is one of my favorite oils to cook with, both stove top and in baking. The flavor, in my opinion, is unbeatable and pairs naturally with popular dessert flavors, such as lemon, vanilla, and chocolate. Look for extra-virgin olive oil, rather than "extra light" or "light tasting," which are generally not 100 percent olive oil or have been filtered several times and are no longer suitable for cooking.

## SHORTENING (NONHYDROGENATED)

My favorite brand of nonhydrogenated shortening is Earth Balance, and I recommend it for the recipes that call for shortening.

Unlike coconut oil, for which it can substitute, nonhydrogenated shortening remains stable at slightly warmer than room temperature and therefore works well in stiffer frostings and icings.

# BINDERS

### APPLESAUCE

Applesauce works well as a fat replacer and egg replacer in baked goods that have a spongy end result, such as muffins. Seek out unsweetened, or better yet, make your own with the recipe on page 229. It works especially well in cakes and pancakes.

1 egg: ¼ cup applesauce

### AVOCADO

As well as a fat replacement, blended avocados also work well in replicating the properties of eggs in baked goods. They work best in darker baked goods, such as chocolate cakes, where their green color is easy to mask.

1 egg: ¼ avocado, blended

### BANANA

Blended bananas are perfect for adding binding power to cakes, cookies, sweet breads, and more. Be sure to seek out slightly browned bananas so that the sugar content is high. Blend bananas until extremely smooth or smash vigorously with a fork; whipped bananas add a nice lift to baked goods, ice creams, and puddings. Also works great as an eggy batter on pan-fried sweets.

1 egg: ½ small banana, blended

### BESAN + WATER

This blend works especially well for thickening sauces and puddings and for adding binding properties to baked goods. Be sure to whisk it together into a very smooth paste before adding into desserts for cooking.

1 egg: 2 tablespoons besan mixed with ¼ cup water

### CHIA MEAL

Ground chia seed is a great egg replacer as it works well as a binder; used in higher amounts, it creates an eggy bendability in baked goods. You will most likely need to grind the chia seed yourself using a small spice or clean coffee grinder. Grind until a fine powder is formed and mix with three times as much water. Let set 5 minutes, until a very sturdy paste is formed.

1 egg: ½ tablespoon ground chia seed mixed with 4 tablespoons water

## FLAXSEED MEAL

Ground flaxseed can be used in a similar fashion as chia, with less water needing to be added to create an egglike texture. You can usually purchase flaxseed preground, but oftentimes it's far less expensive to grind the seeds yourself in a spice grinder in small batches. It also preserves the freshness of the seed when left intact.

1 egg: 1 tablespoon ground flaxseed meal mixed with 2 tablespoons water

## MANGO

Like applesauce and bananas, this fruit puree works well as a binder in spongy-textured baked goods. Be sure to only use ripe mangos, or there won't be enough sugar to make an adequate binder. The best way to tell if a mango is ripe is that it should have a lovely tropical fragrance and the flesh should give a little when pressed with your thumb.

1 egg: ¼ cup blended mango

## POTATO

When a starchy cooking potato—such as a russet or Yukon gold—is baked and then peeled and blended in a food processor, if left to run long enough, you will be delighted to find a tacky, sticky substance that makes a wonderful egg replacer in many recipes, especially those calling for a high amount of eggs—just make sure the consistency is like that of a thick glue, or you won't get a proper bind in the recipes.

1 egg: ¼ cup blended potato puree

## POWDERED EGG REPLACER

Found on your grocer's shelf, these dry mixes are usually made of a few starches and binders and work well as an egg replacer when mixed with water. Powders like EnerG, Orgran, or Bob's Red Mill are good for light-colored doughs or batters where flax or chia may not be appropriate.

1 egg: see package instructions

## PUMPKIN PUREE

This puree works just like applesauce as a binder. Canned is usually the densest and what I recommend, but, if you don't want to use canned pumpkin, you can make your own. Simply roast the pumpkin, cut in half with seeds removed, at 400°F (covered with foil) for about 45 minutes, or until fragrant and tender. Let cool, remove skins, and puree until smooth in a food processor. Strain the puree well with cheesecloth to remove any excess moisture before using.

1 egg: ¼ cup pumpkin puree

## SILKEN TOFU

Silken tofu is oftentimes sold in aseptic packages and located with the shelf-stable food, in either the Asian or natural foods section of a typical chain market. It can also be found in the refrigerated section. This egg replacer works especially well in baked goods, cheesecakes, and puddings and mousses.

1 egg: ¼ cup blended silken tofu

## XANTHAN GUM

I like to use xanthan gum in many of my baked goods where it significantly changes the texture when added. The powdery binder comes in a small package but lasts a very long time if stored in a cool dry place within an airtight container. Use about 1 teaspoon per 3 to 4 cups gluten-free flour blend—I usually call for a touch more in doughs that need to be handled and shouldn't fall apart.

**Substitutions:** In many baked goods, the xanthan can be left out and instead you can make a gel from ground chia or flaxseeds but the texture will be different, and usually drier/crumblier, than if xanthan gum is used. Also try psyllium husk, carob gum, or guar gum.

# MILKS, CREAMS, AND CHEESES

## ALMOND MILK, UNSWEETENED

Almond milk is my favorite type of nondairy milk. You can purchase it store-bought (I recommend unsweetened Almond Breeze) or you can easily make it yourself and avoid additives and any extra ingredients. See page 28 for instructions.

## CASHEW CREAM

Follow the recipe on page 33 for a delectable sweetened whipped cream made from cashews. Use this cream in baked goods, candies, cream sauces, ice cream, and so much more.

Use 1:1 for crème fraîche, sour cream, or whipped cream in recipes

## COCONUT MILK, UNSWEETENED

Coconut milk is available in both a carton—where it resembles a slightly lighter almond milk and is great for topping cereal or drinking—or canned, usually labeled either full fat or "lite." The milk, once shaken lightly, should be smooth, thick, and white and never congealed or overly clumpy/watery. Seek out the highest-quality canned coconut milk possible for best flavor and texture in recipes—generally, but not in all cases, a higher price is indicative of higher quality. Avoid cans that sound or feel overly watery when shaken—you should be able to detect a heavy cream consistency. Coconut cream comes from a can of full-fat coconut milk (see page 11).

## NONDAIRY CREAM CHEESE

There are a few varieties of vegan cream cheeses available, most which are also 100 percent gluten-free. Be sure to check labels just in case. The cream cheeses are pretty great in that they truly replicate the texture, and for the most part the taste, of cream cheese or Neufchâtel.
Use 1:1 like dairy-based cream cheese

## NONDAIRY MAYONNAISE

A few types of nondairy, vegan-friendly mayonnaise exist on the market, and some are better in flavor and texture than others. My favorite brands are Vegenaise and Earth Balance, each for different reasons. Nondairy mayo works well in baked goods such as cakes or muffins or to add a little zing to puddings, ice cream, and more.
Use 1:1 like egg-based mayo

## NONDAIRY SOUR CREAM

You can use nondairy sour cream just as you would dairy-based sour cream. Nondairy sour cream is available at most supermarkets in the United States from a few different brands. Look for it in the natural foods sections or near where other perishable dairy-free items are sold.
Use 1:1 like dairy-based sour cream

## RICE MILK, UNSWEETENED

Rice milk is much thinner than almond or soy milk, closer in texture and taste to skim milk. It doesn't yield very full-bodied sauces or icings but works great as the liquid in baked goods and perfectly for those who have soy or nut allergies.

## SOY MILK, UNSWEETENED

Soy milk has always been one of the most popular nondairy milks and is widely available in US grocery stores. You can use unsweetened soymilk just as you would 2 percent dairy milk in most recipes.

# OTHER NOTEWORTHY INGREDIENTS

## AGAR

This ingredient is derived from red algae and does a remarkable job in replacing gelatin. Agar can be sourced in most Asian groceries or Asian sections of natural foods stores. It is usually available in flakes, powder, or bars; I find the powdered types easiest to work with in recipes.

## KASHA

Kasha is simply toasted buckwheat kernels, or groats. Oftentimes buckwheat groats are sold both toasted (as kasha) and un-toasted. For recipes calling for kasha, seek out toasted buckwheat, which is a medium brown color. Untoasted buckwheat is a pale green color and must be cooked before eating, either by toasting, steaming, boiling, or another method.

## NONDAIRY CHOCOLATE

Many brands of nondairy chocolate are available, usually with a cocoa content of 55 percent or more, listed as semi-sweet, bitter-sweet, or simply "dark." Check ingredient labels. If needed, seek out brands that do not contain soy (usually as lecithin) such as Enjoy Life Brand.

## VINEGAR

Vinegar is best reserved for cakes, waffles, and lighter cookies. It doesn't offer any binding power but does give cakes a proper lift when used in conjunction with baking powder. Apple cider vinegar is my favorite for most desserts; you can make your own (page 30) or seek out raw varieties, such as Bragg, from natural foods stores.

1 egg: 1 tablespoon vinegar—up to 4 eggs' worth in recipes with baking powder

# TOOLS OF THE TRADE

If there's one thing I have learned throughout my years of creating, both in cooking and making art, it's that if you don't have the right tools, you'll never be able to complete your task with good results. Craftsmanship and skill have a lot to do with how well a work of art, or a recipe, turns out. Creativity is of course paramount, but a huge portion of the outcome falls on whether or not you have access to and are using the correct tools to do the job.

On the following pages I've listed the equipment that I recommend keeping in your own kitchen. There are a lot of items listed; however, many of them are commonplace and are probably lurking in your cabinet right now. And, many of them are inexpensive, so the next time you find yourself with an extra $5 burning a hole in your pocket, pick up a small kitchen tool that you do not already own. It will save you so much frustration on subpar desserts for years to come, and over time you'll have a wonderful collection of tools for any and every need. Of course, there are many tools that I have not mentioned that are excellent to have around as well, so I highly recommend browsing through your favorite kitchen supply store for inspiration. If anything, you can always leave with a few inexpensive and adorable paper muffin liners that you didn't have before you stopped in. And of course, don't feel pressured to purchase every single item on the list—it's taken me over fifteen years to collect much of my kitchen arsenal and I always purchase based on need/priority. I'd say at the very least you need to have two sturdy cookie trays, a few wooden spoons, a whisk, a blender or small food processor, and at least three sizes of mixing bowls.

The equipment suggested in the book is made with the ideal outcome in mind; however, I realize that each person's kitchen is stocked differently. In that case, in the directions I will specify a particular appliance and then offer an alternative option. I've chosen the first option based on experience and oftentimes have had better experiences with certain outcomes (retrieving or scooping out thicker batter from a food processor is oftentimes easier than from a high-speed blender, for example), so keep this in mind as you are creating the recipes.

A quick note about cross-contamination: If you share a kitchen with someone who eats and cooks with gluten-containing ingredients, such as bread, etc., be sure to keep the utensils very clean to prevent a cross-contamination disaster! Most of these tools can be cleaned quickly and easily with a little soap and hot water, which will help eliminate the possibility of cross-contamination. If you are using equipment that is difficult to clean all particles from, such as a toaster, sieve, cutting board, or rolling pin, I also recommend keeping a dedicated gluten-free version.

## APRON

No matter how frivolous (or frilly!) you may view an apron, if you're serious about baking or are planning to make more than one recipe in a day, it's best to play it safe and slip on an apron before getting to work. It helps tremendously while washing dishes by keeping your clothes from getting drenched, and hence, flour sticking to your drenched shirt resulting in you being covered in batter. Just slip one on and prevent a mess. I prefer at least one pocket and for the material to have a bib above the waist, but you should find the one that is most functional and fashionable for your needs. If you're into vintage threads, check out secondhand stores and consignment shops for some outstanding deals on cute retro-era baking gear.

## BAKING BANDS

Made from aluminized fabric or even silicone, these bands, also called "cake bands" and "magic bands" are the tool you need if you crave cakes that are totally level. For fabric wraps, be sure to soak them in water and squeeze out all the excess before wrapping your pans. Silicone wraps often need just a minute or so under water, but follow the directions on your band's product label to be sure. Wrap the bands as evenly as you can to maximize their insulation properties, which prevents uneven baking; I often cut mine to size to fit my various sizes of pans. For fabric bands, I recommend Wilton brand. You can make your own by folding a damp sheet of cheesecloth into 2-inch-wide strips wrapped with aluminum foil. Secure with baking twine.

## BENCH SCRAPER

A multitasker in the kitchen, use to transfer chopped fruits and nuts effortlessly, chop and shape dough, and release dough from the rolling surface.

## CAKE DECORATING TURNTABLE

About the size of a serving platter, oftentimes with decorative edging to act as a base for a cake, this plate is used to apply frosting quickly and easily while using a frosting spatula. The plate spins like a Lazy Susan, making the application of frosting easy without the need to walk around the cake.

## CAKE PANS

Recommended sizes for getting started: 9 x 13 inch; 8 x 8 inch; 4 x 8 inch; standard-size muffin pan; two 9-inch circular pans. Muffin or cupcake pans are also good to have around and generally come in mini (1.5 inches diameter), standard size (2.5 inches diameter), and jumbo (3 to 4 inches diameter). I recommend metal pans for best results.

## CANDY THERMOMETER

Every serious candy lover needs to have a candy thermometer. Unless you are really good at temperature estimating or have been making various candies for a long time, it is an essential piece of inexpensive equipment. Although the Cold Water Method (explained on page 232) is helpful, a good-quality candy thermometer removes all guesswork and ensures perfect candy every time, provided you follow the rest of the recipe. Calibrate your thermometer by placing it into a pot of boiling water. Adjust the temperature accordingly if your reading is off from 212°F.

## CHEF'S KNIFE

A good-quality chef's knife is an essential tool for baking as well as cooking. I recommend seeking out a quality knife that will last for years through numerous sharpenings. Having a quality chef's knife will turn the tedious task of chopping an array of fruits or chiffonading delicate herbs into an effortless and fun exercise in knife skills.

## CHOCOLATE MOLDS

These molds are available in various materials, usually silicone or clear plastic. I find silicone is easiest to work with and available in many shapes and sizes. Once you temper the chocolate, pour it into the mold and then tap very gently on the countertop to release any trapped air bubbles in the chocolate. Let rest at room temperature until chocolate has fully resolidified and releases easily from the mold.

## CHOCOLATE THERMOMETER

A chocolate thermometer is designed specifically to test the temperature of chocolate when tempering as it measures in much smaller increments than most cooking or candy thermometers. To get a nice sheen and snap when dipping or coating with chocolate, having the correct temperature at the correct time is essential (the entire process of tempering is explained on page 234).

## COOKIE CUTTERS

Every baker needs a variety of cookie cutters, and a giant collection is even better. They are great for collecting as they are usually very inexpensive and come in a variety of shapes and sizes. Seek out firm, high-quality stainless steel or copper cutters with rounded tops for easy cut-ability.

## COOKIE SHEETS

I advise having a few of these around in various sizes, depending on the structure of your oven. If you have a small oven, it may make sense to purchase two small cookie sheets so that you can fit them both in the oven at once, enabling more cookies to be baked at once; however, if you have a large oven, you'd be better off getting more bang for your buck and opting for two medium pans or one large cookie sheet for baking bigger batches. There are many types available for purchase, some with nifty air pockets inside. I prefer the standard flat metal pans with one side gently lipped.

## COOKIE PANS/MOLDS

Madeleines (page 133) and Ladyfingers (page 131) benefit from cookie molds as the dough is wet enough to be shaped by the molds while baking. And cookies such as Springerles (page 122) utilize the embossing-type molds to create beautiful patterns on the surface of the cookie. Kitchen stores are your best bet for seeking out these specialty items.

## COOKIE PRESS

These relatively small gadgets are a must-have if you want to create festive classic cookies such as Holiday Spritz (page 134) with as little effort as you would a drop cookie. The small contraption is simply a cylinder, usually made of plastic or aluminum, with a "stencil" on one end that you create shaped cookies with by pressing down with a lever on the other end. It is essentially a very controlled piping mechanism for flawless shaped cookies.

## DEHYDRATOR

A dehydrator can be a pricey investment and is revered in the raw food community,

since so many wonderful foods can be created with one. However, if you aren't looking to make breakfast, lunch, and dinner with a dehydrator and won't be running it constantly, or making up big bulk batches of food very often, then I recommend purchasing an inexpensive dehydrator. There are many available with just a few stacks of trays that are about the same size as an ice cream maker, which you can pick up at many household goods stores for about $50. I use my dehydrator often to create easy and stunning garnishes for cakes, pies, cookies, and more. You can also makeshift your own dehydrator by setting your oven on its lowest temperature and placing your foods onto an ungreased cookie sheet. Bake with the oven door slightly ajar for a few hours, or until the food has been thoroughly dried.

## DOUBLE BOILER

You can purchase a double boiler from a kitchen supply store or easily make one yourself by placing a heat-safe glass or metal bowl on top of a 2 or 3 quart saucepan that is filled about 2 inches with water. Heat over medium-low heat to melt chocolates and other temperamental goodies without scorching.

## ELECTRIC MIXER

Although not essential for gluten-free vegan baking, since no gluten needs to be worked, kneaded, or pummeled repeatedly at high speed, I still love my electric mixer for creating smooth and airy frostings, whipped creams, and more. It's also handy to have around for mixing simpler mixes such as batter, or cookie dough that takes a lot of elbow grease to come together as in the Cinnamon Amaretti recipe (page 278).

## FLAT METAL SPATULA

A high-quality flat and sturdy spatula is so helpful when making rolled pastries, cookies, or pies. It makes transferring easier and removing from hot pans effortless with no breakage.

## FONDANT ROLLING PINS

These rolling pins are usually smooth, even, plastic cylinders with detachable rubber rings to allow the user to control the thickness of the fondant. Found next to other fondant decorating supplies, these can also be used to roll out other types of softer dough and malleable fillings.

## FONDANT SPATULA

Use when applying fondant to cakes to smooth out bubbles by gently massaging out the bubble with a little bit of pressure. These tools are usually about the size of your palm and made of flat plastic, with a very shallow handle.

## FOOD PROCESSOR

This appliance is a very wise investment if you find yourself in the kitchen often, as they make quick, clean, and easy work of previously arduous tasks. From slicing fruits, to pureeing nut butters, I find myself using a food processor practically every single day. Seek one out that is at least 7 cups capacity (preferably with an insert for a smaller bowl); the smaller ones are good for some things, but they tend to be too tiny to cater to most recipe quantities.

## FROSTING SPATULA

To apply perfectly even frosting to a cake like they do in bakeries, you must have a frosting spatula. These long offset spatulas (about 1 x 8 inches), combined with a cake decorating turntable, make decorating a breeze as they allow the icing to just glide on. Offset spatulas are similar to a regular spatula except that they are not straight but bent slightly at (or offset from) the handle. Purchase a long slender one for applying frosting and ganache to layer cakes and a larger one for loosening pastry doughs from rolling surfaces without breaking the delicate, gluten-free dough.

## HIGH-SPEED BLENDER

It's not essential to have, but what a difference a high-speed blender can make! I love my Vitamix and recommend it above and beyond all other blenders I have tried. Each recipe calling for a blender was prepared using a Vitamix. It's a great investment you won't regret.

## ICE CREAM MAKER

Although these come in the old-fashioned rock ice variations, I find the newer electric models with the freezable bowls to be superior to the rock ice machines. Not only are they quieter, they are less messy, easy to maintain, and always ready to rock out great ice cream if you have the bowl properly frozen ahead of time. Use to make gelato, sorbet, frozen yogurt, ice cream, semifreddo, and sherbet, all quickly and very easily.

## JELLY ROLL PANS

This is a sturdy pan with a lip, usually about ¾ inch high, used to create jelly rolls or sponge cakes, although they work perfectly for baking cookies or whoopee pies as well. Look for a sturdy metal pan, with a rolled edge, to avoid warping.

## KITCHEN SCALE

A scale is extremely useful when baking with gluten-free flours, as each flour has a different weight, and sometimes even the slightest difference in grams can make or break a baked good. The Escali scale is my top pick for an inexpensive but trustworthy scale. If you get familiar with your scale and get one with a "tare" function, you will be able to dirty less dishes and nix the measuring cups by piling everything into one bowl.

## MANDOLINE

This handy tool will create beautifully even and paper-thin slices that would be quite difficult to achieve with a knife. Slice up perfect pears, apples, peaches, and so much more with a mandoline. Watch your fingers, though! The blades are sharp and can give you a nasty wound before you even realize what you've done. Finger-protecting gloves and/or hand guards are available for use with a mandoline.

## MEASURING CUPS AND SPOONS

This is an essential collection of cups that will aid you in following recipes with accuracy. Seek out high-quality measuring cups and spoons if you bake often, otherwise you will plow through the cheap ones. I like all-stainless-steel nested measuring spoons with an elongated measuring area that fits nicely into small ingredients packaging such as baking powder and jarred spices. When measuring with cups rather than weights, I find a simple "scoop and sweep" method to be the most dependable.

## MICROPLANE

A flat (or sometimes flat on the bottom with a curved top), elongated metal utensil with small perforations used for zesting and grating. I depend on these for quickly grating ginger, nutmeg, and other spices as well as using them when a fine citrus zest is needed.

## MIXING BOWLS

I suggest having a variety of mixing bowls on hand, ranging from 2 inches in diameter to 15 inches. When baking gluten-free, you'll almost always need an extra one on hand for flour mixing, and small ones come in handy for things like premixing flax or chia "eggs." Seek out stainless steel over plastic, as they clean up easier and retain less odor/discoloration.

## OVEN MITT

You will need one of these. In fact, purchase two of them that extend at least three-quarters of the way up your forearm. The higher quality the better.

## PARCHMENT PAPER

Available in natural or bleached, parchment paper can be used for rolling out stiff pie doughs or lining baking pans for non-stick purposes. I always have a big roll of this around for pastry and cookie making.

For gluten-free baking, this is an essential to have on hand, so stock up!

## PARING KNIFE

This tiny knife will help breeze you through all kinds of small tasks, from coring apples to scoring designs into piecrusts with authority. Look for one that fits well in your hand, giving you better control and comfort.

## PASTRY BAGS AND TIPS

An essential for decorating and filling cakes, cookies, doughnuts, quick breads, and more. Seek out a good-quality kit or purchase tips separately. Fabric bags with plastic linings are best and are very durable, lasting about two years with regular use. For inexpensive bags, I like Wilton bags and tips and recommend at the very least two large tips, one star and one flat, and a small circular for decorative piping.

The bags are assembled by inserting the tubular part of the coupler into the bag, exposing about ½ inch of plastic from the small opening in the bag. Slip on the metal tip, and then twist the remaining piece of the coupler to lock into place. Fill the piping bag with a viscous frosting, ganache, or icing and twist the bag until the contents form a tight pouch. This will help you in controlling the piping when repeating various maneuvers, while at the same time keeping the icing/frosting moving freely without any blips.

## PASTRY BLENDER

This small hand-size gadget looks similar to a half-moon-shaped whisk, or an egg slicer, but is in fact used to "cut" dry ingredients (such as flours or sugar) into fat for pastry making. To use, simply combine the required amount of cold fat (coconut oil, margarine, etc.) along with the required flours and chop repeatedly with the tool until the mixture resembles coarse crumbles.

## PASTRY BRUSH

For candy, cookies, and breads, a pastry brush is an essential tool. Reserve a "wet" brush to wash down sugar granules from the saucepan when making candies, to brush on eggless washes for baked goods, to lightly grease bakeware, and to paint layers of chocolate for candy making.

## PLASTIC WRAP

Often referred to as "Saran wrap" because of the common brand name, plastic wrap will make gluten-free dough and pastry rolling effortless and keep desserts fresher longer. Since gluten-free dough tends to be either stickier or stiffer (not very stretchy), plastic wrap enables you to roll out dough without it sticking to a surface or the rolling pin and roll up doughs that would be much too sticky to do by hand, and in cases where

parchment may not be strong enough to withstand the water content.

## RAMEKINS

Small dishes that can go from oven to table with ease, ramekins are often the most important aspect of many recipes, such as baked custards, individual cobblers, and small desserts requiring a water bath. They can also double nicely as small mixing bowls for preparing ingredients like flaxseed or chia "eggs."

## ROLLING PIN

I tend to have several rolling pins around, my favorite being a solid wood tapered version that I've baked with for years. Different rolling pins have different uses, so be sure to choose the one that is best suited for your project. A good all-purpose pin is one that is heavy, wooden, and about 16 inches long. Others have rotating handles that allow easier movement and usability when rolling stiffer, heavy doughs.

## SAUCEPAN (2- OR 3-QUART)

This essential piece of equipment is great to have on hand for making sauces, candies, and other goodies. Be sure to have a good quality pot: copper bottomed or all copper is best, but, if it's not in your price-range, a good stainless steel piece will do the trick.

Make sure the pot's sides are vertical rather than tapered. Also works great as a base for a double boiler, as heat-safe bowls oftentimes fit snugly into the nook of the pot.

## SERRATED KNIFE

A long serrated knife is your best friend when it comes to perfecting layer cakes. Go for knives that have a close-set tooth to prevent tearing of cakes when cutting. With a long, sharp, serrated knife you can easily turn a single layer cake into three or more layers!

## SIEVE

Great for sifting ingredients together as well as dusting cakes and cookies lightly with confectioner's sugar or cocoa powder. I enjoy having a few different sizes for various tasks. These also work as strainers in a pinch, and small sieves fit perfectly over mugs for straining beverages, such as herbal infusions.

## SILICONE MAT

Silicone mats are a staple in my kitchen as they are convenient, easy to clean, and most important, reusable. They don't replace parchment for a few applications, such as rolling out dough or lining odd-shaped pans, but they provide the perfect nonstick surface on cookie sheets or jelly roll pans when needed.

## SILICONE SPATULA

These spatulas are essential in baking for scraping cake batter from bowls and evenly spreading icing or glaze onto baked goods. I enjoy having several different sizes of these on hand so I'm well prepared for various different uses.

## SPRINGFORM PAN

This pan is a lot like a standard cake pan in size and shape, yet it has a detachable base, so that you can easily release pies and cakes that require layering and baking or chilling such as cheesecakes, tiramisu, layered pies, and more. Eight inches is standard size, but I also recommend purchasing a 6-inch pan for when you want to create very tall desserts, such as with some cheesecakes.

## STOCKPOT

As the name suggests, this pot is great for stocks, and it also comes in handy when making desserts. Use for boiling bready dough (such as bagels), blanching peaches, cooking sauces in large batches, and so much more.

## TART AND TARTLETS MOLDS

Often made of aluminum or silicone, these shallow, scaffolded molds are essential for making tarts and tartlets. Press the dough or crumb crusts into the pans and roll over the top with a rolling pin to evenly cut the dough. Blind bake and use for cold fillings or use with baked filled desserts, such as the White Chocolate Peanut Butter Pretzel Tartlets (page 173).

## TUBE PAN

Perfect for making Bundt cakes and to form gelled desserts, these pans are shaped like a donut when viewed from above, and they usually have ornate decorations embossed to impart an elegant touch to the final cake or molded dessert.

## WHISK

Whisks are handy to have around for easy mixing of gluten-free flour blends, and for getting lumps out of gravies and batter; they are the only tool that will get the job done right. I recommend having at least a small (under 6 inches) and a standard-size balloon whisk for convenient and even mixing.

## WOODEN SPOONS

Wooden spoons are essential for candy making, as they are insulated, which means they won't cause a sudden temperature change to the hot liquid like a metal spoon may do, and they are simple to clean. Be sure not to let wooden spoons soak too long in water, and keep them out of the dishwasher to prevent damage.

## ZESTER

This is the perfect tool for removing the flavorful zest of a citrus fruit while leaving the pith behind. Zesters create beautiful strands for flavoring and garnishing recipes. Often confused with a microplane, which also does a fine job of removing zest, this is a small utensil with a curved metal end that has several holes along the top with sharp edges.

**Make sure your oven is calibrated.** You can do this by purchasing an oven thermometer and setting your oven to 350°F. If the oven temperature is off from the thermometer when the oven preheats, you will either need to adjust your temperature throughout when baking, or get your oven serviced so it reads temperature properly.

**Follow the recipe directions very carefully.** Before you begin, read the instructions for the recipe all the way through so you understand the preparation from the beginning. Gather the ingredients at this time and lay out any equipment you will need. There is a reason why I put the steps in the specific order, the ingredients in certain amounts, and the measurements for distribution as they are listed: because they work. Each recipe has been thoroughly tested to ensure accuracy. Of course, certain things like altitude, humidity, and quality of ingredients can affect the end-product as well, so bear this in mind when making a recipe.

**Use good ingredients.** For best results, the quality of your ingredients counts. Splurge on the highest quality ingredients you can afford for high-quality results.

**Reduce the fat.** Use applesauce, banana, canned pumpkin, pureed peaches, and other cooked, pureed stone fruits in place of half the amount of called-for margarine or oil. This works well with quick breads, cookies, and cakes. I wouldn't recommend this method with piecrusts, though.

**Before you start cooking, clean your work area.** It's important to treat your work space as a place you want to create in. Clean, get organized, and have all your ingredients arranged before you begin.

**Clean up as you go.** It makes your kitchen so much more manageable if you clean as you work. I often find myself standing around waiting for a sauté to finish, a piecrust to blind bake, or a sauce to thicken—take advantage of these spare moments to put ingredients away, wipe the countertops, and fill up a mixing bowl with dirty measuring spoons, spatulas, and some hot bubbly water to soak.

**Don't place freshly made cookie dough onto hot or very warm cookie trays.** Be sure to have at least two trays so that in your rotation of baking, one can be room temperature at all times, otherwise the dough will cook inconsistently.

**Don't open the oven door!** Gluten-free vegan baking is extremely sensitive and touchy to even slight temperature changes, not to mention, the need to be undisturbed in the beginning stages of baking so that batters and doughs can set properly while baking.

**Mix your dry ingredients well before incorporating them into the rest of the ingredients.** This goes for the flours, xanthan gum, cream of tartar, baking powder, and baking soda.

**Seal your bags of flours tightly to store and check for freshness when using.** Gluten-free flours have a short shelf life if not stored properly. I recommend keeping flour in an airtight container, and, if possible, storing in the refrigerator for maximum freshness.

**Keep everyone out of the kitchen while a cake is baking.** Because there is no gluten protein in the batter to hold the structure, a strong vibration can cause a cake that is not quite set to flop completely.

**Use your freezer's middle setting.** For frozen treats, the middle setting will give you the most consistent and easy-to-eat frozen desserts.

# HOMEMADE BASICS

## ALMOND MILK

There are lots of nondairy milks to choose from, but almond milk is my favorite. While there are many packaged options available, it's really easy to make yourself—and the bonus is there are no additives or any extra ingredients, plus the flavor is much richer than store-bought.

**2 cups raw almonds**
**6 cups water**

**YIELD: 6 CUPS**

• Blend almonds and water in high-speed blender for about 7 minutes, or until well mixed into a thick liquid. Strain through a cheesecloth. Will keep in the fridge for 3 to 5 days.

You can discard the almond pulp or use it for a flour replacement or a protein fix in your morning smoothies. For flour replacement: Preheat oven to 375°F. Spread an even, thin layer of almond pulp onto an ungreased cookie sheet and bake for 10 to 12 minutes, or until lightly toasted. To dry using a dehydrator, spread the pulp onto a dehydrator sheet in a thin even layer and dehydrate at 130°F, for 5 hours, or until completely dry.

## SIMPLE SYRUP

It may just be sugar and water, but keeping a jar of simple syrup around will make for effortless cocktails, mocktails, coffee drinks, and more! This lasts indefinitely if stored in the fridge. If it begins to crystallize, simply warm again over the stove until once again dissolved.

**1 cup sugar**
**½ cup water**

**YIELD: 1¼ CUPS**

• Over medium heat in a small saucepan, warm the ingredients just until the sugar has dissolved completely and the mixture turns from cloudy to mostly clear. Remove from heat before it reaches a boil. Let cool completely. Use as needed in recipes requiring simple syrup. Store in an airtight container in the refrigerator for up to 4 weeks.

# DATE SYRUP

This makes a fantastic refined sugar–free sweetener that can be used in place of sugar or agave in many recipes. I love having a jar of this around to add to smoothies or plain non-dairy yogurt in the mornings.

**20 Medjool dates**
**Water to soak**
**1⅓ cups additional water**

YIELD: 1½ CUPS

- Place the dates into a medium bowl. Cover with water and top with a salad plate. Let soak for 8 hours, drain, and replace the water, and then allow the dates to soak an additional 4 to 6 hours.
- Drain the dates completely and then remove the seeds and tops of the dates. Place into a blender along with 1⅓ cups water and blend until extremely smooth, scraping down the sides often.
- Store in an airtight container in the refrigerator for up to 1 month.

# THE BESTEST NUT BUTTER

Peanuts are the star of the show below, but this method works well with other roasted nuts, which comes in handy with a peanut allergy. Try toasted or raw almonds, cashews, or sunflower seeds instead. Even though nut butters are widely available in pretty much every grocery store in the United States, I think homemade is much tastier, and it's so much cheaper. And, it's easy! So easy, in fact, that you may wonder why you hadn't tried it sooner.

**3 cups dry roasted peanuts,**
**    unsalted (or nuts or seeds**
**    of your choice)**
**1 teaspoon salt, or to taste**
**1 teaspoon vanilla extract**

YIELD: 3 CUPS

- Place the peanuts into a food processor and blend until very smooth, about 7 minutes, scraping down the sides of the bowl as needed. Add the salt and vanilla extract and mix well. Store in an airtight container for up to 3 months.

# APPLE CIDER VINEGAR

Apple cider vinegar is one of those things that is just *so* much better homemade and can be made much cheaper at home than store-bought. All it takes is some apples and a lot of patience (like 2 months), but the end result is well worth the wait. And, don't be afraid of the gelatinous "mother" or the "yeasties" that float in the jar . . . that's what makes the vinegar good! You'll need a 2-gallon glass jar or vessel with a wide mouth, as well as a piece of cheesecloth, about 16 x 16 inches, and a rubber band.

**10 apples, chopped roughly into large chunks: seeds, stems, and all**
**¼ cup sugar**
**Water**

**YIELD: 2 GALLONS**

- Place the apples into the large jar, pushing down gently with a ladle to pack the apples in. You can also use a clean saucer or small dish to weight down the apples inside the vessel. Next add in the sugar and then cover the apples with water so that they are completely submerged. Cover with the cheesecloth and then secure with a rubber band. This keeps the critters out but still allows air to help the process along. Place the jar carefully into a cool dark place for 1 week.
- Strain the apples from the vinegar and replace the cheesecloth. At this point you may transfer it to a different container, or several. Just be sure the containers are totally clean. Cap again with cheesecloth and rubber band and place back into a cool dark place for 6 to 8 more weeks. And that's it! You have the best darned vinegar money doesn't have to buy. You can bottle it and store as you would any bottle of vinegar. Store in an airtight container for 6 months to 1 year and beyond.

To sterilize containers, a good scrubbing with very hot soapy water, a hot rinse, and preferably a run through the dishwasher—complete with dry cycle—works perfectly.

# VANILLA EXTRACT

Although vanilla extract is fairly easy to come by, the stuff made at home is superior in flavor and will last virtually forever. I like to make up a big batch at once and bottle to give away to friends. Dark vanilla extract bottles work well for storing. Simply scrub off the labels and replace them with new!

**5 cups bourbon**
**(vodka works well, too)**
**12 vanilla beans, split**

**YIELD: 5 CUPS**

• Pour 5 cups of bourbon into a clean jar or bottle. Place the vanilla beans into the bottle of bourbon and reseal tightly. Place in cool dark place, such as a pantry, and store for 3 months. After three months, you can either use it straight from the bottle or bottle individually, leaving at least 1 vanilla bean in each bottle. As the bottle becomes empty, replace with more bourbon. After one year, replace the vanilla beans with new. Store in airtight container.

### SWEET FACT

Vanilla beans are the second most expensive spice after saffron because growing and harvesting the beans is incredibly labor intensive.

# SWEET CASHEW CREAM

This recipe makes a fantastic substitute for dairy-based cream cheeses, whipped cream, and more. Store in an airtight container in the refrigerator for up to 2 weeks. Cashew cream can also be frozen and thawed for later use, with little effect on flavor or color. Just thaw in the fridge overnight before using.

**4 cups raw cashews**
**1 cup water**
**1 teaspoon vanilla extract**
**3 tablespoons maple syrup**
    **or agave**
**⅛ teaspoon salt**

**YIELD: 5 CUPS**

- Before making, place the cashews into a large bowl and cover with 1 inch of water. Let soak 2 to 4 hours and then rinse well. Place cashews into a food processor along with the water, vanilla extract, maple syrup, and salt. Blend until smooth, scraping down sides as needed.
- Continue to blend, about 7 minutes, until very smooth and creamy. Use as a topping for a variety of treats as you would whipped cream, or as directed in recipes. Store in an airtight container in the refrigerator up to 1 week.

# MASCARPONE

True mascarpone is a light, dairy-based cream cheese that has an ever-so-slightly sweet taste. In this version, I've used cashews in place of dairy. Feel free to use your own homemade margarine or coconut oil in this mascarpone. This spread can be stirred into your favorite puddings for an extra dose of creamy, or sandwich in between cake layers for a remarkable filling, as I have in the Tiramisu (page 217).

**1 cup raw cashews**
**2 tablespoons nondairy**
    **margarine or coconut oil**
    **(add ¼ teaspoon salt if**
    **coconut oil is used)**
**1 tablespoon nondairy milk**
**1 tablespoon confectioner's**
    **sugar**

**YIELD: 1 CUP**

- Place the cashews in a bowl and cover with 3 cups of water; soak for 6 hours. Drain the cashews and rinse well. Place the soaked cashews into a food processor and blend until pasty, about 2 minutes, scraping down the sides often. Add the margarine, nondairy milk, and confectioner's sugar and blend an additional 5 minutes, again, scraping the sides often, until a fluffy mixture is made. Store in an airtight container in the refrigerator for up to 5 days.

# SWEETENED WHIPPED COCONUT CREAM

This whipped cream could not be easier. Stash a few cans of coconut milk in your fridge so you are ready to rock when the need arises for whipped cream. Also, use the best-quality coconut milk you can, and be sure it's full fat—with this recipe, quality counts.

**1 (13.5-ounce) can full-fat (organic is best) coconut milk**

**1 tablespoon confectioner's sugar, or 1 teaspoon powdered stevia**

**YIELD: 1 CUP**

• Before you attempt to whip your coconut cream, place the can of coconut milk in your refrigerator and chill overnight. Flip the can upside down and open. Drain all liquid from the can (use it in smoothies or recipes that call for nondairy milk) until you are left with just the thick white cream from the can. Place the cream and confectioner's sugar into a sturdy mixing bowl, and using a whisk attachment, whip until fluffy. Use immediately.

*Chapter 2*

# KILLER CAKES AND TOPPINGS

*Cakes are probably* the most iconic celebration foods, being the ultimate centerpiece at birthdays and weddings, but I enjoy baking them "just because" every now and again, too. On the following pages, I tackle all you need to make the perfect cake, whether it be for a small wedding or a simple Sunday brunch.

## CAKE BASICS

### PREPPING AND ICING A LAYER CAKE

*Making Layers Even*

Ever bake a cake and once decorated, find it's a bit "rounder" than you anticipated? I'm here to let you know that it's not you—it's the nature of the cake! Unless cakes have been leveled, if you try and stack them, you'll end up with a fairly uneven mound of cake that slopes on the sides, which, although tasty, isn't the most aesthetically appealing. Baking bands come in handy, and I absolutely recommend them if you're trying to tackle large projects, such as multilayered cakes.

To make perfectly even layers, be sure to divide your batter evenly among pans. Use baking bands (soaked in water and then squeezed) to increase the odds of even baking. Once the cakes have baked, let them cool in the pans for about 30 minutes. After they are slightly cooled, gently slide a knife around the edges of the cake pan to release, and once the cakes have completely cooled, invert each one once onto a plate and then reposition it so that the top of the cake is facing up. Basically, you're flipping both cakes out of the pans and just making sure the bottom is on the bottom and top is on the top.

Use a long serrated knife to slice off just the tops of the cake so that both cake rounds appear very level. Use excess cake for crumbs . . . or just eat it! Now your cake is ready to be decorated!

## CRUMB COAT

The scenario: You bake a fabulous cake and a perfectly complimentary frosting, and you are so excited to show it off to your family and/or friends. But, once frosted, you are devastated to find that you have speckled your entire cake with pebbles of cake crumbs rather than a silky smooth layer of frosting. This is a common problem, friend, and it can be remedied. Crumb coat to the rescue!

### For an Easy Crumb Coat

Use a small portion of your frosting to create a thin layer of frosting—cover each layer without worrying about keeping crumbs out of the icing; that's what this step is for! Crumb it up.

Now, place one of the layers onto a steady cake dish or icing plate.

Be sure to top each layer liberally with frosting and press gently to set the filling in between cakes. Repeat with as many layers as you have. Freeze the cake briefly, about 15 minutes, or until frosting has totally hardened.

Now you're ready for the final coat of frosting! Frost the entire cake again with a thick layer of frosting and garnish with any fancy piping that you can dream up.

Devil's Food Cake, page 38

# DEVIL'S FOOD CAKE

A classic recipe for birthday parties and other celebrations, this version is as close to authentic, in taste and texture anyhow, as you can get. The surprise ingredient is tahini, the sesame seed paste commonly used in savory dishes like hummus.

1¼ cups sorghum flour

¾ cup extra-dark cocoa powder

½ cup potato starch

¼ cup buckwheat flour

¼ cup sweet white rice flour

2 teaspoons xanthan gum

2 teaspoons baking soda

1 teaspoon baking powder

¼ teaspoon salt

½ cup olive oil

1½ cups sugar

2 tablespoons tahini

1 cup extra-strong coffee, cold

1 cup coconut milk

2 tablespoons apple cider vinegar

YIELD: ONE 9 X 13-INCH CAKE OR 12 CUPCAKES

- Preheat oven to 350°F and grease and lightly flour a 9 x 13-inch cake pan or line 12 cupcake tins with paper liners.
- In medium bowl, combine sorghum flour, cocoa powder, potato starch, buckwheat flour, sweet white rice flour, xanthan gum, baking soda, baking powder, and salt. Whisk well to make sure everything is completely combined.
- In large mixing bowl, combine the olive oil, sugar, and tahini. Add one-third of the flour mix and stir until well combined. Mix in the coffee and coconut milk and the remaining flour mixture a little at a time until all has been incorporated. Stir in the vinegar until the batter is smooth and fluffy.
- Spread the cake batter into a prepared cake pan, or drop about ½ cup of batter into each cupcake liner. Bake for 27 to 30 minutes for sheet cake or cupcakes, or until knife inserted into the middle of the cake comes out clean. Let cool completely before frosting. Store covered for up to 3 days.

### SWEET FACT

Devil's food cake used to describe a type of cake that was red rather than the deep dark chocolate version we are used to. It is speculated to have been interchangeable with what is known as "Red Velvet Cake" today. It wasn't until the 1970s that we started seeing the chocolate version take over.

# GERMAN CHOCOLATE CAKE

The name "German Chocolate Cake" is actually a corruption of "German's Chocolate Cake" . . . meaning the "German's" chocolate bar that was named after their creator, Baker's Chocolate Company employee Sam German. Somewhere along the way, this dessert became known as German Chocolate Cake, even though it is quite American. Whatever you call it, it's tender and lighter in color than traditional chocolate cake; this recipe utilizes chocolate pieces rather than cocoa powder to give it that chocolaty flavor. You can also bake these as cupcakes, just reduce the baking time to 25 minutes, or until a knife inserted into the center comes out clean. Let cool and top with recommended icing.

¾ cup nondairy chocolate pieces or chips

¾ cup water, plus 4 tablespoons water

2 tablespoons flaxseed meal

1¼ cups brown rice flour

½ cup teff flour

2 teaspoons xanthan gum

1 cup potato starch

¼ cup tapioca flour

1 teaspoon baking powder

1 teaspoon baking soda

¾ teaspoon salt

1 cup nondairy margarine

1¾ cups sugar

1 teaspoon vanilla extract

½ cup nondairy milk

2 tablespoons apple cider vinegar

**YIELD: 1 CAKE**

- Preheat oven to 350°F. Lightly grease and dust with cocoa powder two 9-inch round cake pans.
- In a small saucepan over medium-low heat, heat the chocolate and ¾ cup water until the chocolate is melted, stirring often. Remove from heat and set aside.
- In a small bowl, combine the flaxseed meal and 4 tablespoons water and let rest for 5 minutes, until gelled.
- In a large bowl, sift together the brown rice flour, teff flour, xanthan gum, potato starch, tapioca flour, baking powder, baking soda, and salt.
- Add the margarine, sugar, vanilla extract, and nondairy milk to the chocolate mixture and stir well to combine. Mix into the flour mixture along with the prepared flaxseed meal. Stir well, at least fifty strokes or 1 minute, and then stir in the vinegar.
- Divide the cake batter evenly between the two cake pans and bake for 25 to 30 minutes, or until knife inserted into the center comes out clean.
- Let cool completely, invert from pan, and then top each layer with German Chocolate Icing (page 76). Store covered for up to 3 days.

# MARBLED CAKE

This gorgeous cake needs no frosting in my opinion, as it offers plenty of sweet, sweet, goodness all by its lonesome. Plus, served undressed is the best way to show off its striking swirls.

¾ **cup white rice flour**
½ **cup brown rice flour**
¾ **cup besan/chickpea flour**
1 **cup potato starch**
1½ **teaspoons xanthan gum**
2½ **teaspoons baking**
   **powder**
1 **teaspoon baking soda**
1 **cup sugar**
1 **teaspoon salt**
¾ **cup olive oil**
2 **cups very cold water**
2 **tablespoons lemon juice**
¼ **cup cocoa powder**

**YIELD: 10 SERVINGS**

When marbling the batter, be sure to go the whole width of the cake to get the deepest variegation of contrast between the yellow and chocolate swirls. And don't overdo it! A little swirl goes a long way, and too much will muddy the pattern.

- Preheat oven to 350°F. Lightly grease an 8 x 8-inch cake pan. In a large bowl, whisk together the rice flours, besan, potato starch, xanthan gum, baking powder, baking soda, sugar, and salt. Add the olive oil, water, and lemon juice and stir well to achieve a very smooth batter.
- Pour about one-third of the batter into a bowl and whisk in the cocoa powder until evenly blended. Spread the yellow cake batter into the prepared baking pan and then drop dollops of the chocolate batter onto the yellow. Use a butter knife to gently swirl the two batters together into a loose and even pattern.
- Bake the cake for 35 to 40 minutes, or until a knife inserted into the middle comes out clean. Let cool before slicing with a serrated knife. Store covered for up to 3 days.

# PINEAPPLE CHERRY UPSIDE-DOWN CAKE

This cake is a standard in our house on my husband's birthday, as he always requests this over a traditional birthday cake. And, I admit, I'm a pretty big fan of it myself. It definitely increases the appeal that the cake makes its own icing!

⅔ cup cold nondairy margarine

¾ cup sugar

1 teaspoon vanilla extract

⅓ cup tapioca flour

½ teaspoon sea salt

1 teaspoon xanthan gum

3 teaspoons baking powder

¼ cup agave

2 cups besan/chickpea flour

1 cup pineapple juice

½ cup nondairy milk (unsweetened)

4 tablespoons softened margarine

½ cup brown sugar

7 pineapple rings, canned or fresh

7 maraschino cherries

**YIELD: 8 SERVINGS**

If you don't want to use traditional maraschino cherries, fresh will work, too. I recommend soaking them in cherry juice or rum (yum!) for an hour and draining well before using.

- Preheat oven to 350°F and lightly grease the sides of an 8-inch springform pan.
- In a large mixing bowl, cream together the ⅔ cup margarine and sugar until fluffy. Mix in the vanilla extract, tapioca flour, sea salt, xanthan gum, baking powder, and agave until blended. Add the besan a little bit at a time, alternating with the pineapple juice, until all of each has been added. Whisk in the nondairy milk and mix until the cake batter is very smooth, at least fifty strokes. If you are using an electric mixer, let it run on medium for about 1 minute. (The batter will taste unpleasant due to the raw chickpea flour!)
- Spread the additional 4 tablespoons margarine onto the bottom of the springform pan, covering completely. Evenly sprinkle on the brown sugar and arrange the pineapple slices to fit snugly onto the bottom of the springform pan. Place the maraschino cherries into the holes of the pineapple rings for a pop of color. Spread the cake batter gently over the pineapples and place onto the middle oven rack with a large baking pan placed underneath to catch any drips.
- Bake for about 50 to 55 minutes, or until a knife inserted into the middle comes out clean. The edges will be very dark brown, but the middle should be bright and golden. Let the cake cool in the pan for 20 to 30 minutes before releasing the springform and inverting the cake onto a plate. Serve warm or room temperature. Store covered for up to 3 days.

# OLIVE OIL CAKE

This moist and dense cake is a classic Italian American dessert and features the flowery undertones of olive oil rather than coconut oil or margarine. Serve after a delicious plate of pasta and hearty salad, along with a scoop of gelato.

1 cup superfine brown
   rice flour
½ cup potato starch
¼ cup tapioca flour
1 teaspoon xanthan gum
1 teaspoon salt
2 teaspoons baking powder
1 cup sugar
3 tablespoons lemon juice
¾ cup olive oil
½ cup + 2 tablespoons
   nondairy milk
Powdered sugar, for dusting

**YIELD: 1 CAKE, ABOUT
8 SERVINGS**

- Preheat oven to 350°F. Lightly grease and (brown rice) flour an 8-inch round cake pan.
- In a large bowl, whisk together the superfine brown rice flour, potato starch, tapioca flour, xanthan gum, salt, baking powder, and sugar. Add in the lemon juice, olive oil, and nondairy milk and whisk until very smooth. Spread the batter into the prepared cake pan and bake for 40 minutes, or until lightly golden brown on edges and a knife inserted into the center comes out clean. Let cool before dusting lightly with powdered sugar and cut using a serrated knife. Store covered for up to 3 days.

# BANANA CAKE

If you love bananas, you'll adore this cake. I especially enjoy it paired with a Fluffy Chocolate Frosting (page 75) or Dark Chocolate Ganache (page 79).

**3 large very ripe bananas
(peels should be brown)**
**⅔ cup olive oil**
**1 cup sugar**
**⅓ cup brown sugar**
**1 teaspoon vanilla extract**
**1 teaspoon salt**
**1½ cups brown rice flour**
**¾ cup potato starch**
**⅓ cup tapioca flour**
**1 teaspoon xanthan gum**
**2 teaspoons baking powder**
**2 teaspoons baking soda**
**½ cup plain nondairy yogurt**
**3 tablespoons apple cider
vinegar**

**YIELD: ONE 2-LAYER CAKE**

- Preheat oven to 350°F and lightly grease and (brown rice) flour two 8-inch round baking pans.
- In a large bowl, mix up the bananas until they are well mashed. Beat in the olive oil, sugars, and vanilla extract until smooth. Gradually add in the rest of the ingredients, mixing well after each addition. Spread batter between the two prepared baking pans and bake on the center rack for about 30 to 35 minutes, or until a knife inserted into the center comes out clean. Let cool in pans for about 15 minutes, then gently run a knife around the edges of the pans to release. Invert the cakes onto a wire cooling rack and allow to cool completely before frosting. Once cooled, follow the directions for Prepping and Icing a Layer Cake (page 35). Simply cover the tops of one cake with frosting, sandwich with another cake, and top the second layer with frosting. Store in airtight container or cake dish for up to 3 days.

This recipe also makes a delicious sheet cake. Simply grease and lightly flour a 9 x 13-inch pan, spread the prepared batter evenly, and bake for 30 to 35 minutes, or until a knife inserted into the middle comes out clean.

### SWEET FACT

A bunch of bananas is called a "hand" of bananas and a single banana is called a finger.

# BOURBON CARAMEL CUPCAKES

Bourbon is one of my absolute favorite flavors because it pairs so perfectly with my other favorite flavors, vanilla and brown sugar. These bad boys tout all three flavors and make one heck of a fancy addition to a dessert tray. Not so keen on bourbon? You can replace it with apple cider or nondairy milk.

1¼ cups superfine brown rice flour
¾ cup sorghum flour
¾ cup potato starch
¼ cup sweet white rice flour
1½ teaspoons xanthan gum
2 teaspoons baking powder
1 teaspoon baking soda
1 teaspoon salt
¾ cup olive oil
1 cup brown sugar
⅓ cup sugar
2 tablespoons molasses
2 teaspoons vanilla extract
1 tablespoon ground chia seed mixed with ¼ cup water
½ cup bourbon
1 cup ice-cold water

YIELD: 12 CUPCAKES

- Preheat oven to 350°F. Line 12 muffin tins with paper liners.
- In a medium bowl, whisk together the brown rice flour, sorghum flour, potato starch, sweet white rice flour, xanthan gum, baking powder, baking soda, and salt.
- In a separate, larger bowl, combine the olive oil, sugars, molasses, 1 teaspoon of the vanilla extract, and chia mixture. Add a little bit of the flour mixture, the bourbon, and a little bit of the cold water plus the remaining teaspoon of vanilla extract and mix until smooth. Repeat with the flour mixture and the water until all of each has been incorporated completely. Mix the batter on high speed for 1 minute using an electric mixer, or about fifty strokes by hand.
- Drop ⅓ cup of batter into each prepared cupcake tin and bake for 25 to 30 minutes, or until a knife inserted into the middle comes out clean. Let cool completely before frosting with Caramel Frosting (page 76). Store covered for up to 2 days.

# CLASSIC YELLOW CUPCAKES

Perfect for birthday parties, especially when paired with Fluffy Chocolate Frosting (page 75) for a classic combo.

¾ cup white rice flour
½ cup brown rice flour
¾ cup besan/chickpea flour
¼ cup sweet white rice flour
¾ cup potato starch
1½ teaspoons xanthan gum
3 teaspoons baking powder
1 teaspoon baking soda
1 teaspoon vanilla
¾ cup melted nondairy
    margarine
1¼ cups sugar
1¼ cups canned coconut milk
1 cup water
2½ tablespoons apple cider
    vinegar

**YIELD: 24 CUPCAKES**

- Preheat oven to 350°F. Line 24 muffin tins with paper liners, or lightly grease and (brown rice) flour the individual cups.
- In a large bowl, whisk together the white rice flour, brown rice flour, besan, sweet white rice flour, potato starch, xanthan gum, baking powder, and baking soda. Gradually stir in the rest of the ingredients, as they are ordered, and whisk until very smooth. Drop a little less than ⅓ cup batter into the prepared baking trays and bake for about 27 minutes, or until knife inserted into the center comes out clean. Remove cupcakes from the pan and let them cool completely on a rack before frosting. Store covered in airtight container for up to 2 days.

This recipe can also be used to make a sheet cake; bake about 10 to 15 minutes longer, just until a knife inserted into the middle comes out clean.

# BOSTON CREAM PIE CUPCAKES

This tender sponge cake with a tangy filling and topped with ganache is a tribute to the classic dessert Boston Cream Pie. In my opinion, the tangy cream filling is the best part—which comes from the unlikely addition of mayo!

## CAKE

1⅓ cups superfine brown rice flour
¼ cup sweet white rice flour
¾ cup potato starch
⅔ cup besan/chickpea flour
2 teaspoons xanthan gum
3 teaspoons baking powder
1 teaspoon baking soda
1 teaspoon salt
1½ cups packed brown sugar
¾ cup olive oil
1 cup coconut milk
1¼ cups very cold water
2½ tablespoons lemon juice

## FILLING

⅓ cup nondairy margarine
2 cups confectioner's sugar
1 tablespoon nondairy milk
1 tablespoon lemon juice
1 tablespoon nondairy mayonnaise, such as Vegenaise
½ teaspoon xanthan gum

## TOPPING

1 recipe Dark Chocolate Ganache (page 79)

**YIELD: 12 CUPCAKES**

- Preheat oven to 350°F. Line a cupcake pan with 12 paper liners, or lightly grease and (brown rice) flour the individual cups.
- In a large mixing bowl, whisk together the brown rice flour, sweet white rice flour, potato starch, besan, xanthan gum, baking powder, baking soda, and salt.
- In the bowl of electric mixer, cream together the brown sugar, olive oil, and coconut milk. Gently add in the flour mixture, alternating with the water. Add the lemon juice and mix on high speed for about 1 to 2 minutes. Divide batter among the 12 muffin tins and bake for 35 minutes, or until puffed up high and golden brown, and knife inserted into center comes out clean. Let the cupcakes cool completely before filling and topping.
- To make the filling, combine all the ingredients using an electric mixer with a whisk attachment and whip until fluffy. Using a serrated knife, cut off tops of cupcakes just above the papers. Add about 2 tablespoons of filling and replace the top. Place cupcakes in the freezer on a flat surface a few minutes before topping with Dark Chocolate Ganache (page 79). Store loosely covered cupcakes in the refrigerator for up to 1 week.

You can easily make this into a traditional Boston Cream Pie by doubling the recipe and baking for about 30 minutes in two round cake pans, using the same knife test for doneness.

# CAPPUCCINO CUPCAKES

Let these cupcakes transport you to your favorite café with notes of deep dark espresso. The tender moist cake is a perfect complement to the recommended topping of the lighter-than-air Mocha Fluff frosting.

**1 cup besan/chickpea flour**
**½ cup white rice flour**
**⅓ cup potato starch**
**¼ cup tapioca flour**
**1½ teaspoons baking powder**
**1 teaspoon salt**
**1 teaspoon xanthan gum**
**½ cup brown sugar**
**⅔ cup sugar**
**⅓ cup olive oil**
**3 teaspoons instant espresso powder**
**1½ cups water**
**1 tablespoon apple cider vinegar**

**YIELD: 12 CUPCAKES**

- Preheat oven to 350°F and line 12 muffin tins with paper liners, or lightly spray with oil.
- In a large bowl, whisk together the besan, white rice flour, potato starch, tapioca flour, baking powder, salt, xanthan gum, and sugars. Make a well in the center of the flour mixture and add in the olive oil, espresso powder, water, and vinegar. Stir to mix well until batter is smooth. Fill cups about two-thirds full. Bake for 25 to 30 minutes, or until knife inserted into the center of one of the cupcakes comes out clean. Let the cupcakes cool completely on a rack before frosting. Store covered for up to 2 days.
- Top with Mocha-Fluff Frosting (page 77).

# TUBE AND BUNDT CAKES

# APPLE CAKE

Apple Cake is perfect to bake when you want to "wow" without a lot of fuss. This cake is extra moist and flavorful with the addition of fresh apples. The secret is to slice the apples thinly and evenly. You don't want them too thin, but about ¼ x 1 x 1 inch is just right.

¾ cup brown rice flour
¾ cup besan/chickpea flour
½ cup potato starch
1 teaspoon xanthan gum
1 teaspoon baking powder
1 teaspoon baking soda
2 teaspoons cinnamon
¾ cup melted nondairy
    margarine
1 cup sugar
½ cup brown sugar
1 teaspoon vanilla extract
1 cup nondairy milk
1 tablespoon olive oil
4 apples, peeled, quartered,
    and sliced into thin pieces

**YIELD: 1 CAKE**

- Preheat oven to 350°F. Lightly grease a standard-size non-stick tube pan.
- In a medium bowl, whisk together the brown rice flour, besan, potato starch, xanthan gum, baking powder, baking soda, and cinnamon.
- Make a well in the center and add the rest of the ingredients except the apples, stirring well after all has been added. Mix well, about fifty strokes. Fold in the apples until completely incorporated. Spread the cake batter into the prepared pan and bake for 65 to 70 minutes, or until a knife inserted into the center comes out clean. If using a different sized pan, check for doneness around the 40-minute mark by using the knife test.
- Let cool for 1 hour, and then run a knife around the outside and inside of the cake to loosen. Flip over onto a wire rack.
- Dust with confectioner's sugar just before serving. Store covered up to 2 days.

This cake is so chock-full of apples that they become a big part of the cake's structure. Be sure to let your cake cool completely before cutting, or you may have an apple cake avalanche!

# LEMON CAKE

Lemons always seem to put me in a good mood, and they dominate this cake. The tartness of the citrus in this cake pairs gorgeously with the airy texture. I recommend topping with Lemon Glaze or a simple dusting of confectioner's sugar.

1 cup nonhydrogenated
    shortening
1½ cups sugar
⅓ cup + 1 tablespoon
    lemon juice
1 tablespoon lemon zest
1 cup besan/chickpea flour
⅓ cup brown rice flour
½ cup potato starch
½ cup tapioca flour
1 teaspoon xanthan gum
1 teaspoon salt
½ teaspoon baking powder
½ teaspoon baking soda
1 cup nondairy milk

**YIELD: 1 BUNDT CAKE**

- Lightly grease a standard-size Bundt cake pan or two 8-inch round cake pans. Flour very lightly using white rice flour. Preheat oven to 350°F.
- In a large bowl of a stand mixer, combine the shortening, sugar, and lemon juice and mix until smooth and fluffy. Add in the lemon zest.
- In a separate bowl, whisk together the besan through the baking soda and then add the flour mixture into the sugar mixture along with the nondairy milk. Mix on low just until blended and then up the speed to high and mix for about 1 minute. The batter should be soft and fluffy.
- Spread the batter evenly into your prepared Bundt cake pan and bake on the center rack for 40 to 50 minutes, or until a knife inserted into the center comes out clean. Let cool for 1 hour and then run a knife around the outside and inside of the cake to loosen. Flip over onto a wire rack and let cool further. Top with Lemon Glaze (page 78). Store covered for up to 2 days.

# CARROT APPLESAUCE CAKE

This cake is delightfully fragrant and tender with the comforting flavor of apples and a lovely subtle color from the carrots. Use any type of sugar you'd like. I love the standard evaporated cane juice . . . but light brown or coconut palm sugar would bake up nicely, too.

½ cup buckwheat flour
¾ cup sorghum flour
¾ cup potato starch
1 teaspoon xanthan gum
½ teaspoon sea salt
½ teaspoon baking powder
1½ teaspoons baking soda
1 teaspoon cinnamon
1¼ cups sugar
½ cup olive oil
1 cup applesauce
   (unsweetened)
2 tablespoons lemon juice
2 medium carrots, shredded

**YIELD: 1 BUNDT CAKE**

- Preheat oven to 350°F. Lightly grease and (sorghum) flour a standard-size tube or Bundt pan.
- In a large mixing bowl, whisk together the buckwheat flour, sorghum flour, potato starch, xanthan gum, sea salt, baking powder, baking soda, cinnamon, and sugar.
- Stir in the olive oil, applesauce, and lemon juice until well mixed and a thick batter has formed. Fold in the shredded carrots and evenly spread the batter into the prepared cake pan.
- Bake on the center rack for 40 to 45 minutes, or until a knife inserted into the center comes out clean. Let cool for 20 minutes before gently running a knife around the edge and inverting onto a flat serving dish. Store covered for up to 2 days.

# HUMMINGBIRD BUNDT CAKE

A popular treat from the South, which is theorized to have originated in Jamaica, this cake was also widely known at one time as "The Cake That Doesn't Last." A fun play on the traditional Southern classic, this dessert takes the cake with all its scrumptious add-ins like pineapple, banana, and walnuts.

1¼ cups brown rice flour
¾ cup besan/chickpea flour
1 cup potato starch
1 teaspoon xanthan gum
2½ teaspoons baking powder
1 teaspoon baking soda
½ teaspoon salt
½ cup melted nondairy margarine
1 teaspoon cinnamon
1 cup sugar
3 very ripe bananas, mashed
1 cup pineapple juice
½ cup water
1 teaspoon vanilla extract
1⅓ cups small pineapple chunks
1 cup crushed pecans
Cream Cheese Frosting, glaze variation (page 75)

YIELD: 1 BUNDT CAKE

- Lightly grease a standard-size Bundt pan.
- In a large bowl, whisk together the brown rice flour, besan, potato starch, xanthan gum, baking powder, baking soda, and salt. Stir in the margarine, cinnamon, sugar, bananas, pineapple juice, water, and vanilla extract and mix well using a whisk until smooth. Fold in the pineapple chunks. Sprinkle the pecans into the Bundt cake pan and pour the batter over the pecans. Bake for 70 minutes, or until a knife inserted into the cake comes out clean. Let cool in the pan for 20 minutes and invert onto a rack to cool completely. Store covered in the refrigerator for up to 3 days.
- Top with Cream Cheese Frosting, glaze variation (page 75).

# RUM CAKE

This is a gem of a cake that my mother made often when I was a child, and that I didn't appreciate until I was a full-fledged adult. But that could just be the rum talking—I kid, this cake is delicious. Although my mom's original recipe isn't gluten-free or vegan, I can assure you that this version is just as incredible.

## CAKE
¾ cup white rice flour
½ cup brown rice flour
¾ cup besan/chickpea flour
1 cup potato starch
1½ teaspoons xanthan gum
2½ teaspoons baking powder
1 teaspoon baking soda
1 cup sugar
1 teaspoon salt
½ cup rum
1½ cups water
½ cup olive oil
3 tablespoons lime juice
1 cup chopped pecans or walnuts

## RUM SAUCE
½ cup nondairy margarine
½ cup rum
½ cup water
1 cup sugar

**YIELD: 10 SERVINGS**

- Preheat oven to 325°F and lightly grease a standard-size Bundt cake pan. In a large bowl, whisk together the flours, potato starch, xanthan gum, baking powder, baking soda, sugar, and salt.
- Make a well in the center of the flour mixture and add the rum, water, olive oil, and lime juice. Stir well until batter is very smooth. Sprinkle the chopped nuts onto the bottom of the Bundt cake pan and then spoon the batter on top of the nuts. Bake for 60 to 65 minutes on the middle rack of the oven, until risen and golden brown. Once the cake has finished baking, keep it in the pan while you make the rum sauce.
- For the sauce, in a small saucepan, combine the margarine, rum, water, and sugar. Bring the mixture to a boil over medium heat, stirring often. Boil for 5 minutes and then gingerly drizzle the sauce onto the top of the cake while it is still sitting snugly in the pan. Let the cake rest for 45 minutes to 1 hour and then very carefully invert the cake onto a flat plate. Serve at room temperature. Store covered for up to 2 days.

Be sure to let this cake cool completely before handling, as it is very fragile while still warm.

Classic Banana Bread, page 60

# LOAF CAKES AND BREADS

# CLASSIC BANANA BREAD

Banana bread has been a staple in my recipe repertoire ever since I first moved out onto my own in college. The first time I made it, I didn't know *exactly* what I was doing, but I knew I had a hankering for banana bread. Luckily, I had enough baking knowledge under my belt to come up with a fantastic banana bread that my friends (and even professor!) raved about. This is a version of that cake, minus the gluten and eggs. This banana bread pairs awfully well with a cup of crushed walnuts or pecans, so toss a few in the batter right before it hits the pan if you like your loaves a little nutty.

½ **tablespoon ground chia seed**

2 **tablespoons water**

¾ **cup sugar**

2 **teaspoons bourbon or vanilla extract**

4 **very ripe medium bananas (skins should be mostly brown)**

1 **cup superfine brown rice flour**

½ **cup sorghum flour**

½ **cup cornstarch**

¼ **cup tapioca flour**

1 **teaspoon xanthan gum**

1 **teaspoon salt**

1 **teaspoon baking powder**

1 **teaspoon baking soda**

**YIELD: 1 LOAF**

- Preheat oven to 350°F and lightly grease a standard-size loaf pan with margarine or refined coconut oil.
- In a small bowl, mix together the chia seed with the water and let rest for 5 minutes until gelled.
- In a large bowl, use a potato masher to blend together the prepared chia "egg," sugar, bourbon, and bananas until smooth. Large lumps of banana aren't so good; small lumps are encouraged.
- In a separate smaller bowl, whisk together the remaining dry ingredients until blended. Gradually stir into the banana mixture until it comes together into a thick batter.
- Gently spoon the batter evenly into the prepared loaf pan and bake on the middle rack for 60 minutes, or until a knife inserted into the center comes out clean. Once baked, allow to cool for 10 minutes and then run a knife along the edges of the pan to loosen. Transfer to a wire rack to cool completely. Store covered in airtight container for up to 2 days.

# VANILLA BEAN POUND CAKE

Delightfully moist and simple, this cake is fantastic on its own and makes a lovely base for mix-ins, such as ½ cup of sliced almonds, dried berries, or chocolate chips.

1 cup sorghum flour
1 cup besan/chickpea flour
¼ cup tapioca flour
½ cup potato starch
2 teaspoons xanthan gum
2½ teaspoons baking
    powder
½ teaspoon salt
2 tablespoons melted
    coconut oil
1 tablespoon nondairy milk
¼ cup orange juice
2 cups granulated sugar
1 teaspoon vanilla extract
2 teaspoons ground chia
    seed mixed with
    2 tablespoons water
2 tablespoons apple cider
    vinegar
1 teaspoon scraped vanilla
    bean (scraped from inside
    the pod)

YIELD: 1 LOAF

- Preheat oven to 350°F and grease and lightly flour a standard-size metal loaf pan.
- In a large mixing bowl, whisk together the flours, potato starch, xanthan gum, baking powder, and salt until well blended. Add the rest of the ingredients and mix well until a thin, uniform batter forms. Pour it into the prepared loaf pan and bake for 50 minutes, undisturbed. Once finished cooking, turn the oven off, gently open the oven door a crack, and allow the cake to rest in the oven for an additional 45 minutes. Remove from the oven and cool completely before cutting with a serrated knife. Store covered for up to 2 days.

# CHOCOLATE CHIP PUMPKIN BREAD

A fun twist on an old favorite, chocolate chips add an extra touch of sweetness to this moist pumpkin bread. For an extra indulgent treat, use this as the bread base for the Bread Pudding recipe on page 219.

2 tablespoons flaxseed meal
4 tablespoons water
½ cup nondairy margarine
1½ cups sugar
1 cup canned pumpkin puree
¾ cup sorghum flour
⅓ cup buckwheat flour
⅓ cup potato starch
¼ cup sweet white rice flour
1 teaspoon xanthan gum
½ tablespoon baking powder
¾ teaspoon baking soda
⅛ teaspoon salt
1 cup nondairy chocolate
   chips

**YIELD: 1 LOAF**

- Preheat oven to 350°F. In a small bowl, combine the flaxseed meal and water and let rest for 5 minutes, until gelled. Lightly grease and (sorghum) flour a standard-size glass loaf pan.
- In large mixing bowl, cream the margarine with the sugar and then incorporate the pumpkin. Stir in the prepared flaxseed meal.
- In a separate smaller bowl, whisk together the sorghum flour, buckwheat flour, potato starch, sweet rice flour, xanthan gum, baking powder, baking soda, and salt.
- Gradually incorporate the flour mixture into the pumpkin mixture and then mix well until a thick batter forms. Fold in the chocolate chips and spread into the prepared loaf pan.
- Bake in preheated oven for 70 to 75 minutes, or until a knife inserted into the center comes out clean. Store covered in airtight container for up to 2 days.

# CINNAMON RAISIN BREAD

This fragrant bread is a lovely addition to a tea party, with sweet cinnamon and plump raisins dotted throughout. This bread is exceptionally good toasted and slathered with Raspberry Chia Jam (page 294).

**1 tablespoon active dry yeast**
**¼ cup sugar**
**1½ cups warm water, about 105°F**
**3 tablespoons coconut oil**
**1¼ cups buckwheat flour**
**¾ cup sorghum flour**
**2 teaspoons cinnamon**
**1 cup potato starch**
**½ cup tapioca flour**
**2 teaspoons xanthan gum**
**1 teaspoon salt**
**1½ cups raisins**
**¼ cup turbinado sugar**

**YIELD: 1 LOAF**

- Preheat oven to 450°F. Grease a standard-size loaf pan with olive oil.
- In a large bowl, combine the yeast with the sugar and water; proof until foamy, for about 5 minutes. Add the coconut oil.
- In a separate bowl, whisk together the buckwheat flour, sorghum flour, cinnamon, potato starch, tapioca flour, xanthan gum, and salt. Mix the dry ingredients in with the wet ingredients and stir just until blended. Fold in the raisins.
- Pat the dough evenly into the greased loaf pan. Lightly cover with a kitchen towel and allow to rest in a warm place for 1 hour. Sprinkle the top of the bread with the turbinado sugar. Bake the bread for 15 minutes, then reduce heat to 375°F and bake for an additional 30 to 35 minutes, or until the loaf sounds hollow when tapped.
- Let cool for 15 minutes and then remove from pan. Let cool completely before slicing with a serrated knife. Store covered in airtight container for up to 2 days.

# OTHER CAKE TREATS

# PUMPKIN ROLL

This pumpkin roll freezes exceptionally well, allowing you to just take off a bit when a craving strikes and reserve an emergency stash for later. It's my go-to treat for a late night, early autumn sweet fix.

**3 tablespoons flaxseed meal**
**6 tablespoons water**
**⅓ cup sorghum flour**
**2 tablespoons brown**
**    rice flour**
**1 tablespoon potato starch**
**¼ cup tapioca flour**
**1 teaspoon xanthan gum**
**1 teaspoon salt**
**1 teaspoon baking soda**
**1 cup sugar**
**½ teaspoon cinnamon**
**¼ teaspoon cloves**
**¼ teaspoon nutmeg**
**1 cup canned pumpkin puree**
**1 teaspoon lemon juice**
**1 recipe Cream Cheese**
**    Frosting (page 75)**

**YIELD: 8 SERVINGS**

- Preheat oven to 375°F. Line a jelly roll pan with a large silicone baking mat or two sheets of parchment paper. Spray lightly with nonstick oil spray, such as PAM.
- Prepare your flaxseed "egg" mixture by mixing the flaxseed meal with the water and allowing it to rest for at least 5 minutes, or until thick.
- In a large bowl, whisk together all the dry ingredients and then add the pumpkin puree, lemon juice, and prepared flaxseed meal. Stir just until smooth and evenly mixed. Spread the mixture evenly into a rectangular shape on your prepared cookie sheet, about ½ inch thick. Bake for 14 minutes in preheated oven. Let cool for about 5 minutes, and then carefully flip out onto a large piece of plastic wrap on a flat surface. Sprinkle lightly to coat with confectioner's sugar and then place a clean tea towel on top of the cake (or, coat one side of the towel with confectioner's sugar and place sugar side down onto the cake). Roll up lengthwise, tea towel and all, and allow to cool about 20 minutes in a cool place (an open window during fall is perfect for this). Don't let it stay in the towel too long, or it may stick.
- Unroll the slightly cooled roll, and carefully remove the towel. Spread the icing in the middle of the cake and immediately reroll back up lengthwise. Dust with confectioner's sugar. Refrigerate for at least 2 to 3 hours before serving. Store covered in airtight container in refrigerator for up to 1 week, or freeze for up to 3 months.

This recipe is best made on a dry day. Humid or rainy weather can cause the dough to become sticky.

# STRABERRY SHORTCAKE

Nothing says summertime like the taste of sweetened strawberries atop a delicate shortcake. Don't forget the whipped coconut cream! Feel free to adjust the amount of sugar depending on the natural sweetness of your berries. Use more or less sugar as needed.

## SHORTCAKES

1½ cups superfine brown
    rice flour
¼ cup cornstarch
¼ cup tapioca flour
1 teaspoon xanthan gum
2½ teaspoons baking
    powder
⅓ cup sugar
½ cup cold nondairy
    margarine, cut into
    small pieces
½ cup nondairy milk
1 tablespoon flaxseed meal
2 tablespoons water

## STRAWBERRY MIX

3 cups strawberries
½ cup sugar

YIELD: 8 SHORTCAKES

- Preheat oven to 400°F. Line a large baking sheet with parchment paper or a silicone mat. In a large bowl, whisk together the brown rice flour, cornstarch, tapioca flour, xanthan gum, baking powder, and sugar. Use your fingers to crumble in the margarine until the mixture is pebbly. Add the nondairy milk. Mix the flaxseed meal with the water and then stir into the mixture. Knead lightly to form a very soft dough. Roll dough between two sheets of parchment until half an inch thick and using a biscuit cutter, cut into 2-inch rounds. Place 2 inches apart and bake for 17 to 20 minutes, or until lightly golden brown on edges.
- Rinse and slice the strawberries and discard the greens or reserve for another use, such as smoothies or salad greens. Place the strawberries into a bowl and toss with sugar. Cover and let rest for 1 hour. Serve with shortcakes and Sweetened Whipped Coconut Cream (page 33) with proportions of each to suit your fancy.
- Store cakes separately in airtight container for up to 2 days.

# PETITS FOURS

These take a little finesse and time to put together, but the end result is so fun, you'll want to do it all over again! These are an especially good choice to bring along to potlucks, or to serve at a dinner party, a la mode with a little Matcha Cashew Ice Cream (page 191), perhaps?

## CAKE
2 cups sugar
1½ cups olive oil
3 teaspoons vanilla extract
1 teaspoon salt
2 teaspoons baking powder
1¾ cups sorghum flour
¼ cup besan/chickpea flour
½ cup tapioca flour
½ cup potato starch
2 teaspoons xanthan gum
1 cup nondairy milk
2 tablespoons vinegar
3 tablespoons lemon juice

## FILLING
½ cup raspberry preserves
8 ounces Marzipan
    (page 252)

## GLAZE
1 recipe Lemon Glaze
    (page 78) or
    Vanilla Glaze (page 77)
2 ounces nondairy chocolate,
    melted, for drizzling

YIELD: 24 CAKES

- Preheat oven to 350°F. Grease and (sorghum) flour a 9 x 13-inch baking pan.
- In a large mixing bowl, combine the sugar, olive oil, vanilla extract, and salt and mix until smooth. In a separate bowl, whisk together the baking powder, sorghum flour, besan, tapioca flour, potato starch, and xanthan gum. Add about 1 cup of the flour mixture to the sugar mixture and mix well, and then stir in the nondairy milk. Blend in the remainder of the flour mix and mix well, for about 1 minute or fifty-five strokes. Stir in the vinegar and lemon juice. Spread evenly into prepared baking pan.
- Bake at 350°F for 40 to 45 minutes, undisturbed, until knife inserted in middle comes out clean. Let cool for about 30 minutes and gently run a knife around the edge to release. Flip over onto a wire rack and let cool completely, for at least 2 hours.
- Once cake is cool, cut into 1 x 1-inch squares. Cut the squares in half, and then spread a bit of preserves (about ½ teaspoon) onto one of the cakes, and top with another cake to form a sandwich. Repeat until all cakes have been cut and sandwiched together.
- Place the marzipan in between two sheets of parchment paper and roll as thinly as possible without tearing the marzipan. Cut evenly into 1 x 1-inch squares and place one small square on top of the sandwiched cakes until all have been covered.
- Prepare the glaze and immediately dip the cakes into the glaze, one by one, and then place them onto a wire rack with a large cookie sheet underneath. Let the cakes harden briefly and then repeat with another layer. Drizzle with melted chocolate and let rest for at least 1½ hours, or until firm. Store covered in airtight container for up to 2 days.

# CHERRY BOMBS

I adore these little desserts. Crispy, fluffy, chewy cake is topped with caramelized cherries that deliver an explosion of flavor.

1½ teaspoons nondairy margarine or coconut oil

6 tablespoons turbinado sugar

2 cups whole sweet cherries, pitted, stems removed

½ cup besan/chickpea flour

¼ cup superfine brown rice flour

¼ cup potato starch

1 teaspoon baking powder

½ teaspoon xanthan gum

½ cup sugar

½ teaspoon salt

⅔ cup nondairy milk

¼ cup olive oil

2 tablespoons lime juice

**YIELD: 6 CAKES**

When choosing cherries, seek out plump and brightly colored fruits. Avoid any fruit that is bruised or damaged, as the bruised fruit tends to make the good fruit go bad quickly.

- Preheat oven to 350°F and liberally grease a 6-count large muffin tin with the margarine, leaving about ¼ teaspoon spread evenly onto the bottom of the cups. Sprinkle the turbinado sugar into the muffin tin, 1 tablespoon evenly into each cup. Arrange the cherries to fit snugly into the bottoms of the tins, about six cherries per cup, pitted sides facing up.
- In a medium bowl, whisk together the besan, brown rice flour, potato starch, baking powder, xanthan gum, sugar, and salt. Stir in the nondairy milk, olive oil, and lime juice and beat until fluffy, about fifty strokes or 1 minute.
- Divide the batter evenly among the 6 cups and bake for 40 to 45 minutes, until golden brown on tops and baked through. Let cool for 5 minutes, and then gently scoop the cakes out with a large spoon, inverting onto a serving dish. Store covered in refrigerator for up to 2 days.

# CHOCOLATE WHOOPIE PIES

A treat whose roots are from Maine, whoopie pies have grown increasingly popular over the years. They live somewhere in between a cake and a cookie and are traditionally stuffed with a fluffy frosting, but fill them with whatever you please, such as ganache or even a decadent jam.

## PIES
1¼ cups brown rice flour
½ cup potato starch
¼ cup tapioca flour
⅓ cup cocoa powder
1 teaspoon xanthan gum
1 teaspoon baking soda
1 cup sugar
2 tablespoons flaxseed meal
4 tablespoons water
½ cup nondairy margarine, melted
¾ cup nondairy milk

## FILLING
1 recipe Fluffy Bakery-Style Frosting (page 74)

YIELD: 12 PIES

- Preheat oven to 350°F. Line a cookie sheet with a silicone baking mat or lightly grease.
- In a large bowl, whisk together all of the ingredients up until the flaxseed meal.
- In a small bowl, mix the flaxseed meal with the water and let rest for 5 minutes to form a gel.
- Mix in the prepared flaxseed, melted margarine, and nondairy milk and mix well to form a foamy batter.
- Drop by evenly rounded tablespoons onto the cookie sheet about 2 inches apart. Bake for 11 minutes and let cool completely before carefully removing from the cookie sheet. Once cookies are cooled, spread 2 tablespoons Fluffy Bakery-Style Frosting onto one of the cookies and then gently press another cookie on top and gently smoosh to combine. Repeat until all cakes have been assembled. Store covered in airtight container for up to 3 days.

A tasty berry-ation: Add a couple tablespoons Strawberry Preserves (page 229) into the fluffy frosting to make Strawberry Chocolate Whoopie Pies.

Marshmallow Fondant, page 72

# TOPPINGS: FROSTINGS, GLAZES, AND SAUCES

# MARSHMALLOW FONDANT

Fondant is one of those wonderful things that can help transform a cake from "meh" to "marvelous!" It is easy to use and can be made into multiple colors. You can also use fondant to make cute cutout shapes to paste onto your cake. Once you've covered your cake, roll out a thin layer and then cut out using cookie cutter—see Rolling Fondant (page 73). Lightly brush one side with water and paste it to the cake.

1 bag (10 ounces) vegan marshmallows, such as Dandies
¼ cup warm water
1 teaspoon vanilla extract (optional)
½ tablespoon refined coconut oil, plus ¼ cup for kneading and greasing
2 to 3 drops food coloring (optional)
1½ cups confectioner's sugar + about ½ cup extra for kneading

**YIELD: COVERS ONE 2-LAYER CAKE**

- Thoroughly grease a silicone spatula and mixing bowl.
- Place the marshmallows into a medium saucepan and heat over medium-low heat until sticky, for about 5 minutes, stirring often. Add the water, vanilla extract, ½ tablespoon coconut oil, and food coloring, if desired. Continue to cook over medium-low heat until completely smooth, for about 7 minutes, stirring often with the greased silicone spatula.
- Transfer to a very well greased mixing bowl. Carefully beat in 1½ cups confectioner's sugar until tacky. There most likely will be confectioner's sugar remaining in the bottom of the bowl. It's okay, just leave it.
- Using greased hands, remove from the bowl and knead in about ½ tablespoon coconut oil and more confectioner's sugar until the dough is no longer sticky. It should take quite a few small additions of confectioner's sugar, about ½ cup total, to get it to the right consistency.
- Wrap in plastic wrap and chill overnight. Remove the fondant from the refrigerator about 10 to 15 minutes before using. Store in airtight container in refrigerator for up to 2 weeks.

## Rolling Fondant

Whether you use my recipe for Marshmallow Fondant (page 72), or opt for store-bought, such as Satin Ice brand, working with fondant is easier than it looks; in fact, I think it's the easiest way to make a spectacular-looking cake with little fuss. You simply need to have a few inexpensive tools on hand to make it look flawless.

Always keep a small container of coconut oil handy for greasing your hands as fondant tends to dry out quickly but can easily be saved by massaging a touch of coconut oil or shortening into it.

When working with fondant, I recommend having a few special tools on hand to make the experience easier. A fondant roller and rubber rolling rings are handy, as well as a fondant spatula, which will enable a smooth application onto your cake.

The most important tip I can offer is to make sure that the cake you are covering is even. Use a serrated knife to carve the cakes into even layers (usually only the very top needs to be trimmed) and fill in gaps with a little extra frosting. Use the method on page 36 to create a crumb coat, and, if desired, add a final layer of frosting to the outside of the cake. Now you are ready to cover the cake.

When rolling out fondant, be sure to roll out onto a very clean, flat, and lightly confectioner's sugared surface. Use plastic rings on a fondant roller to determine the thickness of your fondant, which will ensure an even layer on your cake. Use the fondant roller to help lift the rolled fondant and transfer it evenly onto the cake. Mend any tears or cracks with a touch of water and/or coconut oil. Finally, smooth out the cake with the fondant spatula, gently moving the spatula over the fondant in a circular motion to remove any large bumps or bubbles. You can insert a clean pin into any small bubbles to "pop" them before smoothing over, if needed. Seal edges with fondant balls or piped icing.

# BUTTERCREAM FROSTING

A standard in any dessert lover's arsenal, this recipe works exceptionally well with either margarine or coconut oil. If you opt for the latter, add a pinch of salt and keep slightly chilled.

**6 tablespoons nondairy margarine or coconut oil (cold)**
**6 cups confectioner's sugar**
**2 to 3 teaspoons vanilla extract**
**6 tablespoons nondairy milk**
**2 additional tablespoons softened nondairy margarine or coconut oil**

**YIELD: 4 CUPS**

- Cream together the 6 tablespoons margarine and about ½ cup of the confectioner's sugar. Gradually add in other ingredients, except the softened margarine. Once all the other ingredients have been combined and are fairly smooth, add in softened margarine.
- Mix on very high speed, using a whisk attachment, whipping until fluffy.
- Use immediately on cake, or chill in fridge for later use. If refrigerated, make sure you let it soften slightly by setting the icing out at room temperature just until it is softened enough to spread easily onto cake. If you find the icing too thick, add a touch more nondairy milk to thin. Store in airtight container in refrigerator for up to 2 weeks.

# FLUFFY BAKERY-STYLE FROSTING

Use this classic frosting to fill Whoopie Pies (page 70), cupcakes, and more. This frosting can easily be made up to 1 week ahead of time and stored in the refrigerator before using. Be sure to thaw to room temperature before using.

**2 cups confectioner's sugar**
**1 cup nonhydrogenated shortening**
**¼ cup nondairy margarine**

**YIELD: 2 CUPS**

- Beat together the ingredients in an electric mixing bowl, or by hand, until fluffy. Store refrigerated and allow to warm slightly at room temperature before piping or spreading onto cakes or cookies. Store in airtight container in refrigerator for up to 1 week.

# CREAM CHEESE FROSTING

A foolproof recipe with a tangy twist. Feel free to sub in 1 cup Sweet Cashew Cream (page 32) + 1 teaspoon lemon juice in place of the vegan cream cheese. To make a drizzly glaze rather than a fluffy frosting, simply thin with 2 to 3 tablespoons nondairy milk and 1 teaspoon agave or corn syrup.

**8 ounces nondairy cream cheese**
**2 cups confectioner's sugar**

**YIELD: 1¼ CUPS**

• Make the icing by mixing the ingredients vigorously by hand, or using an electric mixer, until fluffy. Chill before using. Store in airtight container in refrigerator for up to 1 week.

# FLUFFY CHOCOLATE FROSTING

Better than the stuff from a can, but just as addictive. Top your favorite cupcakes or use as a filling in between cookies, like the Vanilla Wafers (page 108).

**⅔ cup cocoa powder**
**⅓ cup nonhydrogenated shortening**
**¼ cup softened nondairy margarine**
**¼ cup nondairy milk**
**2½ cups confectioner's sugar**

**YIELD: 2 CUP**

• In a large mixing bowl fitted with a whisk attachment, combine the cocoa powder, shortening, and margarine until smooth. Gradually add the nondairy milk and confectioner's sugar and then beat on high speed until fluffy, scraping down the sides as needed. Makes enough for one sheet cake; double recipe if making for a layer cake. Store in airtight container in refrigerator for up to 2 weeks.

# GERMAN CHOCOLATE ICING

This sweet coconutty icing makes an apropos topper for German Chocolate Cake (page 39), but it's just as scrumptious in other applications as well! Try it atop a big scoop of Vanilla Soft Serve, page 188.

½ cup agave
¾ cup powdered sugar
2 tablespoons nondairy milk
1 cup pecans, finely chopped
2 tablespoons coconut oil, softened
2 cups sweetened shredded coconut

**YIELD: TOPS 1 GERMAN CHOCOLATE CAKE (PAGE 39)**

• In a medium bowl, whisk together the agave, powdered sugar, and nondairy milk until smooth. Add the rest of the ingredients and mix well. Spread onto cakes while they are still warm, or pipe onto cupcakes using a bag with no tip. Store in airtight container in refrigerator for up to 2 weeks.

# CARAMEL FROSTING

This rich and velvety frosting is reminiscent of sweet and salty caramel candies, without the need to slave over the stove. Even though this frosting goes stunningly with the recommended Bourbon Caramel Cupcakes (page 45), this also tastes fantastic on chocolate cake. For an over-the-top treat, try it slathered on top of my Ultimate Fudgy Brownies (page 138), and sprinkled with toasted pecans.

2 cups confectioner's sugar
½ teaspoon vanilla extract
1 tablespoon molasses
¼ cup nondairy milk
⅛ teaspoon salt
1 tablespoon nondairy margarine

**YIELD: COVERS 12 CUPCAKES**

• Combine all ingredients, in the order given, into a small electric mixing bowl and mix on high speed until smooth and tacky. Spread generously onto the tops of cooled cupcakes or layer cake. Store in airtight container in refrigerator for up to 2 weeks.

# MOCHA-FLUFF FROSTING

This frosting is best used right after preparing, since as it cools, it hardens into a fantastically light and airy, candy-like topping.

1 cup vegan marshmallows, such as Dandies
1 tablespoon nondairy margarine
2 teaspoons instant espresso powder
2 cups confectioner's sugar
1 tablespoon nondairy milk

YIELD: 1½ CUPS

• In a small saucepan, heat the marshmallows, margarine, and espresso powder over medium-low heat until the marshmallows and margarine have melted. Stir constantly and then immediately transfer into a mixing bowl equipped with a whisk attachment. Blend on low as you add in the sugar and nondairy milk and then increase speed to high and whip just until fluffy. Quickly transfer into a piping bag fitted with a large round tip and pipe onto cupcakes.

You can double the batch of this recipe and make a confection a lot like a vegan meringue. Just pipe onto parchment or waxed paper and let air-dry for about 6 hours.

# VANILLA GLAZE

Particularly nice for glazing one-half of a Black and White Cookie (page 103), this glaze also works well for cakes, Blondies (page 139), and pretty much any treat you can think of.

1 cup confectioner's sugar
1 tablespoon + 1 to 2 teaspoons nondairy milk
1½ teaspoons light corn syrup
⅛ teaspoon vanilla extract
Dash salt

YIELD: 1 CUP

• In a small bowl, whisk all the ingredients together until very smooth, ensuring no lumps remain. Use immediately after making and let set for at least 1 hour before handling.

# CHOCOLATE GLAZE

This super-easy glaze tastes just like the icing on popular chocolate snack cakes and makes a perfect alternate glaze for Petits Fours (page 68).

⅓ cup melted nondairy chocolate coins or chips
1 teaspoon coconut oil
⅓ cup confectioner's sugar
1 teaspoon corn syrup
1 tablespoon nondairy milk

YIELD: 1 CUP

- In a small bowl, whisk together the chocolate and coconut oil until smooth. Gradually add the confectioner's sugar, corn syrup, and nondairy milk, stirring continuously to blend. Stir vigorously until very smooth. Use immediately to top cookies and cakes. Let set for 2 hours before handling.

# LEMON GLAZE

Perfect atop Lemon Cake (page 55) or drizzled onto Sugar Cookies (page 110), this glaze sets quickly and should be prepared right before using.

1 large lemon, sliced thinly
1 cup sugar
1½ to 2 cups confectioner's sugar
1 teaspoon corn syrup

YIELD: 1 CUP

- In a 2-quart saucepan over medium heat, bring the lemon slices and sugar to a gentle boil and let cook for 1 minute. Remove from heat and strain the liquid into a medium bowl. Mix in the confectioner's sugar and corn syrup until smooth and creamy. Drizzle onto cooled cakes or cookies and let rest for 1 hour before serving.

# ROYAL ICING

This icing has numerous uses, from piping intricate decorations on cookies, to gluing gingerbread houses together. Make this icing right before using for easiest application. For best results, use a piping bag equipped with a small round tip.

2 cups confectioner's sugar
3 tablespoons nondairy milk
1 tablespoon corn syrup

YIELD: 2 CUPS

- Place all ingredients into a medium bowl and whisk together until very smooth. Use immediately.

# RAINBOW SPRINKLES

DIY sprinkles for cakes and cookies are very simple, and it gives you the option to make your own sprinkles using all-natural food dyes.

**1 recipe Royal Icing
(page 78)
4 or 5 different colors of food
coloring, paste, or drops**

YIELD: 2 CUPS

• Prepare the Royal Icing according to recipe directions and divide evenly among four or five small mixing bowls. Place 1 or 2 drops of each color into the individual bowls until the desired colors are achieved. Place one color of icing into a piping bag fitted with a very small round tip (or you can use a plastic storage bag with just the tip of one corner cut off). Pipe a long skinny stream of icing onto a silicone mat or sheet of waxed paper. Repeat with all colors and let dry completely. Once dried, use a sharp knife to cut into small jimmies.

# DARK CHOCOLATE GANACHE

This delicious cake topper couldn't be easier to make, and it only contains two ingredients. Use the best-quality chocolate you can get your hands on for exceptional flavor. Ganache makes a lovely filling in between cakes and cookies, too, especially the Vanilla Wafers (page 108).

**¾ cup full-fat coconut milk
1½ cups nondairy chocolate
chips**

YIELD: 2 CUPS

• Heat the coconut milk in a small saucepan over medium heat just until it begins to bubble. Remove from heat. Place chocolate chips in small bowl and then stir in hot coconut milk to melt the chips. Let cool until slightly thickened.

# DEVILISHLY DARK CHOCOLATE SAUCE

Espresso and cocoa powders combine for a sinfully rich sauce. Easy to make, it is great served warm over ice cream, or drizzled onto cheesecakes for an extra-special touch.

⅔ cup dark cocoa powder
½ teaspoon espresso powder
1⅔ cups sugar
1¼ cups water
1½ teaspoons vanilla extract

YIELD: 1 CUP

- In a medium saucepan, whisk together the cocoa powder, espresso powder, sugar, and water. Over medium heat, bring the mixture to a boil and let cook for 1 minute, while stirring constantly. Remove from heat and stir in vanilla extract. Let cool before transferring to an airtight container. Store in refrigerator for up to 2 weeks and reheat to serve warm or use cold.

# HOT FUDGE SAUCE

Better than the kind you can buy from the store, this hot fudge sauce keeps for up to 1 month if stored in an airtight container in the fridge. Or, eat it right away on anything and everything you can; I won't judge.

1 cup sugar
⅓ cup cocoa powder
2 tablespoons brown rice
    flour (superfine is best)
2 tablespoons coconut oil
1 cup nondairy milk
1 teaspoon vanilla extract

YIELD: 1½ CUPS

- In a small saucepan, whisk together all of the ingredients and heat over medium heat. Continue to stir as the mixture heats, ensuring no lumps remain as the mixture gets hot. Reduce the temperature slightly and continue to cook until thickened, for about 3 to 4 minutes. Stir well right before serving and enjoy hot.
- Store in airtight container in the refrigerator for up to 1 month, and reheat as needed to top ice cream and other goodies.

# BUTTERSCOTCH SAUCE

Salty and sweet butterscotch sauce was always my favorite topper for ice cream. I like having a jar stowed away in the fridge for those inevitable ice cream sundae cravings.

¼ cup nondairy margarine
1 cup packed brown sugar
¾ cup canned full-fat
   coconut milk
½ teaspoon vanilla extract

**YIELD: 2 CUPS**

- Place the margarine into a 2-quart saucepan over medium heat and melt slightly. Add in the brown sugar and heat until the margarine and sugar have mostly melted.
- Once liquefied, add the coconut milk and vanilla extract and stir well. Continue to cook over medium heat for 9 minutes, stirring often. Turn off heat and let cool slightly. Whisk together well and transfer to a glass jar. Let cool completely before capping and transferring to the refrigerator. This will keep for up to 3 weeks.

# CARAMEL SAUCE

This easy caramel sauce was created for topping the Caramel Chai Cheesecake but is also incredible over ice cream, especially with sprinkles.

1 cup brown sugar, packed
½ cup nondairy margarine
¼ cup almond or coconut
   milk
1¼ teaspoons vanilla extract

**YIELD: 1 CUP**

- In a 2-quart saucepan, whisk together the ingredients and warm over medium heat. Cook, stirring, just until the mixture has thickened to a creamy caramel sauce consistency, for about 5 minutes. Store in airtight container in refrigerator for up to 2 weeks.

*Chapter 3*

# CAPTIVATING COOKIES AND BARS

*Who doesn't love* a cookie? They come in all shapes, sizes, textures, flavors, and colors, are easy to prepare, and are always a crowd-pleaser—especially when they are free of a few common allergens, like dairy, eggs, and gluten!

You may want to invest in a few cookie jars to house all these cookies and bars. If the baking bug hits you hard, cookies do make wonderful gifts.

# DROP COOKIES

# CLASSIC CHOCOLATE CHIP COOKIES

Crispy, chewy, and crunchy, these chocolate chippers are just like the ones the corner cookie shop makes. Be sure to let these rest for at least 30 minutes before transferring from cookie sheet.

2 tablespoons flaxseed meal
4 tablespoons water
1 cup nondairy margarine
1 cup sugar
1 cup packed brown sugar
1 teaspoon vanilla extract
1 teaspoon baking soda
2 teaspoons warm water
2 cups sorghum flour
1 cup brown rice flour
½ cup tapioca flour
1 teaspoon xanthan gum
1 cup semi-sweet nondairy
　　chocolate chips

**YIELD: 24 COOKIES**

- Preheat oven to 375°F.
- In a small bowl, mix the flaxseed meal with the water and allow it to rest for at least 5 minutes, or until thick. Cream together the margarine and sugars until smooth. Add in the vanilla extract and prepared flaxseed meal. Blend together the baking soda and water and add into the creamed margarine mixture.
- In a separate bowl, whisk together the rest of the ingredients up to the chocolate chips. Gradually stir the flours into the margarine mixture until a clumpy dough forms. It should be doughy, but not sticky. If it is too sticky, you will need to add more sorghum flour, about 1 tablespoon at a time, until it becomes a soft dough.
- Shape the dough into rounded spoonfuls and place onto an ungreased cookie sheet about 2 inches apart. Bake on the middle rack about 11 minutes, or until slightly golden brown on edges.
- Store in airtight container up to 1 week.

# OATMEAL RAISIN COOKIES

Addictively easy, these are always a welcome addition to a standard cookie tray. If you're like I was as a kid, feel free to sub in chocolate chips for the raisins.

2 tablespoons flaxseed meal
¼ cup water
1 cup nondairy margarine
1 cup brown sugar
1 teaspoon vanilla extract
1 cup brown rice flour
½ cup potato starch
¼ cup tapioca flour
1 teaspoon xanthan gum
1 teaspoon baking powder
3 cups certified gluten-free
    oats
1 cup raisins

**YIELD: 24 COOKIES**

- Preheat oven to 350°F. In a small bowl, combine the flaxseed meal with the water and let rest for 5 minutes, until gelled.
- In a large mixing bowl, cream together the margarine and sugar until smooth. Add in the vanilla extract and the prepared flaxseed.
- In a medium bowl, whisk together the brown rice flour, potato starch, tapioca flour, xanthan gum, and baking powder. Stir into the creamed sugar mixture. Fold in the oats and raisins.
- Shape the dough into about 1½-inch balls and place onto an ungreased cookie sheet about 2 inches apart. Flatten slightly and bake on middle rack for 15 minutes. Let cool completely before serving. Store in airtight container for up to 1 week.

# PRETENTIOUSLY PERFECT PEANUT BUTTER COOKIES

To be able to call oneself "perfect" takes a good bit of gusto, but man oh man, do these cookies deliver! Chewy, but crunchy, and baked until gloriously golden, these can also be perfect almond, cashew, or sunflower butter cookies if you have a peanut allergy. Simply swap in another nut or seed butter.

½ **cup nondairy margarine**
¾ **cup smooth peanut butter**
½ **cup sugar**
½ **cup packed light brown sugar**
1 **tablespoon flaxseed meal**
2 **tablespoons water**
¾ **cup sorghum flour**
¼ **cup tapioca flour**
½ **cup potato starch**
¾ **teaspoon xanthan gum**
¾ **teaspoon baking soda**

**YIELD: 24 COOKIES**

- Preheat oven to 375°F.
- In a large mixing bowl, cream together the margarine, peanut butter, and sugars until smooth. In a small bowl, mix the flaxseed meal with the water and allow it to rest for at least 5 minutes, or until thick. Add into the peanut butter mixture.
- In a separate bowl, whisk together the rest of the ingredients and then gradually incorporate into the peanut butter mixture until all has been added and a clumpy dough forms. Roll dough into 1-inch balls and flatten the cookies using a fork, forming a crisscross pattern and pressing down gently but firmly. Place 2 inches apart onto an ungreased cookie sheet.
- Bake for 11 minutes. Remove from the oven but let remain on cookie sheet until completely cooled. Store in airtight container for up to 2 weeks. These also freeze nicely.

# SNICKERDOODLES

Some speculate that Snickerdoodles have German roots, while others believe that the name "Snickerdoodle" was just another whimsical cookie name made in the nineteenth-century New England tradition. Regardless of the source of the name, these cookies are another childhood favorite.

2 tablespoons flaxseed meal
4 tablespoons water
½ cup nondairy margarine
½ cup nonhydrogenated shortening
1½ cups sugar, plus 4 tablespoons for rolling
1 teaspoon vanilla extract
2 teaspoons cream of tartar
2 teaspoons baking soda
½ teaspoon salt
1 cup sorghum flour
1 cup millet flour
¾ cup potato starch
1 teaspoon xanthan gum
1 tablespoon cinnamon, for rolling

**YIELD: 24 COOKIES**

- Preheat oven to 375°F.
- In a small bowl, mix the flaxseed meal with the water and allow it to rest for at least 5 minutes, or until thick.
- Cream together the margarine, shortening, and 1½ cups sugar until smooth. Mix in the prepared flaxseed meal, vanilla extract, cream of tartar, baking soda, and salt.
- In a separate bowl, combine sorghum flour, millet flour, potato starch, and xanthan gum. Slowly combine the flour mixture with the sugar mixture and mix vigorously (or use an electric mixer set on medium-low speed) until a stiff dough forms.
- In another small bowl combine the 4 tablespoons sugar with the cinnamon.
- Roll dough into 1-inch balls and then roll each dough-ball into the cinnamon sugar mixture.
- Place 2 inches apart on an ungreased cookie sheet and bake for 9 minutes.
- Remove from oven, sprinkle with a touch more sugar, and let cool on cookie sheet for about 5 minutes.
- Transfer the cookies to a wire rack and let cool for at least 20 more minutes before handling. Store in airtight container for up to 1 week.

These tender cinnamon sugar–speckled cookies need a lot of space when baking. Be sure to place them at least 2 inches apart on a cookie sheet or the cookies will merge together.

# TRAIL MIX COOKIES

These cookies feature all my favorite flavors of trail mix baked right into a scrumptious cookie. The options for mix-ins are endless. Try pepitas, dried blueberries, or even your favorite spice blend to shake things up!

½ cup smooth peanut butter
½ cup nondairy margarine
1½ cups turbinado sugar
1 teaspoon vanilla extract
3 tablespoons flaxseed meal
6 tablespoons water
¼ teaspoon salt
1 cup sorghum flour
½ cup brown rice flour
¼ cup almond meal
½ cup potato starch
¼ cup tapioca flour
1 teaspoon xanthan gum
1 teaspoon baking powder
½ cup shredded coconut
  (sweetened)
1 cup nondairy chocolate
  chips
½ cup sliced almonds
½ cup raisins

**YIELD: 24 COOKIES**

If you use a sugar other than turbinado, you may need to add 1 to 2 tablespoons of nondairy milk to get a proper dough to form.

- Preheat oven to 375°F. In a large bowl, cream together the peanut butter, margarine, sugar, and vanilla extract until smooth. In a small bowl, mix the flaxseed meal with the water and allow it to rest for at least 5 minutes, or until thick. Add in the prepared flaxseed meal.
- In a separate bowl, whisk together the salt, sorghum flour, brown rice flour, almond meal, potato starch, tapioca flour, xanthan gum, and baking powder. Gradually add the flour mixture into the peanut butter mixture and mix until a dough forms.
- Fold in the coconut, chocolate chips, almonds, and raisins until incorporated.
- Drop by rounded tablespoonfuls onto an ungreased cookie sheet 2 inches apart. Flatten slightly with the back of a spoon and bake for 12 minutes, or until bottoms are golden brown. Let cool completely on the rack before enjoying. Store in airtight container for up to 1 week.

# SUPER-SOFT CHOCOLATE CHIP PUMPKIN COOKIES

(S) (N) (C) (B)

Just as the name implies, these cookies are super soft and chock-full of pumpkin goodness. I love making these for Halloween parties, as they are always quick to get gobbled up!

½ cup nondairy margarine
1⅓ cups sugar
1¼ cups canned (or fresh, drained well in cheesecloth) pumpkin puree
1 teaspoon vanilla extract
1 teaspoon baking powder
½ teaspoon baking soda
1 teaspoon sea salt
1¼ cups sorghum flour
¾ cup brown rice flour
½ cup potato starch
¼ cup tapioca flour
1 teaspoon xanthan gum
1 cup nondairy chocolate chips

**YIELD: 20 COOKIES**

- Preheat oven to 350°F.
- Cream together the margarine and sugar. Once smooth, mix in the pumpkin.
- In separate bowl, mix together the rest of the ingredients except for the chocolate chips. Slowly fold the flour mixture into the pumpkin mixture just until mixed. Fold in the chocolate chips.
- Drop by tablespoonfuls onto an ungreased cookie sheet about 2 inches apart. Bake for 17 minutes. Remove from oven and let cool completely before enjoying. Store in airtight container for up to 1 week.

If using fresh pumpkin with these, be sure to strain the pumpkin very well so that very little liquid remains before adding to the cookies.

# GARAM MASALA COOKIES

If you think garam masala is only good for savory dishes, these cookies will open your eyes! With warming notes of brown sugar, vanilla, and the delicious Indian spice blend, what's not to love?

1 cup cold nondairy
    margarine
¾ cup sugar
¾ cup brown sugar
1 teaspoon vanilla extract
2 teaspoons baking powder
2 teaspoons garam masala
1 teaspoon xanthan gum
2 tablespoons apple cider
    vinegar
¼ cup almond flour
1 cup buckwheat flour
½ cup sweet white rice flour
2 tablespoons cocoa powder,
    for dusting

**YIELD: 18 COOKIES**

- Preheat oven to 375°F. Cream together the margarine and sugars. Add the vanilla extract, baking powder, garam masala, and xanthan gum. Add the vinegar and then gradually mix in all of the flours a little at a time until well blended.
- Using a tablespoon, scoop out round balls onto an ungreased cookie sheet about 3 inches apart. Bake for about 10 minutes, or until the cookies have flattened out completely.
- While they are still warm, sprinkle a touch of cocoa powder on each cookie. Store in airtight container for up to 1 week.

# MAPLE COOKIES

Crispy on the inside and cakey in the middle, these irresistible cookies will have you reaching in the cookie jar again and again with their seductive maple flavor. For an extra-indulgent treat, top with the glaze from Mini Maple Donuts (page 180).

1 tablespoon flaxseed meal
2 tablespoons water
½ cup nondairy margarine
½ cup brown sugar
½ cup maple syrup
1 teaspoon maple extract
1 teaspoon baking soda
1¾ cups superfine brown
    rice flour
1 cup potato starch
¼ cup cornstarch
¼ cup tapioca flour
1 teaspoon xanthan gum
½ teaspoon salt
½ cup turbinado sugar

YIELD: 24 COOKIES

- Preheat oven to 350°F. Line a cookie sheet with parchment paper. Mix the flaxseed meal with the water in a very small bowl. Let rest for 5 minutes, or until gelled.
- In a large mixing bowl, cream together the margarine, sugar, and maple syrup until fluffy. Mix in the prepared flaxseed meal and maple extract.
- In a medium bowl, whisk together the remaining ingredients, except for the turbinado sugar, and then gradually incorporate into the creamed margarine until a soft dough is formed. Do not overmix.
- Form into 1-inch balls and roll in the turbinado. Flatten slightly with the back of a fork and bake for 15 minutes, rotating the cookie tray after 10 minutes' baking time. Let cool completely before removing from cookie sheet. Store in airtight container up to 1 week.

# PECAN SANDIES

It took a little effort to come up with a cookie that rivals the store-bought version I so fondly remember from my childhood, but I think I've captured it with this recipe. Be sure to serve with a tall cold glass of almond or rice milk!

1 tablespoon flaxseed meal
2 tablespoons water
½ cup nondairy margarine
½ cup olive oil
½ cup confectioner's sugar
½ cup sugar
1¼ cups brown rice flour
½ cup potato starch
¼ cup tapioca flour
1 teaspoon xanthan gum
½ teaspoon baking soda
½ teaspoon cream of tartar
½ teaspoon salt
1 cup chopped pecans,
    plus 24 whole pecans
    for topping

**YIELD: 24 COOKIES**

- Preheat oven to 375°F.
- Mix the flaxseed meal with the water in a very small bowl. Let rest for 5 minutes, or until gelled. In a large bowl, mix together the margarine, oil, sugars, and prepared flaxseed meal until blended.
- In a separate bowl, whisk together the brown rice flour, potato starch, tapioca flour, xanthan gum, baking soda, cream of tartar, and salt. Add the flour mixture to the sugar mixture and stir well to combine into a slightly oily dough. Add the chopped pecans.
- Form into 1-inch balls, place 2 inches apart onto an ungreased cookie sheet, and place a single pecan on top of each cookie. Bake for 11 minutes, or until lightly golden on the edges.
- Let cool completely before serving. Store in airtight container for up to 1 week.

# COCOA MACAROONS

These simple cookies are ooey, gooey, and chewy with a crispy crunchy outer shell. Perfect for snacking. If you want to change it up a bit, try the Australian method and place a small bit of jam or a fruit—such as a dried cherry—inside the coconut dough before baking.

**3 tablespoons flaxseed meal**
**¼ cup + 2 tablespoons water**
**4 cups sweetened shredded coconut**
**¼ cup cocoa powder**
**½ cup sugar**
**½ teaspoon salt**

**YIELD: 24 COOKIES**

- Preheat oven to 350°F and line a cookie sheet with a silicone mat or parchment paper.
- In a small bowl, whisk together the flaxseed meal and water and let set for 5 minutes, until gelled. In a medium bowl, stir together the remaining ingredients until blended. Fold in the prepared flaxseed meal and stir well until completely incorporated. The batter will be slightly tricky to squeeze together but will hold well once baked. Drop by tablespoons onto the prepared cookie sheet and bake for 15 to 18 minutes, until fragrant and slightly darkened.
- Let rest for at least 1 hour before serving.

# FLORENTINES

Even though the name sounds wholly Italian, these cookies most likely originated in French kitchens, with the name simply a nod to the Tuscan city. As beautiful as they are tasty, don't be intimidated by the Florentine; they are a snap to make. Be sure to leave extra space in between each cookie, as they spread! Aim for about six per standard-size cookie sheet.

1¼ cups sliced almonds
¼ cup superfine brown
    rice flour
⅓ cup sugar
4 tablespoons nondairy
    margarine
¼ cup agave
¼ teaspoon salt
⅓ cup nondairy chocolate,
    melted
2 tablespoons finely chopped
    Candied Orange Peels
    (page 266) or orange zest

YIELD: 12 COOKIES

- Preheat oven to 350°F.
- In a medium bowl, combine the almonds and the brown rice flour. In a small saucepan, mix together the sugar, margarine, agave, and salt and bring to a boil, stirring often. Remove immediately from heat and stir mixture into the almond mixture. Mix until totally combined and drop by heaping tablespoons onto a parchment-lined cookie sheet, about 3 inches apart. Using a lightly greased fork, press down cookies into a flat circle, so that the almonds are in a single layer.
- Bake for 5 minutes, rotate the cookie sheet, and bake for 4 to 5 minutes more, until the edges of the cookies are golden brown. Let cool completely and then drizzle with melted chocolate and sprinkle with orange peel. Let chocolate firm up before serving. Store in airtight container for up to 1 week.

# THUMBPRINT COOKIES

A lovely cookie that is simple to make and easy on the eyes. Sprinkle with confectioner's sugar once cooled for an elegant presentation. This cookie works best with low-sugar preserves (my favorites are apricot and raspberry!) or a high-pectin jam. Other types of jams can cause the filling to spread.

**1 tablespoon flaxseed meal**
**2 tablespoons water**
**1 cup nondairy margarine**
**1 cup sugar**
**1 teaspoon vanilla extract**
**1 teaspoon baking powder**
**1 cup sorghum flour**
**1 cup potato starch**
**1 cup almond meal**
**1 teaspoon xanthan gum**
**⅓ cup preserves**
**(1 teaspoon per cookie)**

**YIELD: 24 COOKIES**

- Preheat oven to 350°F.
- Mix the flaxseed meal with the water in a very small bowl. Let rest for 5 minutes, or until gelled. Line a cookie sheet with parchment paper or a silicone baking mat.
- Cream together the margarine and sugar until smooth. Add in the prepared flaxseed meal and vanilla extract and mix well.
- In a separate bowl, combine the baking powder, sorghum flour, potato starch, almond meal, and xanthan gum.
- Gradually add the flour mixture into the sugar mixture until a stiff dough forms.
- Shape into 1-inch balls and place onto cookie sheet. Use the back of a ½ teaspoon (or your thumb) to make an indent in the cookies while slightly flattening them.
- Fill each cookie with a little less than a teaspoon of preserves. Bake for 15 minutes in preheated oven and then let cool completely. Store in airtight container for up to 4 days.

# MEXICAN WEDDING COOKIES

These delicately crunchy cookies practically melt in your mouth. Also known as Russian Tea Cakes or Polvorones, it doesn't matter what name you use—once you try them, you'll never forget them.

¾ cup nondairy margarine
½ cup confectioner's sugar,
     plus ¼ cup for rolling
½ teaspoon salt
1 cup almond meal
1½ teaspoons vanilla extract
¾ cup sorghum flour
½ cup potato starch
¼ cup tapioca flour
1 teaspoon xanthan gum

**YIELD: 15 COOKIES**

- Preheat oven to 325°F.
- In a large mixing bowl, cream together the margarine and ½ cup confectioner's sugar until smooth. Add the salt, almond meal, and vanilla extract and mix well. In a separate bowl, whisk together the sorghum flour, potato starch, tapioca flour, and xanthan gum.
- Gradually incorporate the flour mixture into the margarine mixture until a clumpy dough forms. Shape into 1-inch balls and place onto an ungreased cookie sheet.
- Bake for 17 to 20 minutes in a preheated oven. Let cool for 2 to 3 minutes, then coat the entire cookie with the additional confectioner's sugar. Let cool completely before serving. Store in airtight container for up to 2 weeks.

# CRANBERRY WHITE CHOCOLATE ORANGE CLUSTERS

These soft clusters of fragrant citrus, tangy cranberry, and creamy white chocolate will have you reaching in the cookie jar again and again!

2 tablespoons flaxseed meal
4 tablespoons water
½ cup nondairy margarine
½ cup unsweetened
     applesauce
1 cup sugar
1 teaspoon vanilla extract
½ teaspoon orange zest
1 teaspoon salt
1 teaspoon baking soda
1½ cups superfine or regular
     brown rice flour
1 cup cornstarch
½ cup tapioca flour
1 teaspoon xanthan gum
½ cup dried cranberries
½ cup nondairy white
     chocolate chips

**YIELD: 24 COOKIES**

- Preheat oven to 375°F.
- In a small bowl, mix together the flaxseed meal and the water and let rest until gelled, for about 5 minutes.
- In a large mixing bowl, cream together the margarine, applesauce, sugar, vanilla extract, and orange zest until smooth. In a medium bowl, whisk together the salt, baking soda, brown rice flour, cornstarch, tapioca flour, and xanthan gum. Gradually incorporate into the sugar mixture until a soft dough forms. Fold in the cranberries and white chocolate chips.
- Drop by the tablespoonful onto a parchment-lined cookie sheet, about 2 inches apart. Bake for 12 to 15 minutes, until golden brown on edges. Let cool completely before serving. Store in airtight container for up to 1 week.

# DATE DROP COOKIES

Sticky sweet centers are enveloped in a soft cookie to bring you an ultimate treat. My husband, who is admittedly a cookie fanatic, raves about these guys and their irresistible texture. I particularly like them because they are simple to prepare but look so beautiful when baked. For soy-free cookies, use soy-free yogurt.

## FILLING
1¼ cup dates, pitted and
    finely chopped
½ cup water
Pinch salt

## COOKIES
2 tablespoons ground
    flaxseed
4 tablespoons water
1 cup nondairy margarine
¾ cup sugar
¾ cup brown sugar
⅓ cup plain unsweetened
    nondairy yogurt
1 teaspoon vanilla extract
1¼ cups sorghum flour
1 cup superfine brown
    rice flour
¾ cup cornstarch
¼ cup sweet white rice flour
1 teaspoon xanthan gum
1¼ teaspoons baking soda
½ teaspoon salt

YIELD: 24 COOKIES

- Place filling ingredients into a 2-quart saucepan and heat over medium heat, stirring often. Cook mixture for 5 minutes, or until thickened. Set aside.
- Preheat oven to 400°F.
- In a small bowl, combine the flaxseed meal with water and allow to gel for 5 minutes, or until thick. In a large mixing bowl, cream together the margarine and sugars until smooth. Add in the prepared flaxseed meal, yogurt, and vanilla extract.
- In a separate bowl, whisk together the rest of the ingredients. Gradually incorporate the flour mixture into the sugar mixture until a clumpy dough forms.
- On an ungreased cookie sheet, drop a tablespoon of the dough. Next, place a teaspoon of the date filling on top of the dough, and then top with a teaspoon more cookie dough. Repeat with all dough and filling. Bake for 11 minutes; let cool completely before serving. Store in airtight container for up to 1 week.

# PEANUT BUTTER CHOCOLATE NO-BAKE COOKIES

This is one of the very first recipes I learned to make as a kid, and boy did I make them a lot! These were always a favorite due to their quickness and ease and irresistible chocolate peanut butter combo.

¼ cup cocoa powder
2 cups sugar
½ cup almond milk
½ cup nondairy margarine
½ cup + 3 tablespoons creamy peanut butter
1 teaspoon vanilla extract
3½ cups certified gluten-free oats

**YIELD: 24 COOKIES**

- Line a large cookie tray with parchment paper.
- In a 2-quart saucepan, combine the cocoa powder, sugar, almond milk, and margarine. Bring to a boil over medium heat, stirring often. Boil for exactly 2 minutes and then remove from heat. Immediately stir in the peanut butter and vanilla extract. Fold in the oats and then drop by spoonfuls on prepared cookie tray. Let rest until firm, for about 1 to 2 hours. Store in airtight container for up to 1 week.

# CHERRY COCONUT NO-BAKE COOKIES

Tart cherries work so nicely with the base of these no-bakes—perfect for when you're craving cookies, but don't want to turn on the oven.

2 cups sugar
¼ cup coconut oil
2 teaspoons vanilla extract
½ cup nondairy milk
3 cups certified gluten-free oats
⅔ cup dried cherries
½ cup unsweetened flaked coconut
¼ cup almond meal

**YIELD: 24 COOKIES**

- Line a large cookie tray with parchment paper.
- In a 2-quart saucepan, over medium heat, combine the sugar, coconut oil, vanilla extract, and nondairy milk. While stirring often, bring the mixture to a boil. Once boiling, continue cooking over medium heat, stirring occasionally, for 1½ to 2 minutes. Remove the mixture from heat and stir in oats, cherries, coconut, and almond meal.
- Drop by heaping tablespoonfuls onto the prepared cookie sheet. While the cookies are still warm, guide them into an evenly round shape using lightly greased fingertips.
- Let the cookies cool for about 1 hour at room temperature. They will harden up nicely.
- Store in airtight container for up to 2 weeks.

# BLACK AND WHITE COOKIES

If you've never tried a black and white cookie, you are in for a treat. These ginormous lemony beasts boast not one, but two flavors of icing: chocolate *and* vanilla.

½ cup + 1 tablespoon
   nondairy margarine
¾ cup sugar
½ teaspoon lemon oil or
   extract
2 teaspoons egg replacer
   powder (such as Orgran)
   mixed with 2 tablespoons
   water
1 cup besan/chickpea flour
½ cup white rice flour
½ cup potato starch
1 teaspoon xanthan gum
½ teaspoon baking powder
¼ teaspoon salt
⅔ cup nondairy milk
1 recipe Chocolate Glaze
   (page 78)
1 recipe Vanilla Glaze
   (page 77)

**YIELD: 12 COOKIES**

- Preheat oven to 350°F. Line a large baking sheet with parchment paper.
- Cream together the margarine and sugar in a large mixing bowl. Add in the lemon oil and prepared egg replacer. In a separate bowl, whisk together the besan, white rice flour, potato starch, xanthan gum, baking powder, and salt. Add it to the margarine mixture and then add in the nondairy milk. Stir well to combine until a fluffy cookie dough is formed. Using an ice cream scoop, drop dough in 3-ounce balls onto the prepared cookie sheet, leaving about 4 inches between each cookie. You will have to make these in multiple batches as they need room to spread.
- Bake for 22 minutes, or until edges are light golden brown. Remove from the oven and let cool completely. Prepare the Vanilla Glaze (page 77) and frost one half of each of the cookies with the vanilla glaze. Let harden for about 20 minutes, and prepare the Chocolate Glaze (page 78). Frost the other half of each cookie with the chocolate glaze. Let harden completely, for about 2 hours, before serving. Store in airtight container for up to 3 days.

# GINGER SNAPPERS

Crispier than gingerbread, these snappers pack a big ginger flavor into such a small little snack.

1 tablespoon flaxseed meal
2 tablespoons water
1 cup packed light brown sugar
¾ cup olive oil
¼ cup molasses
1 cup sorghum flour
¼ cup superfine brown rice flour
½ cup potato starch
¼ cup tapioca flour
1 teaspoon xanthan gum
2 teaspoons baking soda
1 teaspoon salt
1 teaspoon cinnamon
2 teaspoons fresh grated ginger
½ teaspoon cloves
⅓ cup turbinado sugar, for rolling

**YIELD: 24 COOKIES**

- In a small bowl, combine the flaxseed meal with water and let rest until gelled, for about 5 minutes. Preheat oven to 375°F.
- In a large bowl, mix together the brown sugar, olive oil, molasses, and prepared flaxseed meal.
- In a smaller bowl, whisk together the rest of the ingredients except for the turbinado sugar, and, once mixed, gradually incorporate into the sugar mixture until a stiff dough forms.
- Roll into 1-inch balls and then coat with turbinado sugar. Flatten slightly using the bottom of a glass and bake for 13 minutes in preheated oven. Let cool completely before serving. Store in airtight container for up to 2 weeks.

# LEMON OLIVE OIL COOKIES

Tender and bright, these cookies are sure to delight! Use freshly squeezed lemon juice and extra-virgin olive oil for best results. If the dough seems a little soft, be sure to chill for about 20 minutes in the refrigerator before baking to prevent excessive spreading.

**1 cup sorghum flour**
**¾ cup brown rice flour**
**½ cup potato starch**
**¼ cup almond meal**
**1 teaspoon xanthan gum**
**1¼ cups sugar**
**2 teaspoons baking soda**
**½ teaspoon salt**
**2 teaspoons lemon zest**
**½ cup olive oil**
**½ cup lemon juice**
**Granulated sugar for garnishing**

**YIELD: 24 COOKIES**

- Preheat oven to 350°F.
- In a large bowl, whisk the sorghum flour, brown rice flour, potato starch, almond meal, xanthan gum, sugar, baking soda, and salt. Mix in the lemon zest, olive oil, and lemon juice until a thick cookie dough forms.
- Drop the dough by heaping tablespoonfuls, or roll dough into walnut-size balls and place about 2 inches apart onto an ungreased baking sheet.
- Flatten slightly with a fork (like you would with a peanut butter cookie) and sprinkle lightly with granulated sugar.
- Bake in your preheated oven for 12 minutes, or until edges are slightly golden brown.
- Remove from oven and let cool completely before serving. Store in airtight container for up to 1 week.

*Pizzelles, page 114*

# ROLLED AND SHAPED COOKIES

# VANILLA WAFERS

A vanilla wafer is always a good cookie to have around for basic reasons, like making into cookie crumbs, using in trifles, and simply snacking. Use the highest-quality vanilla extract you can get your hands on for these, or better yet, make your own (page 31).

1 tablespoon flaxseed meal
2 tablespoons water
5 tablespoons nondairy
   margarine
1 cup sugar
1 tablespoon vanilla extract
¼ cup nondairy milk
¾ cup sorghum flour
½ cup white rice flour
½ cup potato starch
¼ cup tapioca flour
1 teaspoon xanthan gum
2 teaspoons baking powder
¼ teaspoon salt

**YIELD: ABOUT 36 COOKIES**

- Preheat oven to 350°F and line a cookie sheet with parchment paper.
- In a small bowl, stir together the flaxseed meal and water and let rest until gelled, for about 5 minutes.
- In a separate bowl, cream together the margarine, sugar, and vanilla extract until smooth. Mix in the prepared flaxseed meal and nondairy milk.
- In a medium bowl, whisk together the remaining ingredients and then combine well with the margarine mixture until a soft dough forms. Place into a large freezer bag and snip off the tip. Pipe out 1-inch circles onto the parchment-covered cookie sheet about 1 inch apart. Bake for about 20 minutes, or until golden brown on edges. Let cool completely before serving. Store in airtight container for up to 2 weeks.

# CHOCOLATE WAFERS

Just as versatile as their vanilla cousins, these wafers can wear many hats. Sandwich a little Caramel Frosting (page 76) in between two cookies or add 1 teaspoon mint extract and dip them in melted chocolate for easy thin mints.

¾ cup cold nondairy margarine

1 cup sugar

1 cup sorghum flour

¾ cup cocoa powder

½ cup potato starch

1 teaspoon xanthan gum

¼ teaspoon baking soda

2 tablespoons strong coffee

¼ cup additional cocoa powder

**YIELD: 36 COOKIES**

- Preheat oven to 350°F. Line a large cookie sheet with parchment paper or a silicone baking mat.
- In a large bowl, cream together the margarine and sugar until smooth. In a separate bowl, whisk together the sorghum flour, cocoa powder, potato starch, xanthan gum, and baking soda. Fold the dry ingredients into the sugar mixture and mix until crumbly. Add the coffee and mix until a soft dough forms.
- Gradually fold in the ¼ cup cocoa powder and mix just until dough is workable. Chill in freezer for 5 to 10 minutes and then pinch off sections large enough to create 1-inch balls. Place dough balls onto the prepared baking sheet and flatten with the bottom of a glass to about ¼ inch thick. Bake for 16 minutes. Allow to cool completely before serving. Store in airtight container to keep crisp for up to 2 weeks.

# SUGAR COOKIES

Sometimes a basic sugar cookie is the best dessert! The secret to these cookies is to keep the dough chilled. I like them best rolled to ¼ inch thick, but you can roll them a touch thinner if you prefer a crispier sugar cookie.

¾ cup nondairy margarine
½ cup sugar
½ cup confectioner's sugar
3 teaspoons powdered egg replacer + 2 tablespoons hot water, frothed with fork
2 tablespoons apple cider vinegar
1 teaspoon vanilla extract
1 cup sorghum flour
½ cup white rice flour
¾ cup potato starch
½ cup tapioca flour
1 teaspoon xanthan gum
1 teaspoon baking powder

**YIELD: 24 COOKIES**

- Cream together the margarine and sugars until smooth. Mix in the prepared egg replacer along with the vinegar and vanilla extract.
- In a separate bowl, whisk together the sorghum flour, white rice flour, potato starch, tapioca flour, xanthan gum, and baking powder. Gradually combine the flour mixture with the margarine mixture until a clumpy dough forms. If the dough seems too sticky to handle, add a little more sorghum flour . . . it should be easily workable with your hands, yet a little bit sticky. Form into a patty, wrap in plastic wrap, and chill until cold, for about 1 hour in the refrigerator and 15 minutes in the freezer.
- When your dough is chilled, preheat oven to 400°F. Lay countertop or other work area with parchment paper, and using a lightly floured (any kind of flour will do) rolling pin, roll dough anywhere between ⅓ to ½ inch thick. Cut out using your favorite cookie cutters, and use a flat metal spatula to gently lift the cookies and place them onto an ungreased cookie sheet. Repeat until all dough is used. If the dough seems to be getting a little soft and sticks to your pin, rechill until once again workable.
- Bake cookies for 7 to 8 minutes, or until slightly golden brown on edges. Remove from oven and let cool completely before handling. Store in airtight container for up to 1 week.
- Once they have fully cooled, eat as is or cover them with icing! Royal Icing (page 78) works beautifully here. Pipe a ring around the cookie's exterior and let harden before filling it in with icing. This will ensure an even layer of icing on the tops with no drips.

# BUTTERY SHORTBREAD

Shortbread used to be considered a delicacy and was reserved for special occasions, such as Christmas or weddings. But no need to wait for a holiday, whip some of these cookies up anytime a craving strikes. This simple cookie can be made extra fancy if you bake them in shortbread molds and dip the ends in melted chocolate.

1 tablespoon flaxseed meal
2 tablespoons water
½ cup + 2 tablespoons nondairy margarine
½ cup sugar
1 teaspoon vanilla extract
¾ cup sorghum flour
¼ cup brown rice flour
¼ cup tapioca flour
½ cup arrowroot starch
¼ cup sweet white rice flour
1 teaspoon xanthan gum
½ cup nondairy chocolate chips, melted, for dipping (optional)

**YIELD: ABOUT 20 COOKIES**

- In a small bowl, combine the flaxseed meal with water and let rest until gelled, for about 5 minutes. In a large mixing bowl, cream together the margarine and the sugar until smooth. Add in the prepared flaxseed meal and vanilla extract and mix until combined.
- In a separate bowl, whisk together the sorghum flour, brown rice flour, tapioca flour, arrowroot starch, sweet white rice flour, and xanthan gum. Gradually mix into the sugar mixture until a clumpy dough forms. The dough may be crumbly at first, but allow enough mixing time for it to come together.
- Wrap the dough in parchment paper and chill for about 30 minutes in the freezer. The dough should be cold, but workable; if it is too crumbly once removed from the freezer, work it a bit with your hands to soften it up.
- Preheat oven to 350°F.
- Create a disk with the dough and place in between two sheets of plastic wrap and roll out to a ¼ inch thickness. Cut using a bench scraper into 2-inch squares, or use a circle cookie cutter, and place onto an ungreased cookie sheet. Bake for 12 minutes, or until bottoms are slightly golden brown. Let cool completely before removing from cookie sheet. At this point, if desired, the cookies can be dipped in melted chocolate and allowed to set back up on a sheet of waxed paper. Store in airtight container for up to 2 weeks.

# CHOCOLATE SHORTBREAD

Just like the traditional shortbread, only much more chocolaty. I like to cut these into bars, but feel free to shape them as you desire with metal cookie cutters.

**1 cup nondairy margarine**
**½ cup + 2 tablespoons sugar,**
     **plus ¼ cup for rolling**
**½ cup cocoa powder**
**¾ cup sorghum flour**
**¾ cup brown rice flour**
**½ cup potato starch**
**1 teaspoon xanthan gum**

**YIELD: 12 COOKIES**

• Cream together the margarine and ½ cup + 2 tablespoons sugar until smooth. Using an electric mixer, or mixing quickly with a spoon, gradually add the cocoa powder.

• In a separate bowl, combine the sorghum flour, brown rice flour, potato starch, and xanthan gum. Add the flour mixture into the sugar mixture (a little bit at a time) until all is incorporated.

• Keep mixing until a stiff dough forms, scraping down the sides as necessary. It will look crumbly at first, but will come together nicely with a little mixing. Using your hands, pat dough into a disk on a lightly sugared surface and then chill the dough in the refrigerator for 2 to 3 hours.

• When you're ready to bake the cookies, preheat oven to 300°F.

• Use a large knife to cut the dough into even rectangles, about 1 x 4 inches. Using a flat metal spatula, scoop up cookies and place them onto an ungreased cookie sheet. Sprinkle with granulated sugar and then poke a few holes in the tops with a fork. Bake for 30 to 35 minutes. Let cool completely before serving. Store in airtight container for up to 2 weeks.

# SPECULOOS

These cookies have been a favorite of mine long before I ever knew what a speculoos was. I learned this term from the vegan blogging world but soon realized it had been one of my favorites since childhood, only I knew these spicy treats as "windmill cookies." Feel free to roll these out flat and cut with windmill cutters to share in my nostalgia.

1 tablespoon flaxseed meal
2 tablespoons water
1 cup sorghum flour
¼ cup tapioca flour
¼ cup potato starch
½ cup + 2 tablespoons almond meal
1 teaspoon xanthan gum
1 teaspoon baking powder
1 teaspoon cinnamon
¼ teaspoon cloves
¼ teaspoon nutmeg
¼ teaspoon fresh ground ginger
¼ teaspoon salt
½ cup nondairy margarine
¾ cup packed light brown sugar
Extra sugar for sprinkling (optional)
Sliced almonds for topping

YIELD: 24 COOKIES

- In a small bowl, combine the flaxseed meal with water and let rest until gelled, for about 5 minutes.
- In a large bowl, whisk together all the flour ingredients (up until the margarine) until well blended. In a separate mixing bowl, cream together the margarine and brown sugar until smooth. Mix in the prepared flaxseed meal until a smooth mixture is formed. Gradually add in the flour mixture and mix for about 45 seconds at medium speed until the dough clumps together. Chill in the freezer for 40 minutes, or until stiff—or alternatively, chill in refrigerator overnight.
- Preheat oven to 350°F.
- Once the dough is chilled, use your hands to roll into 1-inch wide balls and place onto an ungreased cookie sheet. Flatten with the bottom of a glass—slightly damp and dipped in granulated sugar. Top with a few sliced almonds and bake in preheated oven for 15 minutes. Let cool on the cookie sheet before attempting to move. Once cool, transfer to wire rack to fully harden.
- Store in airtight container for up to 5 days.

# SPECULOOS BUTTER

This cookie butter has taken over the nation from suppliers such as Trader Joe's popularizing it to the extreme . . . but I've never found one in stores that is gluten-free! So, I had to make my own, and boy am I glad I did. Try this "butter" on top of cupcakes, more cookies, ice cream, or simply a spoon.

**24 Speculoos cookies
    (page 113)
3 tablespoons water
½ cup coconut oil, melted**

**YIELD: ABOUT 2 CUPS**

- Place the cookies into a food processor and pulse until very crumbly. Make sure the crumbles are finely chopped. Add in the water, one tablespoon at a time and pulse until well blended. Drizzle in the coconut oil and let blend until very smooth, for about 5 minutes, scraping the sides as needed. Transfer into a jar and store in refrigerator. Keep for up to 2 weeks.

# PIZZELLES

These cookies are delicious on their own but also make a fabulous accompaniment to ice cream, especially when shaped into waffle cones. To make these cookies into homemade waffle cones you will need a Pizzelle press, which can be sourced from any typical home goods store. When hot to the touch, shape the cookie disks into cones, fit inside a small bowl to make waffle bowls; or, leave them flat for classic pizzelle cookies.

**3 tablespoons flaxseed meal
6 tablespoons water
1 cup white rice flour
½ cup potato starch
¼ cup tapioca flour
2 teaspoons baking powder
1 teaspoon xanthan gum
1 teaspoon vanilla extract
1 cup melted nondairy
    margarine
¼ cup water**

**YIELD: 18 COOKIES**

- Preheat the pizzelle press and grease lightly with oil or non-stick spray just before the first batch, and repeat sparingly as needed.
- In a small bowl, mix the flaxseed meal with water and let rest for 5 minutes, until gelled. In a medium bowl, whisk together the rice flour, potato starch, tapioca flour, baking powder, and xanthan gum. Make a well in the center of the flours and add in the vanilla extract, melted margarine, prepared flaxseed meal, and water. Mix until smooth. Place about 1 tablespoon batter onto the hot press and clamp down to close. Cook until golden brown and then gently remove.
- To make waffle cones: Using an oven mitt or heat-safe gloved hands, gently shape the cookie into a cone and snugly place in a safe spot to cool, for about 1 hour. Watch that they don't unravel before cooling or they will become stuck in that shape. Let cool completely, and then serve with your favorite frozen treat. Store in airtight container for up to 3 weeks.

# SNOW CAP COOKIES

These cookies are a classic right up there next to Chocolate Chip and Peanut Butter. This version includes teff flour, which boasts a pretty impressive nutritional profile for such a tiny grain, being high in protein, iron, calcium, and potassium!

**3 tablespoons flaxseed meal**
**6 tablespoons water**
**1 cup cocoa powder**
**½ cup teff flour**
**¾ cup sorghum flour**
**¼ cup tapioca flour**
**½ cup potato starch**
**1 teaspoon xanthan gum**
**2 teaspoons baking powder**
**½ teaspoon salt**
**2 cups sugar**
**½ cup melted**
**   nonhydrogenated**
**   shortening**
**¼ cup nondairy milk**
**½ cup confectioner's sugar**

**YIELD: 24 COOKIES**

- In a small bowl, combine the flaxseed meal with water and let rest until gelled, for about 5 minutes.
- In a large bowl, whisk together the cocoa powder, teff flour, sorghum flour, tapioca flour, potato starch, xanthan gum, baking powder, salt, and sugar. While stirring constantly, or set on medium speed of an electric mixer, add in the prepared flaxseed meal and shortening until a crumbly dough forms. Mix well to blend. Add in the nondairy milk while continuing to stir and keep mixing until the dough clumps together easily.
- Wrap dough in parchment or foil and chill in refrigerator for 2 hours.
- Once chilled, roll into small balls about 1½ inches wide and flatten slightly to resemble small pucks.
- Preheat oven to 350°F.
- Dip the tops only in confectioner's sugar and place onto an ungreased cookie sheet. Bake for 12 minutes, or until spread out and crackled. The centers will still be gooey while warm. Allow to cool completely before enjoying. Store in airtight container for up to 1 week.

# TUXEDO SANDWICH COOKIES (S) (N) (C) (B)

These cookies taste just like America's favorite sandwich cookie; a touch of orange adds an elegant note. You can even twist off the tops and just enjoy the filling! Dunked in almond milk they become the perfect remedy to the midday slumps.

## COOKIES

1 cup nondairy margarine
¾ cup sugar
¼ cup brown sugar
1 teaspoon vanilla extract
¾ cup dark cocoa powder
½ cup superfine brown
    rice flour
1 cup sorghum flour
½ cup potato starch
1½ teaspoons xanthan gum
1 teaspoon salt
1 teaspoon baking powder
½ teaspoon baking soda

## FILLING

1½ tablespoons orange zest
½ cup very cold coconut-
    based buttery spread
    (shortening will also
    work)
½ cup nondairy margarine
3½ cups confectioner's sugar

**YIELD: ABOUT 20 COOKIES**

- Cream together the margarine and sugars and then mix in the vanilla extract. In a separate bowl, whisk together the cocoa powder, superfine brown rice flour, sorghum flour, potato starch, xanthan gum, salt, baking powder, and baking soda.
- Gradually incorporate the flours with the margarine mixture until a clumpy dark dough is formed. Divide and pat into two disks. Chill in the refrigerator for 2 hours, or briefly in freezer, for about 10 minutes.
- After dough is chilled, preheat oven to 350°F and line two cookie sheets with parchment paper.
- On a flat surface, place each chilled disk of dough between two separate sheets of parchment paper and roll each disk to about ⅛ inch thickness. Using a round 2-inch cookie cutter, cut out circles of dough and transfer onto prepared cookie sheets. Bake for 13 minutes and let cool completely before piping filling in between two of the cookies.
- To make the filling, simply mix together all frosting ingredients using an electric mixer with whisk attachment. Whip until fluffy and then pipe a ring onto one cookie and smoosh down with another until an even layer of frosting is snugly set in the middle. Store in airtight container for up to 1 week.

# COCONUT CARAMEL COOKIES

Similar to the coconut-topped Girl Scout Cookies that are both chewy and crisp, these brilliant bites utilize Medjool dates to stand in for the caramel, adding a little extra goodness.

## COOKIES
1 cup nondairy margarine
1 teaspoon vanilla extract
½ cup sugar
1 cup sorghum flour
¾ cup superfine brown
    rice flour
¾ cup potato starch
1½ teaspoons xanthan gum

## TOPPING
20 Medjool dates, pits
    removed
4 tablespoons nondairy
    margarine
1 teaspoon vanilla extract
½ teaspoon sea salt
3 tablespoons water
2 cups toasted coconut
    shreds
2 cups chopped nondairy
    chocolate

**YIELD: 24 COOKIES**

- Cream together the margarine, vanilla extract, and sugar until smooth. In a separate bowl, mix together sorghum flour, brown rice flour, potato starch, and xanthan gum.
- Using an electric mixer, slowly incorporate flour mixture into the margarine mixture and beat on medium-low speed for about 2 minutes, scraping sides as needed to form a stiff dough. Press dough into a disk and chill in refrigerator for an hour or so, or chill in the freezer for about 30 minutes.
- Preheat oven to 300°F.
- Once dough has chilled, roll out gently onto parchment paper. The warmer the dough becomes the softer it will get. Roll to about ½ inch thick. Using a 1½-inch circular cookie cutter, cut out as many circles as possible, saving the scraps, rechilling and rerolling until no dough remains. Cut the centers of the cookies out using a small circular cookie cutter, or the back of an icing tip.
- Place cookies gently onto a parchment-covered cookie sheet and bake for 30 to 35 minutes, or until very lightly golden on edges. Let cool completely before removing from cookie sheet.
- Put dates, margarine, vanilla extract, sea salt, and water into a food processor and blend until very smooth, scraping down sides often. Stir in the toasted coconut. Transfer the mixture into a piping bag fitted with a very wide tip. Pipe a ring of filling carefully onto the cookies and press gently into place using slightly greased fingers. Place upside down onto a piece of waxed paper or silicone mat.
- In a double boiler, place the chocolate into the bowl and warm over medium-low heat until melted. Brush the tops of the inverted cookies with melted chocolate to completely coat. Let the chocolate harden and then flip the cookies over. Drizzle with stripes of chocolate and let harden again. Store in airtight container for up to 1 week.

# LEMON SANDWICH COOKIES

These dreamy cookies, with crispy wafers and creamy filling, make a wonderful accompaniment to chamomile or green tea.

## COOKIES

1 tablespoon flaxseed meal
2 tablespoons water
1⅓ cups superfine brown
    rice flour
½ cup sorghum flour
¼ cup tapioca flour
½ cup potato starch
1½ teaspoons xanthan gum
¾ teaspoon baking powder
½ teaspoon salt
1 cup sugar
½ cup nondairy margarine
¼ cup lemon juice
Zest of 1 lemon

## FILLING

1 teaspoon lemon zest
1 tablespoon lemon juice
½ cup shortening
½ cup nondairy margarine
3½ cups + 2 tablespoons
    confectioner's sugar

**YIELD: 24 COOKIES**

- In a small bowl, combine the flaxseed meal with water and let rest until gelled, for about 5 minutes.
- In a medium bowl, whisk together the superfine brown rice flour, sorghum flour, tapioca flour, potato starch, xanthan gum, baking powder, and salt.
- In a large bowl, cream together the sugar and the margarine until smooth. Add the prepared flaxseed meal, lemon juice, and lemon zest and mix well. Slowly incorporate the flour mixture and stir well until a stiff dough forms. Divide dough into two equal-size disks and chill for at least 1 hour in refrigerator.
- When dough is chilled, preheat oven to 375°F. Roll out one section of dough in between two sheets of parchment paper until about ¼ inch thick. Using a circular cookie cutter, cut out cookies and place onto an ungreased cookie sheet. Repeat until all dough has been used, rechilling the dough if it becomes too soft to work with.
- Bake in preheated oven for 9 minutes. Let cool completely. Make the filling by mixing together all the ingredients in a mixer at high speed until very well combined. Pipe filling onto the back of one cookie and sandwich together with another cookie. Repeat until all cookies have been filled.
- Allow cookies to set for at least 1 hour for best flavor and texture. Store in airtight container for up to 1 week.

# ROLLED GINGERBREAD COOKIES

Freshly grated ginger really makes these cookies sparkle. Feel free to cut these little guys (or gals) into any shape your heart desires. Roll them thicker for softer cookies, and thinner for crispier.

**1 tablespoon flaxseed meal**
**2 tablespoons water**
**½ cup nondairy margarine**
**½ cup sugar**
**½ cup molasses**
**1 teaspoon freshly grated ginger**
**1 teaspoon cinnamon**
**½ teaspoon nutmeg**
**½ teaspoon cloves**
**1¾ cups buckwheat flour, divided**
**¾ cup potato starch**
**¼ cup tapioca flour**
**1 teaspoon xanthan gum**
**½ teaspoon salt**

**YIELD: 24 COOKIES**

- In a small bowl, stir together the flaxseed meal and water and allow to rest for 5 minutes, until gelled.
- In a large mixing bowl, cream together the margarine, sugar, molasses, ginger, and prepared flaxseed meal. In a separate bowl, whisk together the spices, 1 cup buckwheat flour, potato starch, tapioca flour, xanthan gum, and salt. Add into the sugar mixture and mix until a dough forms. Add up to ¾ cup additional buckwheat flour, until a soft dough that is easy to handle forms. Gently pat the dough into a disk and wrap in parchment paper. Place in freezer and chill for 30 minutes.
- When the dough is chilled, preheat oven to 350°F. Divide dough in half, and roll out one half of dough (while chilling the other half) to about ¼ inch thick. Work fast so the dough stays chilled; the warmer the dough gets, the stickier it becomes. Once rolled, use your favorite cookie cutters to cut out shapes and place the cut cookies directly onto a parchment-covered baking sheet. Bake for 9 minutes. Repeat with the remaining dough and then let cool.
- Decorate with Royal Icing (page 78). Store in airtight container for up to 2 weeks.

# FIGGY FILLED COOKIES

These delightful cookies, similar to commercial fig bars, are hearty and not-too-sweet. The key to these cookies is keeping the dough super cold. I advise chilling after each rolling and shaping to ensure stick-free, evenly rolled cookies with no frustration.

## COOKIE DOUGH

1½ tablespoons flaxseed meal
3 tablespoons water
⅔ cup cold nondairy margarine
1 cup sugar
1 teaspoon vanilla extract
1⅔ cups brown rice flour
⅔ cup potato starch
⅓ cup tapioca flour
1 teaspoon xanthan gum
2½ teaspoons baking powder
⅓ cup nondairy milk
Additional brown rice flour for rolling

## FILLING

2¼ cups dried mission figs, tops removed
¼ cup raisins
1 teaspoon orange zest
1 small apple, diced
½ cup pecans
3 tablespoons sugar
1 teaspoon cinnamon

**YIELD: 24 COOKIES**

- In a small bowl, combine the flaxseed meal with the water and let rest for about 5 minutes, until gelled.
- In a large mixing bowl, cream together the margarine and sugar until smooth. Mix in the vanilla extract and prepared flaxseed meal.
- In a separate, smaller, bowl, whisk together the brown rice flour, potato starch, tapioca flour, xanthan gum, and baking powder. Gradually add the flour mixture to the sugar mixture and stir well to combine. Add the nondairy milk and mix until a soft dough forms. Dust lightly with brown rice flour if sticky. Wrap in parchment paper and chill in freezer for about 15 minutes, until cold.
- Place all ingredients for the filling into a food processor and pulse until finely crumbled and sticky, scraping down the sides of the bowl as needed.
- Preheat oven to 375°F.
- Take about one-third of the chilled dough and roll it out (in between two sheets of parchment paper) into a rectangle about 3½ inches wide and about ¼ inch thick. Chill briefly, for about 5 minutes in freezer. Roll out a long snake of filling, as you would clay, about 1 inch wide, and place into the center of the rectangle. Fold over each side of the dough, like wrapping a present, using parchment to help roll it up and over, and seal gently using your fingertips. You should have a slightly flat, long enclosed dough tube of figgy filling.
- Chill again briefly, for about 5 minutes. Flip filled dough over to hide the seam on the bottom.
- Using a very clean, sharp, flat blade, cut into 2-inch sections, so that you end up with shapes that look like a popular store-bought variety of fig cookies. Place 2 inches apart onto a parchment-lined cookie sheet. Bake for 15 to 17 minutes or until slightly golden brown on edges. Store in airtight container for up to 1 week.

# SPRINGERLES

These lovely cookies have become a favorite of mine ever since my husband's dear grandmother, Lulu, made him a box when we were first dating and I was lucky enough to get a taste. Spiked with the fragrant flavor of anise, these unforgettable cookies taste just like the holidays to me, and I'm pleased to have a version that I can enjoy again. These cookies taste wonderful with or without the use of a Springerle mold, so feel free to let them remain flat on top if you don't have molds handy.

¾ cup nondairy margarine
1 cup sugar
1 teaspoon anise extract
2½ teaspoons powdered egg replacer, such as Orgran or EnerG, mixed with 3 tablespoons water
1 cup superfine brown rice flour
½ cup millet flour
1 cup potato starch
¼ cup tapioca flour
1 teaspoon xanthan gum
1 teaspoon baking powder
½ teaspoon baking soda
¼ teaspoon salt

**YIELD: 30 COOKIES**

- Preheat oven to 350°F. In a large bowl, cream together the margarine, sugar, and anise extract. Add the prepared egg replacer.
- In a separate bowl, whisk together the rest of the ingredients. Gradually add into the margarine mixture and mix very well until a clumpy dough forms. Roll dough out to about ½ inch thickness. Lightly dust a Springerle mold with superfine brown rice flour, emboss a pattern into the tops of the dough, and then cut cookies to size with a knife. Carefully transfer onto an ungreased baking sheet. Let rest for 1 hour, and then bake for 15 minutes, until very lightly browned on edges and bottoms. To prevent cracking, prop your oven door open an inch or so while baking. Let cool completely before using a spatula to remove. Store in airtight container for up to 1 week.

# CINNAMON GRAHAM CRACKERS

A perfect base for so many recipes, such as s'mores or cheesecake crusts, these crispy crackers are also pretty great on their own. These are especially good slathered with a bit of almond or coconut butter.

1 cup buckwheat flour
1 cup superfine brown
    rice flour
¼ cup tapioca flour
¾ cup cornstarch
2 teaspoons xanthan gum
1 teaspoon baking powder
½ teaspoon baking soda
1 teaspoon cinnamon
½ cup cold nondairy
    margarine
½ cup packed brown sugar
1 teaspoon vanilla extract
⅓ cup nondairy milk
¼ cup agave
¼ cup molasses
3 tablespoons turbinado
    sugar mixed with
    ½ teaspoon cinnamon

**YIELD: 30 CRACKERS**

- In a large bowl, whisk together the buckwheat flour, superfine brown rice flour, tapioca flour, cornstarch, xanthan gum, baking powder, baking soda, and cinnamon until thoroughly mixed.
- In a separate bowl, cream together the margarine and sugar until smooth. Mix in the vanilla extract, nondairy milk, agave, and molasses. Gradually add in the flour mixture until all are incorporated and continue to mix until a stiff dough is formed. Add a touch more buckwheat flour if it is sticky.
- Divide into two sections and pat into disks. Preheat oven to 350°F. Chill each disk briefly (about 15 minutes in freezer), and then roll out in between two pieces of parchment paper until a little less than ¼ inch thick. Cut into squares and poke holes in the top (I used the tip of a chopstick) to poke holes and also to perforate the cracker. For easy rolling and transferring, keep the dough cold. If it starts to lose shape easily, pop it back in the freezer (still on the rolling parchment) for a few minutes, and then go back to shaping the crackers.
- The dough will be quite flexible and very easy to pull off the parchment. Use a flat metal spatula to help you if needed. Place onto an ungreased cookie sheet, sprinkle lightly with the mixture of turbinado and cinnamon, and bake in preheated oven for about 12 to 14 minutes, or until firm and a touch darker on edges.
- Let cool completely. Store in airtight container for up to 1 week.

# RUGELACH

My mother knows how to make some killer rugelach. While it's a traditional Jewish pastry that is enjoyed year-round, the cookies' fragrant fruit filling and crispy pastry crunch always marked the start of the holiday season in our house.

¼ cup soft dried apricots
½ cup dates, not too soft
1¼ cups walnuts
½ teaspoon cinnamon
¼ teaspoon nutmeg
¼ teaspoon salt
¼ cup sugar
1 to 1½ tablespoons apricot
   or strawberry jam
1 recipe Puff Pastry
   (page 147)

**YIELD: 20 COOKIES**

- Preheat oven to 400°F. Place the apricots, dates, walnuts, cinnamon, nutmeg, salt, and sugar into a food processor and pulse until well combined. Add in the jam, 1 tablespoon at a time until the mixture clumps together.
- Roll out one-half of the puff pastry in between two sheets of parchment paper into a 12-inch circle. Using a pizza cutter, cut about ten even triangles. Place a small ball of the filling at the small tip of the triangle. Beginning at the opposite side, roll dough up to cover, sealing the tip when the filling is all bundled up. Repeat with the other half of the dough. Place the cookies onto an ungreased cookie sheet on the middle rack of the oven, about 1 inch apart, and bake for 20 minutes, or until golden brown. Store in airtight container for up to 2 weeks.

# CRISPY GLAZED LIME COOKIES

These zingy cookies are delicious on their own and make an exceptional treat served with a scoop of Strawberry Ice Cream (page 191). Or, cut them slightly larger, then stuff with your favorite ice cream and freeze for an irresistibly sweet and tangy treat.

## COOKIES
**¾ cup cold shortening**
**⅓ cup powdered confectioner's sugar**
**¼ cup sugar**
**Zest of 1 lime (about 1 teaspoon)**
**2 tablespoons lime juice**
**½ teaspoon salt**
**1¼ cups sorghum flour**
**½ cup arrowroot starch**
**¼ cup tapioca flour**
**1 teaspoon xanthan gum**

## GLAZE
**1 cup confectioner's sugar**
**5 tablespoons freshly squeezed lime juice**
**Lime zest to garnish**

**YIELD: ABOUT 12 COOKIES**

- Cream together the shortening, sugars, lime zest, and lime juice until smooth. In a separate bowl, whisk together the salt, sorghum flour, arrowroot starch, tapioca flour, and xanthan gum and then gradually incorporate into the sugar mixture while mixing just until a firm dough is formed. Flatten into a disk and chill in the freezer for about 15 minutes. While the dough chills, preheat oven to 350°F.
- Roll out dough in between two sheets of plastic cling wrap onto a flat surface until about ¼ inch thick. Cut into 2-inch squares and place onto an ungreased cookie sheet.
- Bake for 15 minutes. Let cool and add glaze to the tops. To make the glaze, simply whisk together the glaze ingredients until completely smooth and runny. Spoon onto the tops of the cookies and let dry about 10 minutes. Spoon on another layer and top with lime zest. Let glaze completely harden before serving. Store in airtight container for up to 1 week.

# PALMIERS

These prim and proper cookies are sure to impress at your next gathering with friends. They are so elegant and gorgeous, you won't believe how easy they are if you already have puff pastry on hand.

**1 recipe Puff Pastry
 (page 147)**
**1 cup turbinado sugar**
**1 tablespoon cornstarch
 mixed with 3 tablespoons
 water**

**YIELD: 18 COOKIES**

- Preheat oven to 450°F. Line a large baking sheet with parchment paper.
- Divide the puff pastry in two sections and roll each out into two rectangles, about 12 inches by 6 inches. Dust the tops of each rectangle with ½ cup turbinado sugar to evenly cover. Starting from the edges of the two longest sides of the rectangle, roll the edges of the cookie inward, rolling two separate coils so that they face each other and eventually meet. You will have a long tube with two distinct sections. Cut into ½-inch-wide cookies and place directly onto the prepared cookie sheet. Brush with cornstarch mixture. Sprinkle with additional turbinado. Bake for 12 minutes, or until golden brown. Let cool completely before serving. Store in airtight container for up to 1 week.

# LAVENDER ICEBOX COOKIES

Fresh lavender buds are best for these, but, if you don't have fresh, dried will certainly do. You can source dried lavender either online or in specialty herb stores; look for buds that have a nice deep lavender color on the tips. I like to place dried buds in an airtight glass container with an orange or lemon peel for about 1 hour before using to soften them up a bit.

1¼ cups sorghum flour
½ cup brown rice flour
     (superfine is best, but
     either can be used)
½ cup potato starch
¼ cup tapioca flour
1⅓ cups confectioner's sugar
1 teaspoon xanthan gum
1 cup very cold nondairy
     margarine
1 tablespoon flaxseed meal
2 tablespoons water
½ cup granulated sugar
     for rolling
3 tablespoons fresh or dried
     lavender buds for rolling

**YIELD: ABOUT 30 COOKIES**

- In a food processor, combine all the ingredients up through the xanthan gum and pulse several times to combine thoroughly. Add in the margarine, about a tablespoon at a time, and continue to pulse until crumbly. In a small bowl, combine flaxseed meal with water and let rest until gelled, for about 5 minutes. Add in the prepared flaxseed meal and mix well until a tacky dough forms.
- Divide dough into two sections and shape each as best you can into a log using two pieces of parchment paper. To make perfectly round logs, freeze each log for about an hour, then roll (while still in the parchment) onto a flat surface to create a more even cylinder. Return to freezer and chill at least an additional hour and up to overnight.
- Once ready to bake, preheat oven to 350°F and spread another piece of parchment or foil with a mixture of the granulated sugar and lavender. On a flat surface, roll the log gently but firmly into the mixture to coat, making sure not to be too rough to break the dough. Slice using a sharp knife into ½-inch-thick rounds and place onto an ungreased cookie sheet.
- Bake for 15 to 17 minutes, or until puffy and bottoms are light golden brown. Let cool completely before eating. Store baked cookies in airtight container for up to 1 week.

# MOCHA CRUNCHERS

Espresso and chocolate meet for a dark and delightful cookie that is easy to roll out and even easier to indulge in! These cookies freeze well both as a dough or prebaked. Simply thaw at room temperature for 30 minutes before baking or enjoying.

2 tablespoons flaxseed meal

¼ cup water

⅔ cup nonhydrogenated shortening

1 cup sugar

1 teaspoon baking soda

1 teaspoon salt

1 teaspoon xanthan gum

1¼ cups brown rice flour

⅓ cup cocoa powder

½ cup teff flour

½ cup tapioca flour

2 teaspoons instant espresso powder

1 tablespoon nondairy milk

⅓ cup nondairy chocolate chips

**YIELD: 36 COOKIES**

- Preheat oven to 375°F. In a small bowl, mix the flaxseed meal with the water and allow to rest until gelled, for about 5 minutes.
- In a large mixing bowl, cream together the shortening and sugar along with the prepared flaxseed meal. Mix until smooth.
- In a separate bowl, whisk together the baking soda, salt, xanthan gum, brown rice flour, cocoa powder, teff flour, tapioca flour, and instant espresso powder. Bring together the shortening mixture and flour mixture until a crumbly dough forms and, while still mixing, add in the 1 tablespoon nondairy milk until the dough comes together. Form into two even disks and roll out in between two sheets of parchment paper until ¼ inch thick. Cut out using a cookie cutter and transfer to an ungreased cookie sheet using a flat metal spatula. Bake for 9 minutes. Remove from the oven and sprinkle chocolate chips over the hot cookies. Let set for 1 minute and then spread chocolate thinly over the tops of the cookies. Let cool completely before serving. Store in airtight container for up to 1 week.

# MATCHA COOKIES

Matcha is the powder of finely milled green tea leaves, most often used as a ceremonial tea. Seek out the highest-quality matcha you can for the best flavor. Matcha can be sourced from tea shops, online, and in many grocery chains that offer specialty items, such as Whole Foods.

1 tablespoon flaxseed meal
2 tablespoons water
¼ cup + 3 tablespoons nondairy margarine
⅓ cup confectioner's sugar
2 tablespoons sugar
¾ cup sorghum flour
¼ cup tapioca flour
¼ cup potato starch
⅓ cup + 1 tablespoon almond meal
1 teaspoon xanthan gum
2 tablespoons matcha powder

**YIELD: 24 COOKIES**

- In a small bowl, mix together the flaxseed meal and water and let rest until gelled, for about 5 minutes.
- In a separate bowl, cream together the margarine and sugars until smooth. Add in the prepared flaxseed meal.
- In another bowl, whisk together the flours, potato starch, almond meal, xanthan gum, and matcha powder and then combine with the margarine mixture to form a soft, but workable dough. If the dough is too sticky, add a touch more sorghum flour until easy to handle. Wrap in plastic wrap and chill in freezer for about 15 minutes. While the dough chills, preheat oven to 350°F and line a cookie sheet with parchment paper or a silicone mat.
- Roll out the chilled dough to a thickness of ¼ inch in between two sheets of parchment paper. Remove top piece of parchment and cut into desired shapes using cookie cutters. Slide the bottom piece of parchment and the cookies onto a cookie sheet and chill for an additional 5 minutes in the freezer, or 15 minutes in the fridge. Using a flat metal spatula, carefully transfer the cut cookies to a parchment-covered baking sheet. Sprinkle with sugar and bake for 12 minutes. Let cool completely before serving. Store in airtight container for up to 1 week.

Have a matcha latte while the cookies bake! To make a simple latte, simply add 1 teaspoon matcha powder to 1 cup very hot nondairy milk. Froth with fork, add a touch of stevia or agave to taste. Voilà! Matcha bliss.

# LADYFINGERS

Use these as the base for Tiramisu (page 217) or eat alone. When mixing, be sure to measure exactly as even a little too much liquid can cause these cookies, which are chickpea-based, to spread and become flatter than desired. If you have one available, a nonstick, lightly greased ladyfinger pan comes in handy for baking perfect ladyfingers.

½ cup brown rice flour

½ cup + 3 tablespoons besan/chickpea flour

2 tablespoons tapioca flour

2 tablespoons potato starch

2½ teaspoons baking powder

¼ teaspoon salt

½ teaspoon xanthan gum

¾ cup sugar

1 teaspoon apple cider vinegar

½ cup nondairy margarine, softened

⅔ cup nondairy milk

**YIELD: ABOUT 36 LADYFINGERS**

- Preheat oven to 375°F. Lightly spray a ladyfinger pan with a nonstick cooking spray or line a heavy cookie tray with parchment.
- In a large bowl, whisk together the dry ingredients until well mixed. Add the vinegar, margarine, and nondairy milk and mix vigorously until fluffy. Place into a piping bag fitted with a wide round tip and pipe about 1 tablespoon batter into the ladyfinger pan template or in a straight line, about 2 inches apart, straight onto the parchment paper. Be careful not to pipe too much batter or the cookies will spread.
- Bake for 13 to 15 minutes, or until golden brown on edges. Let cool completely before serving. Store in airtight container for up to 1 week.

# MADELEINES

These light and crisp cookies are perfect any time you want a treat but want to avoid anything that's overly heavy or dense. You'll want to pick up a madeleine pan or two to make these, but these can easily be sourced for under $10 at most kitchen supply stores or online.

**3 teaspoons baking powder**
**¼ teaspoon salt**
**½ cup white rice flour**
**½ cup + 2 tablespoons besan/chickpea flour**
**2 tablespoons tapioca flour**
**3 tablespoons potato starch**
**½ teaspoon xanthan gum**
**1 cup confectioner's sugar**
**1 teaspoon apple cider vinegar**
**½ cup nondairy margarine**
**½ cup nondairy milk**

**YIELD: 24 COOKIES**

- Preheat oven to 375°F. Lightly spray a madeleine pan with a nonstick cooking spray or grease lightly with olive oil.
- In a large mixing bowl, whisk together the baking powder, salt, white rice flour, besan, tapioca flour, potato starch, and xanthan gum.
- Add the confectioner's sugar, apple cider vinegar, margarine, and nondairy milk and mix on high speed (or very fast using a sturdy balloon whisk) for 2 minutes using a whisk attachment until the batter is fluffy and smooth.
- Spoon about 2 teaspoons of batter into the madeleine molds and spread evenly using a small knife. The cookie molds should be three-quarters full. Rap the pan on an even surface a few times to remove any air pockets.
- Bake for 11 to 13 minutes, or until dark golden brown on seashell side and light blond on the bottoms. Let cool before gently removing from the molds. Store in airtight container for up to 1 week.

# HOLIDAY SPRITZ

These small, classic holiday cookies can be easy to make, but a little finesse is always appreciated. I recommend a metal cookie press over any others as the dough tends to stick less to them. Also, make sure the dough is chilled before piping for perfect results.

**2 teaspoons egg replacer powder (such as Orgran)**
**2 tablespoons water**
**1½ cups brown rice flour**
**½ cup white rice flour**
**⅔ cup potato starch**
**1 teaspoon xanthan gum**
**1 cup nondairy margarine**
**1 cup confectioner's sugar**
**1½ teaspoons vanilla extract**

**YIELD: 48 COOKIES**

- In a small bowl, whisk together the egg replacer powder and the water. In a large bowl, whisk together the brown rice flour, white rice flour, potato starch, and xanthan gum. Cream together the margarine, sugar, and vanilla extract and then add the egg replacer mixture. Gradually add the flour mixture until a stiff dough forms. If dough seems too soft, add up to 2 tablespoons brown or white rice flour. Chill for 2 hours in refrigerator, until very cold.
- Preheat oven to 400°F.
- Place in cookie press and fit with disk of choice. Assemble press as instructed and press cookies into desired shapes onto a parchment-covered cookie sheet. Work quickly and be sure to keep the dough cold; this is key! Bake cookies for 7 minutes or until lightly golden brown on edges. Let cool completely before serving. Store in airtight container for up to 3 weeks.

*Ultimate Fudgy Brownies, page 138*

# BARS

# CHERRY ALMOND BISCOTTI

This tart and slightly sweet cookie complements tea or coffee beautifully with its fruity notes. Not only is it pleasing to the taste buds, your eyes are in for a treat with deep red cherries studded throughout.

2 tablespoons flaxseed meal
4 tablespoons water
⅓ cup nondairy margarine
¾ cup sugar
1½ teaspoons almond
    extract
½ teaspoon salt
2 teaspoons baking powder
1 cup sorghum flour
¾ cup brown rice flour
½ cup potato starch
1 teaspoon xanthan gum
¼ cup nondairy milk
1 cup dried cherries

**YIELD: 20 BISCOTTI**

- Preheat oven to 325°F. Combine the flaxseed meal and water into a bowl and let rest for 5 minutes, until gelled.
- In a large bowl, cream together the margarine and sugar until smooth. Add the prepared flaxseed meal, almond extract, and salt.
- In a separate bowl, whisk together the baking powder, sorghum flour, brown rice flour, potato starch, and xanthan gum. Gradually incorporate into the sugar mixture. Add nondairy milk, 1 tablespoon at a time, until a soft dough forms. It should be just dry enough to handle and shape into two balls. Add a touch more sorghum flour or milk to create the right consistency. The dough shouldn't crumble apart, but it also shouldn't be too sticky. Fold in the dried cherries until even distributed.
- Directly on an ungreased cookie sheet, shape the cookie dough into two ovals, about 2.5 inches wide and 1.25 inches tall. Bake in preheated oven for about 30 minutes, until lightly golden on edges. Let cool and then slice cookies diagonally. Place freshly cut cookies on their sides and bake an additional 8 minutes. Turn cookies over and bake another 8 minutes. And one more time . . . flip, and bake a final 8 minutes. Let cool completely before enjoying. Store in airtight container for up to 3 weeks.

# MARBLE BISCOTTI

Chocolate and vanilla mingle in this delightful-looking cookie. Dip into piping hot coffee or hot chocolate for the ultimate biscotti experience. If you're sharing, these make great gifts once you wrap them up in shiny plastic wrap and adorn them with a bow, especially when paired with your favorite blend of coffee.

3 tablespoons flaxseed meal
6 tablespoons water
½ cup sugar
½ cup nondairy margarine
½ teaspoon vanilla extract
1 cup sorghum flour
¾ cup brown rice flour
½ cup potato starch
¼ cup tapioca flour
1 teaspoon xanthan gum
1½ teaspoons baking
   powder
½ teaspoon salt
½ cup nondairy chocolate
   chips, melted, plus 1 cup
   chocolate chips, melted,
   for drizzling

**YIELD: 18 BISCOTTI**

- Preheat oven to 325°F.
- In a small bowl, combine flaxseed meal with water and let rest until gelled, for about 5 minutes. In large mixing bowl, cream together the sugar and the margarine. Add the prepared flaxseed meal and vanilla extract and mix well. In a separate bowl, combine the sorghum flour, brown rice flour, potato starch, tapioca flour, xanthan gum, baking powder, and salt. Stir well to evenly incorporate.
- Slowly combine the flour mixture with the margarine mixture until clumpy. Divide dough into two sections, leaving half in the mixing bowl and setting the rest aside. Gently stir in the ½ cup melted chocolate chips with one-half of the dough until very well combined, scraping bowl as needed.
- Now you will have two sections of dough: one chocolate and one vanilla. Shape the vanilla dough into two balls. Shape the chocolate mixture into two balls as well. Then, roll each section into long ropes, so that you have four long ropes of both chocolate and vanilla—about 10 inches long each.
- Working on an ungreased baking sheet, place one chocolate rope and one vanilla rope side by side and then twist over one another, pressing together to form a flat log about 3 inches by 10 inches and then repeat with other two ropes.
- Bake for 28 minutes, until lightly golden brown on edges, and then remove from the oven and place onto a wire rack to let completely cool. Using a serrated knife, slice diagonally into 3 x 1-inch cookies and place freshly cut cookies on their sides on the cookie sheet.
- Bake cookies for 10 minutes. Flip and bake for 10 more minutes. Flip one more time and bake for 5 more minutes. Let cool completely and then drizzle or coat one side with melted chocolate.
- Store in airtight container for up to 1 month.

# ULTIMATE FUDGY BROWNIES

I can't think of one recipe I've made that has received more acclaim from friends, family, and readers than these brownies. They boast a crispy, flaky, paper-thin layer atop a chewy, gooey perfect square of brownie bliss. Even though these brownies are pretty delicious all by their lonesome, they do take kindly to a thin layer of frosting on top, too. Try them topped with Fluffy Chocolate Frosting (page 75) or Caramel Frosting (page 76) for an extra-indulgent treat!

¾ cup superfine brown rice flour
¼ cup almond meal
¼ cup potato starch
¼ cup sorghum flour
1 teaspoon xanthan gum
½ teaspoon baking soda
1 teaspoon salt
3 cups chopped nondairy chocolate or chocolate chips
1 cup sugar
¼ cup nondairy margarine
½ cup strong coffee
2 tablespoons ground chia seed mixed with 5 tablespoons hot water
1 teaspoon vanilla extract
1 cup nondairy white chocolate chips (optional)

**YIELD: 12 BROWNIES**

- Preheat oven 325°F and lightly grease a 9 x 13-inch metal pan.
- In a large electric mixing bowl, whisk together the superfine brown rice flour, almond meal, potato starch, sorghum flour, xanthan gum, baking soda, and salt.
- Place the chocolate chips into a large heat-safe bowl.
- In a 2-quart saucepan over medium heat, combine the sugar, margarine, and ¼ cup of the coffee and bring to a boil, stirring often. Once boiling, immediately remove from the heat and pour the hot sugar mixture directly onto the chocolate chips, stirring quickly to combine thoroughly. Transfer to the mixing bowl containing the flour mixture along with the prepared chia gel and vanilla extract and mix on medium-high speed until smooth. Add in the additional ¼ cup coffee and mix well. If you're using them, fold in white chocolate chips.
- Spread the batter in the prepared baking pan—the batter will be tacky. Bake for 45 to 50 minutes. Let cool completely before cutting into squares and serving. Store in airtight container for up to 3 days.

# BLONDIES

Blondies are lighter than brownies in taste, texture, and color but still bear a delicious resemblance to their chocolate pals. Try these topped with Peanut Butter Banana Ice Cream (page 292).

2 tablespoons flaxseed meal
4 tablespoons water
⅓ cup coconut palm sugar
1 teaspoon vanilla extract
1 cup brown rice flour
½ cup almond meal
¼ cup potato starch
1 teaspoon xanthan gum
½ teaspoon salt
½ cup nondairy margarine
1 tablespoon coconut oil
1½ cups nondairy white chocolate chips or pieces
½ cup nondairy mini chocolate chips

**YIELD: 12 BLONDIES**

- Preheat oven to 350°F. Lightly grease an 8 x 8-inch baking pan.
- In a small bowl, combine the flaxseed meal and water and let rest until gelled, for about 5 minutes. Stir in the coconut palm sugar and vanilla extract. In a separate bowl, whisk together the brown rice flour, almond meal, potato starch, xanthan gum, and salt.
- Over a double boiler, on medium-low heat, melt the margarine, coconut oil, and white chocolate until smooth. Remove from heat. Stir white chocolate mixture into the flour mixture along with the flaxseed meal mixture until a batter forms. Fold in the mini chocolate chips. Press the batter into the prepared baking pan and bake for 27 minutes, or until golden brown on edges. Let cool completely, for at least 2 hours, before serving. Store in airtight container for up to 1 week.

# LIGHTEN UP LEMON BARS

These are a lightened-up version of traditional lemon bars, leaving out the eggs and butter and opting for plant-based ingredients instead. Agar can easily be sourced at local health food stores or Asian markets. If you can only source agar bars or flakes, simply run them through a spice grinder until powdered.

## CRUST
2 tablespoons flaxseed meal
4 tablespoons water
1½ cups almond meal
¼ teaspoon salt
3 tablespoons sugar

## FILLING
2 cups water
1½ tablespoons agar powder
1¼ cups sugar
1 cup freshly squeezed lemon
    juice (about 6 lemons'
    worth)
1 drop natural yellow food
    coloring
¼ cup cornstarch dissolved
    completely in ¼ cup water
Confectioner's sugar,
    for dusting

**YIELD: 16 BARS**

- Preheat oven to 400°F.
- In a small bowl, mix the flaxseed meal with the water until gelled, for about 5 minutes. In a medium bowl, whisk together the rest of the crust ingredients and then massage the prepared flaxseed meal into the almond meal mixture until well blended. Press crust into a lightly greased 8 x 8-inch baking pan. Bake for 12 to 15 minutes, until golden brown on edges. Remove from oven and let cool while you make the filling.
- To make the filling, bring the 2 cups water and agar powder to a boil over medium heat, stirring constantly with a whisk. Let boil for 3 to 5 minutes, until thickened and all agar has dissolved. (Be sure that all agar has dissolved or your lemon bars won't set correctly.) Stir in the sugar, lemon juice, food coloring, and cornstarch slurry. Continue to cook over medium heat, bringing back up to a boil. Let boil for about 3 minutes, until thickened. Pour the mixture on top of the crust and chill immediately on a flat surface in your refrigerator. Chill 2 hours, or until firm. Cut into squares. Dust with confectioner's sugar before serving. Store in refrigerator for up to 1 week.

# BLUEBERRY BARS

These delicious bars are similar to boxed cereal bars, only tastier and without any added preservatives or chemicals! If blueberry's not your favorite, feel free to use any other type of preserves for endless flavor variations.

1½ cups pecans
1½ cups sorghum flour, plus more as needed for rolling and shaping
⅓ cup potato starch
1 teaspoon baking powder
1 teaspoon xanthan gum
¾ cup nondairy margarine
1 cup sugar
2 tablespoons flaxseed meal
4 tablespoons water
1 cup high-quality blueberry preserves

**YIELD: 16 BARS**

- Preheat oven to 400°F. Lightly grease and flour the bottom and sides of an 8 x 8-inch baking pan.
- Lay pecans in an even layer on a standard cookie sheet so that they do not overlap. Toast pecans for about 10 minutes, or until fragrant and flavorful. Watch carefully so that they do not burn. Once toasted, remove from cookie sheet and set aside until cool. Toss the toasted pecans into a food processor and pulse just until crumbly. Don't overmix.
- In a medium bowl, sift together sorghum flour, potato starch, baking powder, and xanthan gum. Stir in the pulsed pecans.
- In a separate mixing bowl, cream together the margarine and sugar until smooth.
- In a small bowl, combine the flaxseed meal with the water and let rest until gelled, for about 5 minutes. Fold in prepared flaxseed meal with the margarine mixture and mix until combined. Gradually add in the flour mixture, adding up to ⅓ cup additional sorghum flour until the dough can be easily handled. Shape into two separate disks and chill until cold.
- Once the dough is well chilled, take one of the disks and place it in between two pieces of parchment paper and roll until large enough to cover the baking pan.
- Transfer the dough to cover the bottom of the pan, gently pushing down the edges to form a wall around the crust. Spread the blueberry preserves evenly over the layer of crust.
- Take the second disk of dough and crumble into small pieces. Top the jam liberally with dough crumbles. Chill the pan in your freezer while you preheat oven to 350°F.
- Bake for about 35 minutes or until crust becomes golden brown.
- Let cool, then slice into squares. Store bars in an airtight container in refrigerator for up to 1 week.

# PEANUT BUTTER
# MAPLE CRISPY TREATS

Ⓑ

I never tire of crispy rice treats. These feature peanut butter and are lightly painted with melted chocolate to give them extra oomph! Try these with chocolate hazelnut butter (Justin's is a great choice) instead of peanut butter. Then just try not to eat the whole pan yourself.

**3 tablespoons coconut oil**
**4 cups vegan marshmallows, such as Dandies**
**1 teaspoon maple extract**
**2 tablespoons maple syrup**
**½ cup smooth peanut butter**
**6 cups gluten-free crispy rice cereal**
**1 cup nondairy chocolate chips**

**YIELD: 12 BARS**

- Lightly grease an 8 x 8-inch baking dish using either margarine or coconut oil.
- In a large saucepan over medium heat, melt the 3 tablespoons coconut oil slightly so that the bottom of the saucepan is coated. Add the marshmallows and heat over medium heat until mostly melted, stirring often to prevent burning. Stir in the maple extract, maple syrup, and peanut butter and continue to stir until completely incorporated.
- Place crispy rice cereal into a large bowl and pour hot marshmallow mixture over the crispy rice cereal. Mix quickly to ensure that all the cereal is coated with marshmallow mixture. Spread mixture into the prepared pan and press down firmly using greased hands. Let set until hardened, for about 2 hours. Cut into 2 x 2-inch squares.
- Melt chocolate over double boiler and drizzle the chocolate onto all sides of the bars and place onto waxed paper or a silicone mat. Let chocolate harden completely before enjoying. Store in airtight container for up to 1 week.

# TOFFEE CRACKER COOKIES

Utilizing crunchy crackers, these cookie bars have a salty and sweet flavor with a candy-like crunch. Out of crackers? You can also use plain cookies to make these; opt for a crunchy cookie such as vanilla wafers or graham crackers.

**4 to 5 ounces (about 25 crackers) gluten-free, egg-free crackers, such as Glutino's table crackers**

**½ cup nondairy margarine**

**½ cup brown sugar**

**1 cup semi-sweet nondairy chocolate chips**

**½ cup sliced toasted almonds or pecans**

**YIELD: 24 COOKIES**

- Preheat oven to 400°F. Line a medium (about 9 x 13 inches) lipped cookie sheet or baking pan with parchment paper.
- Arrange the crackers on the parchment, as best as you can, in a single layer. Small gaps in between are fine.
- In a 2-quart saucepan, bring together the margarine and brown sugar over medium heat. Stir often, and bring to a boil. Once it hits a boil, let cook for 3 minutes, without stirring. Carefully and strategically pour the hot candy syrup over the crackers to cover. Bake for 5 minutes. Immediately remove from the oven and sprinkle the chocolate chips to cover. Let set for about 4 minutes, and then spread the chocolate to evenly cover the candy. Sprinkle with the almonds. Let rest for 1 hour in a cool place. Freeze briefly until candy has hardened and then cut into squares. Store in airtight container for up to 1 week.

## Chapter 4

# LUSCIOUS PIES, PASTRIES, TARTS, AND CHEESECAKES

*Baking pies is* a favorite hobby of mine because with just a little bit of extra effort, you end up with a dessert that is so impressive it just begs to be shared. I recommend not trying to bake pies that use the Flakey Classic Piecrust or Puff Pastry on especially humid days, as the tendency for the dough to stick will be much greater, resulting in a frustrating pie baking experience. Shoot for cooler or dry summer days instead for perfect pies every time.

# BASICS

## FLAKEY CLASSIC PIECRUST  Ⓢ Ⓝ Ⓒ Ⓑ

This piecrust is a staple in this chapter. With a flaky, buttery consistency, it truly does make a pie stand out!

1 cup superfine brown
   rice flour
¾ cup white rice flour
½ cup potato starch
½ cup tapioca flour
1½ teaspoons xanthan gum
½ teaspoon baking powder
3 tablespoons sugar
10 tablespoons cold
   nondairy margarine
3 tablespoons lemon juice
½ cup ice-cold water

**YIELD: 2 STANDARD-SIZE
PIECRUSTS, OR ENOUGH
FOR 1 LATTICE-TOPPED
OR COVERED PIE**

- In a large bowl, whisk together the superfine brown rice flour, white rice flour, potato starch, tapioca flour, xanthan gum, baking powder, and sugar.
- Drop the margarine into the flour mixture by tablespoons. Use fingers or pastry blender to quickly mix into an even crumble. Using a large fork, stir in the lemon juice and cold water until a soft dough forms. If the dough seems too sticky, add a touch more brown rice flour. Wrap in plastic wrap and chill in the freezer for 15 minutes, or refrigerator for at least 1 hour before using.
- Keeps tightly covered in refrigerator for up to 1 week, and frozen for up to 3 months.

This crust freezes well, so feel free to shape the unbaked dough into a patty and place into two freezer-safe bags (double layered), and, the day before using, allow to thaw in refrigerator overnight before rolling out to use in a recipe. Or roll it out onto two aluminum pie pans, cover in plastic wrap, and freeze. Pie makin' is easy if you already have the crusts prepared ahead of time!

# PUFF PASTRY

The key to this super-flakey pastry is keeping the dough cold! Be sure to chill adequately between rotations to ensure a workable dough. I also recommend chilling all ingredients before getting started.

¾ cup **superfine brown rice flour**
¾ cup **white rice flour**
⅔ cup **potato starch**
⅓ cup **tapioca flour**
2 teaspoons **xanthan gum**
1¼ cups **very cold nondairy margarine**
½ cup **ice-cold water**

**YIELD: 20 SERVINGS**

### EASY PUFF COOKIES

Preheat oven to 400°F. Dust a sheet of parchment with turbinado sugar. Place the puff pastry dough onto the sugared surface and dust with more sugar. Place another sheet of parchment onto the dough and roll out to ⅓ to ½ inch thick. Use a fun cookie cutter to cut out shapes.

Bake on a parchment-covered cookie sheet for about 20 minutes, until golden brown.

- In a large bowl, whisk together the brown rice flour, ½ cup of the white rice flour, potato starch, tapioca flour, and xanthan gum. Drop in the margarine by the spoonful. Using clean hands, quickly cut the margarine into the flour until the mixture resembles pebbles.
- Add in the cold water and mix quickly to form a slightly sticky dough. Punch down into the bowl to flatten the dough and sprinkle with 2 tablespoons white rice flour; pat into the dough to make it less sticky. Flip and repeat with the additional 2 tablespoons white rice flour.
- Chill the dough for 20 minutes in the freezer.
- In between two sheets of parchment paper, roll out the dough into a rectangle about 5 x 9 inches. Use a straight edge to square up the edges, forming a solid rectangle. Work quickly so that the dough stays cold!
- Fold the dough into thirds (like folding a letter) and rotate a quarter of a turn. Use the parchment to help fold the dough over evenly. Roll it out again into another rectangle 5 x 9 inches. Fold it into thirds once again. Wrap loosely in parchment and chill in the freezer for an additional 20 minutes.
- Repeat the steps again, exactly as described above. Wrap and chill the puff pastry until ready to use. When working with the pastry, be sure not to roll it out too thin, ⅓ to ½ of an inch is just right.
- Use as directed in recipes calling for puff pastry. To deepen the color of the pastry, mix 2 teaspoons cornstarch with ½ cup water—bring to a boil over medium heat and cook until translucent. Brush a little of the paste onto the surface before baking. Keeps frozen for up to 1 month.

# PIES

# SUGAR CRUNCH APPLE PIE

I discovered a recipe similar to this apple pie years ago that utilized a unique technique I was immediately drawn to. It was the first pie I made in this fashion and has since become my favorite way of making apple pie. Adding the sugary syrup to the assembled pie is fun and delicious, as it creates a crisp sugar topping, not unlike the candy crunch from crème brûlée.

**1 recipe Flakey Classic Piecrust (page 146)**

**APPLES**
**8 medium Granny Smith apples**
**½ teaspoon cardamom**
**1 teaspoon cinnamon**
**½ teaspoon cloves**

**SAUCE**
**½ cup nondairy margarine**
**4 tablespoons superfine brown rice flour**
**¼ cup water**
**1 cup packed brown sugar**

**YIELD: 8 SERVINGS**

- Prepare the pie dough according to recipe directions, divide into two disks and chill for 2 hours in your refrigerator. Core and peel the apples. Slice thinly and lightly toss with cardamom, cinnamon, and cloves.
- Once piecrusts are chilled, roll out one section of dough in between two sheets of parchment paper to a ¼ inch thickness. Use the parchment paper to help flip the rolled out crust into a lightly greased pie pan. Cut off excess dough and reserve.
- Heap the sliced apples into a mound on top of the crust in the pie pan.
- Take the second chilled dough disk and roll to same thickness in between two sheets of parchment paper. As you did with the first crust, use the parchment to help you flip the dough over on top of the mound of apples. If any dough rips, simply use your fingertips dipped in water to help seal it back together. Build up the sides with excess dough to form a shallow wall as the outer crust. Make a few ¼-inch-wide slits in the top crust to vent.
- Whisk the ingredients for the sauce together into a 2-quart saucepan on medium heat and let it come to a boil, while stirring occasionally. After it has come to a boil, reduce heat to simmer and let cook for 2 minutes. Remove the sauce from the heat.
- Preheat your oven to 425°F. Pour the sugar mixture on top of piecrust, aiming mostly for the slits in the center, and allow any excess to drip over sides. Once all sauce has been added to the pie use a pastry brush to gently brush the remaining syrup evenly over the pie.
- Bake for 15 minutes, then reduce oven temp to 350°F and bake for an additional 35 to 45 minutes. Remove from oven, and let cool for at least 2 hours before serving. Store in airtight container for up to 2 days.

# BANANA CREAM PIE

Up until the Great Depression, bananas were practically unheard of in desserts. Apparently, it was the frugalness of using the overripe bananas that led to incorporating them into sweets. With its rich, cream filling, this pie is the very opposite of frugal! It is best enjoyed right after cooling as the bananas tend to discolor after a day or so; one very good way to remedy this is to freeze the pie immediately after it cools and serve mostly frozen.

½ recipe Flakey Classic
   Piecrust (page 146)

**FILLING**
¾ cup sugar
⅓ cup white rice flour
¼ teaspoon salt
2 cups nondairy milk
3 tablespoons cornstarch
   mixed with 3 tablespoons
   water
2 tablespoons nondairy
   margarine
2 teaspoons vanilla extract
4 large bananas

**YIELD: 10 SERVINGS**

- Preheat oven to 400°F.
- Prepare the piecrust according to recipe directions and then blind bake in oven for 10 minutes. Reduce oven temperature to 350°F.
- In a 2-quart saucepan, whisk together the sugar, white rice flour, salt, nondairy milk, and cornstarch slurry. Add the margarine and vanilla extract. Heat over medium heat until the mixture comes to a boil, stirring constantly. Let cook for 1 minute, still stirring constantly, until the mixture thickens considerably.
- Slice the bananas into the baked piecrust forming an even layer. Pour the hot sugar mixture over the bananas to cover and bake in preheated oven for 15 minutes. Remove from oven and let cool. Chill and serve with fresh banana slices and Sweetened Whipped Coconut Cream, page 33. Store in airtight container in refrigerator for up to 2 days.

# KEY LIME PIE

Sweet yet sour, this creamy pie will transport you straight to the Florida Keys. I recommend using bottled key lime juice for ease and availability.

## CRUST

1 cup gluten-free cookie crumbs (use hard cookie such as Pizzelles (page 114), Cinnamon Graham Crackers (page 123), Vanilla Wafers (page 108), etc.)

1 cup ground pecans

3 tablespoons sugar

2 tablespoons ground chia seed mixed with 4 tablespoons water

1 tablespoon coconut oil

## FILLING

1 (350 g) package extra-firm silken tofu

1 cup key lime juice

1 cup canned full-fat coconut milk

½ cup coconut cream from the top of a can of full-fat coconut milk

1 cup sugar

2 tablespoons confectioner's sugar

¾ teaspoons salt

¼ cup besan/chickpea flour

¼ cup white rice flour

2 tablespoons cornstarch

1 teaspoon lime zest, plus more for topping

**YIELD: 10 SERVINGS**

- Preheat oven to 375°F.
- Mix together all the crust ingredients, in order given, and press into a standard-size pie pan.
- In the bowl of a food processor, place the filling ingredients, pulsing a few times after each addition, until smooth. Be sure to scrape down sides as needed.
- Pour the filling mixture into the crust and carefully transfer to the middle rack of your oven. Bake for 20 minutes. Reduce heat to 300°F and bake for an additional 40 to 45 minutes, until very lightly golden brown on edges. Let cool at room temperature and then chill in refrigerator overnight. Top with lime zest and Sweetened Whipped Coconut Cream (page 33). Store in airtight container in refrigerator for up to 2 days.

### ALLERGY NOTE

If you have a nut allergy and would like to make this pie, simply swap out the pecans in the crust for toasted sunflower or pumpkin seeds.

# PUMPKIN PIE

Popular during the autumn months, pumpkin pie didn't become the traditional dessert of Thanksgiving until the early 1800s. This pumpkin pie is just like the ones my mother used to make for the holiday—with a crust that's softer on the bottom and crispy on the sides. Strange as it sounds, that was always my favorite part of the pie!

½ recipe Flakey Classic
   Piecrust (page 146)
1 cup sugar
1 teaspoon cinnamon
1 teaspoon ginger
½ teaspoon ground cloves
¼ teaspoon ground nutmeg
1 teaspoon salt
1 (350 g) package extra-firm
   silken tofu
1½ teaspoons vanilla extract
⅓ cup superfine brown
   rice flour
2 cups canned pumpkin
   puree
¼ cup apple cider or
   nondairy milk

YIELD: 10 SERVINGS

- Prepare the piecrust according to recipe directions. Shape the dough into a disk and chill in the refrigerator for at least 1 hour.
- Preheat oven to 425°F. Roll out the crust in between two pieces of parchment and then flip over to lay the piecrust evenly into the bottom of a standard-size pie pan. Pinch the top to make the pie fancy, or flute.
- Combine all the ingredients for the pie filling in a food processor and blend until very smooth. Spread pie filling into unbaked crust and bake for 15 minutes.
- Reduce your oven temperature to 350°F and bake for an additional 40 minutes, or until the crust is golden brown. Let pie cool completely and refrigerate for at least 4 hours before serving. This pie is best when chilled overnight. Store in airtight container in refrigerator for up to 5 days.

# STRAWBERRY PIE

Strawberry Pie always reminds me of the beginning of summertime, right when the weather gets warm enough to start craving cold desserts. This is a great recipe to make the night before as it needs to firm up for quite some time, plus it is excellent served very cold.

**½ recipe Flakey Classic Piecrust (page 146)**

**FILLING**
**4 cups strawberries, sliced**
**1 cup granulated sugar**
**4 tablespoons cornstarch**
**¼ cup water**
**Pinch salt**
**2 or 3 sliced strawberries for a garnish**

**YIELD: 10 SERVINGS**

- Preheat oven to 425°F. Lightly grease a standard-size pie pan and dust with brown rice or sorghum flour.
- Prepare the piecrust according to recipe directions.
- Roll out the dough in between two pieces of parchment paper until it is about ¼ inch thick. Carefully invert onto a pie pan, shaping to fit and make a lip on the crust. Using a fork, poke about twenty small holes evenly over the crust. Bake for 20 minutes, or until crust is firm. Let cool completely before filling.
- Filling: Place 1½ cups of the strawberries plus the sugar into a 2-quart saucepan and mash gently with a potato masher. Cook over medium heat just until sugar dissolves completely.
- In a medium bowl, whisk together the cornstarch and water until smooth and add to the cooked strawberry mixture along with the salt. Bring to a boil over medium heat and allow to cook for about 2 minutes. Remove from heat and let cool slightly, but not completely, for about 15 minutes. Arrange the remaining 2½ cups strawberries evenly into the piecrust. Pour the cooked filling into prepared pie pan and let chill in fridge until firm, for about 12 hours. Garnish with additional strawberry slices. Serve cold. Store in airtight container in refrigerator for up to 2 days.

# CHERRY PIE

I recommend using Bing or sour cherries for this pie to achieve that lovely deep red color that we're so accustomed to with cherry pie. I particularly love this pie served warm from the oven à la mode.

**1 recipe Flakey Classic Piecrust (page 146)**
**4 cups fresh cherries, pitted**
**¼ cup tapioca flour**
**1 cup sugar**
**¼ teaspoon salt**
**1 teaspoon vanilla extract**
**4 teaspoons nondairy margarine**

You can use frozen cherries if fresh aren't in season; simply thaw them out and drain thoroughly before using.

- Prepare the piecrust according to recipe directions and divide crust evenly into two sections. Refrigerate one disk while you roll out the other in between two sheets of parchment paper, to about ¼ inch thickness. Flip over into a deep-dish pie pan and shape to fit the pan.
- In a large bowl, toss the cherries with the tapioca flour, sugar, salt, and vanilla extract until evenly coated. Place into the pie shell and spread evenly. Dot with margarine. Roll out the other half of the crust in between two sheets of parchment paper to ¼ inch thickness. Drape over the top of the pie, inverting using one sheet of parchment to assist, and top the pie with the second crust. Flute the edges to seal and then slice a few small slits in the crust to vent. Bake for 45 to 50 minutes, until piecrust is golden brown. Let pie cool slightly before serving. Store in airtight container for up to 2 days.

# ANY BERRY PIE

Blackberry, blueberry, raspberry . . . any type of berry can be used in this pie and it will still be delicious. My favorite is a solid tie between blackberry and blueberry.

**1 recipe Flakey Classic Piecrust (page 146)**
**½ cup brown sugar**
**¼ cup sugar**
**3 tablespoons cornstarch**
**½ teaspoon salt**
**1 teaspoon vanilla extract**
**4 cups blackberries, blueberries, or raspberries**
**1 tablespoon nondairy margarine**

**YIELD: 10 SERVINGS**

- Preheat oven to 425°F.
- Prepare the crust according to recipe directions and roll out half of the crust in between two sheets of parchment to ¼ inch thick, while keeping the other half chilled. Place one half of crust into a deep-dish pie pan and shape to fit the pie pan.
- In a medium bowl, toss together the brown sugar, sugar, cornstarch, and salt until well mixed. Add in the vanilla extract and berries and gently stir until the berries are completed covered. Place berries into the piecrust and dot evenly with margarine.
- Roll out the other half of piecrust in between two sheets of parchment until about ¼ inch thick. Work fast! Have a pizza cutter handy and slice 1 x 9-inch strips of piecrust. Use your hands to gently peel up the tip of the strip and drape on top of the blueberries to form a crosshatch pattern until pie is covered to your liking. You can also use a cookie cutter to cut out shapes to top the pie.
- Bake for 40 minutes, or until the piecrust is deep golden brown, but not burned. Serve hot à la mode or room temperature. Store in airtight container for up to 2 days.

# TARTE TATIN

This recipe is super simple but requires a pan that can safely, and effectively, go from stove top to oven, such as cast iron. For a perfect Tarte Tatin, choose a variety of apple that will hold its shape while cooking, such as Granny Smith or Gala.

½ recipe Flakey Classic
    Piecrust (page 146)
¼ cup nondairy margarine
½ cup brown sugar
5 small apples, peeled,
    cored, and quartered

YIELD: 8 SERVINGS

- Preheat oven to 425°F. Shape the piecrust dough into a disk and chill until ready to use.
- Over medium heat, in a 9-inch cast-iron pan, melt the margarine until liquid. Sprinkle on the brown sugar and then place the apples directly on top of the sugar, arranging snugly and evenly so that the domed sides are facing down. Try to eliminate any excess spaces in between the apples. Let the apples cook, completely undisturbed over medium heat for 20 minutes.
- Transfer the hot pan to the oven and bake on the middle rack for 20 more minutes.
- Remove from oven and let rest briefly.
- Roll the piecrust out in between two sheets of parchment paper, just wide enough to cover the cast-iron pan with about 1 inch excess. Flip the piecrust over the apples to cover, and push the dough gently down to form a rustic top crust. Bake for an additional 20 minutes, and then remove from oven and let cool for 10 minutes.
- Flip the pie out onto a lipped plate, roughly the same size as the tart. The dough will invert to form a lovely crust. If any apples happen to stick to the pan, carefully remove and place them back onto the tart.
- Serve warm or room temperature. Store in airtight container for up to 2 days.

# CHOCOLATE SILK PIE

This is one of my favorite desserts to bring to potlucks because of its simplicity and versatility. The secret ingredient is silken tofu, which creates a base that's both firm and silky. Top each individual piece with Sweetened Whipped Coconut Cream (page 33) just before serving.

½ **recipe Flakey Classic Piecrust (page 146)**

2 **(350 g) packages extra-firm silken tofu**

2 **teaspoons vanilla extract**

2 **tablespoons cocoa powder (I like extra-dark)**

½ **cup sugar**

1½ **cups chopped nondairy chocolate or chocolate chips**

**YIELD: 10 SERVINGS**

- Preheat oven to 400°F.
- Prepare the piecrust according to recipe directions and roll out in between two sheets of parchment paper until about ¼ inch thick.
- Flip over the parchment to gently place the crust into a standard-size glass pie pan. Fold or flute the crust and pierce bottom several times evenly with fork. Bake for 20 minutes, or until light golden brown. Remove from oven.
- To prepare the filling, blend the tofu, vanilla extract, cocoa powder, and sugar in a food processor until completely smooth, scraping down sides as needed.
- In a double boiler, melt the chocolate and drizzle into the tofu mixture and blend until completely incorporated. Spread filling into baked pie shell and let cool at room temperature for 1 hour before transferring to the refrigerator to chill until slightly firm, 4 hours up to overnight. Store in airtight container in refrigerator for up to 3 days.

# SKY-HIGH PEANUT BUTTER PIE

If you love peanut butter you're going to flip over this pie. Rich peanut butter and chocolate combine for a luscious base, while fluffy coconut cream gives the pie its name. You can also switch this up and use almond or cashew butter if you have a peanut allergy.

½ **recipe Flakey Classic Piecrust (page 146)**

4 **ounces semi-sweet chocolate**

3 **(350 g) packages firm silken tofu**

2 **cups creamy peanut butter**

2 **cups confectioner's sugar**

3 **tablespoons ground chia seed**

½ **teaspoon sea salt**

1 **recipe Sweetened Whipped Coconut Cream (page 33)**

2 **ounces nondairy chocolate chips or chunks, melted, for drizzling**

¼ **cup crushed roasted and salted peanuts**

**YIELD: 10 SERVINGS**

- Preheat oven to 400°F and prepare the piecrust according to recipe directions. Roll out in between two sheets of parchment until ¼ inch thick. Drape over a deep-dish pie pan and press down evenly to cover. Flute edges and bake for 20 minutes, or until lightly golden brown. Remove from oven and place on wire rack to cool. Sprinkle 4 ounces of the chocolate chips evenly onto the piecrust and let rest for 5 minutes. Spread the melted chocolate, using a silicone spatula, to coat the inside of the piecrust. Let cool completely until chocolate is rehardened—once the crust is at room temperature, place in the refrigerator to speed up the process.
- In a food processor combine the tofu, peanut butter, sugar, chia seed, and salt. Blend until completely smooth, for about 5 minutes. Spread into the prepared piecrust, and freeze for at least 3 hours. Transfer to refrigerator and chill overnight. Before serving, top with whipped coconut cream and drizzle with chocolate. Sprinkle with crushed peanuts. Store in an airtight container in the refrigerator for up to 2 days.

# PECAN PIE

The first time I tasted Pecan Pie, I was smitten. Even today when I get around one, it takes a bit of restraint for me to stop eating the whole darned thing! Best to share with others, or just make two pies, and save yourself the heartache.

**½ recipe Flakey Classic Piecrust (page 146)**
**2 tablespoons flaxseed meal**
**¼ cup water**
**1¼ cups packed brown sugar**
**2 tablespoons superfine brown rice flour, or white rice flour**
**2 teaspoons vanilla extract**
**½ cup melted nondairy margarine**
**1½ cups chopped pecans**

**YIELD: 10 SERVINGS**

- Preheat oven to 400°F. Prepare the piecrust according to recipe directions and press into a standard-size pie pan, making the crust slightly shorter than the top edge of the pan. Flute or use a spoon to make a design in the top of the crust.
- In a large bowl, stir together flaxseed meal and water and let set for 5 minutes, until gelled. Transfer to a mixing bowl and whip on high speed using a whisk attachment for 1 minute (or using elbow grease and a whisk), until fluffy. Add the sugar, brown rice flour, vanilla extract, and margarine. Fold in 1 cup of the chopped pecans. Stir well. Spoon filling into unbaked crust and then top with remaining chopped pecans.
- Bake for 35 to 40 minutes, until crust is golden brown and filling is bubbly. Carefully remove from the oven and let cool completely, for at least 4 hours, before serving. Store in airtight container in refrigerator for up to 2 days.

# NEW YORK–STYLE CHEESECAKE

This cheesecake takes a little added patience as it absolutely must be left in the oven 1 to 2 hours to finish baking and then it must be chilled overnight, but it is so worth it. This classic dessert is just perfect plain but pairs exceptionally well with fruit topping. Try it with Cherry Vanilla Compote (page 228), Broiled Persimmons (page 226), Blueberry Lavender Jam (page 228), or even plain fruit such as strawberries.

¼ cup almond meal

4 (8-ounce) tubs nondairy cream cheese, such as Tofutti brand

1¾ cups sugar

½ cup nondairy sour cream or coconut cream

½ cup besan/chickpea flour mixed with ½ cup water

¼ cup superfine brown rice flour or white rice flour

1 teaspoon vanilla extract

**YIELD: 12 SERVINGS**

- Preheat oven to 350°F and lightly grease an 8-inch springform pan. Sprinkle the bottom of the pan evenly with the almond meal. You may use a larger pan, but your cheesecake will be thinner and may need to cook less time.
- Place all the remaining ingredients into a food processor and blend until very smooth, for about 2 minutes, scraping down the sides as needed. Don't taste the batter as the besan will make it unpleasant until baked!
- Bake for 45 minutes at 350°F and then reduce heat to 325°F. Bake for an additional 35 minutes, and then turn off oven. Let the cheesecake cool, inside the closed oven, for about 1 to 2 hours. Chill overnight before serving. Store in airtight container in refrigerator for up to 4 days.

# PISTACHIO ROSE CHEESECAKE

This fragrant cake is delightful when served with a dollop of Sweetened Whipped Coconut Cream (page 33) and a dry white wine, or sparkling grape juice for the kids. Rose water can be located in most specialty grocers near other similar extracts and flavorings. Certainly, if you cannot locate this particular flavoring, equal amounts of spiced rum or vanilla extract would replace it just fine, albeit without the floral undertones.

## CRUST

1 tablespoon flaxseed meal
2 tablespoons water
1 cup pistachios, pulsed until crumbly
2 tablespoons sugar
1 tablespoon almond or canola oil
¼ cup almond meal, plus extra for sprinkling

## FILLING

2 cups (20 ounces) silken tofu
1 to 1½ teaspoons rose water (the more the rosier!)
3 (8-ounce) containers nondairy cream cheese, such as Tofutti
¾ cup sugar
¼ teaspoon salt
3 tablespoons white rice flour
2 drops pink food coloring (optional)

**YIELD: 10 SERVINGS**

- Preheat oven to 400°F. Lightly grease only the sides of an 8-inch springform pan. You may use a larger pan, but your cheesecake will be thinner and may need to cook less time.
- In a small bowl, combine flaxseed meal with water and let rest until gelled, for about 5 minutes. In a large bowl, mix together the pistachios, sugar, almond oil, almond meal, and prepared flaxseed meal until clumpy. Use very lightly greased hands and press firmly into the bottom of the springform pan and cover as best as you can. Once it is spread out covering as much surface as possible, sprinkle lightly with almond meal and then press down to cover completely and evenly.
- In a food processor, combine all the ingredients for the filling and blend until completely smooth, for about 5 minutes, scraping down sides often. Spread the filling evenly into the prepared springform pan and then bake for 15 minutes.
- Reduce heat to 250°F, without removing the cheesecake from the oven, and bake for an additional 60 minutes. Turn oven off and let cheesecake remain for 1 more hour. Let cool for 1 hour at room temperature on a wire rack and then transfer to the refrigerator to cool overnight. Store in airtight container in refrigerator for up to 4 days.

# CARAMEL CHAI CHEESECAKE

This version of the classic dessert is pure decadence. If you really love cinnamon, cloves, and allspice, serve it with a piping-hot mug of chai for the ultimate spicy indulgence.

## CRUST

6 ounces (170 g) pecans
3 tablespoons melted nondairy margarine
3 tablespoons sugar
2 tablespoons superfine brown rice flour

## FILLING

1 (350 g) package extra-firm silken tofu
3 (8-ounce) tubs nondairy cream cheese, such as Tofutti
⅔ cup packed light brown sugar
5 tablespoons superfine brown rice flour
¼ teaspoon sea salt
1 teaspoon cinnamon
⅛ teaspoon allspice
¼ teaspoon ground black pepper
¼ teaspoon ground cloves
⅛ teaspoon cardamom
1 teaspoon vanilla extract
1 recipe Caramel Sauce (page 81)

**YIELD: 10 SERVINGS**

### For the Crust

- Preheat oven to 400°F. Pulse the pecans in a food processor, just until crumbly. Stir in the rest of the crust ingredients and press (using hands dusted with superfine brown rice flour) into an 8-inch springform pan.
- Bake for 10 minutes and then remove from the oven.

### For the Filling

- Place all the ingredients for the filling into a food processor and blend until very smooth, for at least 5 minutes. Spread onto the prepared crust and bake in preheated oven for 15 minutes.
- Reduce heat to 250°F and allow cheesecake to bake for an additional 60 minutes. Turn oven off and let cool for up to 2 more hours while remaining in the oven. Chill in refrigerator overnight and then make the Caramel Sauce (page 81) just before serving, so that you have hot caramel sauce on a cold cheesecake. Top with Sweetened Whipped Coconut Cream (page 33). Store in airtight container in refrigerator for up to 4 days.

# PUMPKIN PECAN CHEESECAKE

What could be more apropos for autumn than this flavor combo? If you're looking for a wonderful alternative (or addition!) to Pumpkin Pie on Thanksgiving, look no further.

## CRUST
1 tablespoon flaxseed meal
2 tablespoons water
2 cups pecans
¼ teaspoon salt
¼ cup brown sugar

## FILLING
1 block firm silken tofu
2 (8-ounce) tubs nondairy
   cream cheese, such as
   Tofutti
1 cup sugar
¼ cup plus 2 tablespoons
   brown rice flour
¼ cup lemon juice
1 (15-ounce) can pumpkin
   puree
⅓ cup brown sugar
1 teaspoon cinnamon
½ teaspoon pumpkin
   pie spice

**YIELD: 12 SERVINGS**

- Preheat oven to 400°F. Lightly grease the sides of an 8-inch springform pan.
- In a small bowl, mix together the flaxseed meal and the water. Let rest for 5 minutes, until gelled. In a food processor, pulse together the pecans, salt, and brown sugar until the mixture resembles coarse crumbles. Add in prepared flaxseed meal and pulse again until pecans come together into a loose dough. Press into the bottom of the prepared springform pan and bake for 10 minutes.
- In the meantime, clean the food processor and mix together the tofu, nondairy cream cheese, sugar, ¼ cup brown rice flour, and lemon juice. Blend until completely smooth, for about 2 minutes, scraping down sides as needed. Scoop out about 1 cup of this mixture and spread evenly onto the crust to form a thin white layer.
- Add the canned pumpkin, brown sugar, cinnamon, pumpkin pie spice, and remaining 2 tablespoons brown rice flour. Blend again until completely smooth, scraping down sides as needed. Spread on top of white layer.
- Bake for 15 minutes. Reduce oven temperature to 325°F and bake for an additional hour. Turn oven off and let cheesecake remain for about 1 hour. Chill completely overnight before serving. Store in airtight container in refrigerator for up to 3 days.

# CHOCOLATE BROWNIE CHEESECAKE Ⓒ

This cheesecake has a super-secret special ingredient: black beans! But you can't tell—in gluten-free baking, oftentimes beans and legumes can be our best friends, providing a little bit of rise and a lot of binding power, along with a totally neutral flavor, so you won't taste anything but chocolaty goodness.

## CRUST
1 cup hazelnut meal
    (finely ground hazelnuts)
2 tablespoons cocoa powder
3 tablespoons sugar
3 tablespoons melted
    nondairy margarine or
    coconut oil

## FILLING
⅔ cup sugar
3 (8-ounce) tubs nondairy
    cream cheese, such as
    Tofutti
1 cup canned black beans,
    drained and rinsed
½ cup nondairy milk
¼ cup brown rice flour
2 cups nondairy chocolate
    chips, melted

**YIELD: 10 SERVINGS**

- Grease the sides of an 8-inch springform pan and preheat oven to 400°F.
- In a small bowl, stir together the hazelnut meal, cocoa powder, and sugar. Drizzle in the melted margarine and stir to combine. Press the mixture onto the bottom of the springform pan to form an even layer. Bake for 9 minutes. Remove from oven and decrease temperature to 375°F.
- In a food processor, combine all the ingredients for the filling, one at a time, in the order listed, making sure that all the ingredients have been completely blended before adding in the melted chocolate chips.
- Spread filling mixture evenly on top of the prebaked crust. Bake for 30 minutes, and then reduce oven temperature to 325°F. Bake for an additional 40 minutes. Turn oven off and allow cheesecake to remain for 2 hours. Chill completely—overnight is best—before serving. Store in airtight container in refrigerator for up to 4 days.

# TARTS, COBBLERS, AND PASTRIES

# CHOCOLATE PISTACHIO TART

I love the contrast of the deep chocolate filling against the salty pistachio crust. This pie freezes beautifully and can be thawed in the refrigerator overnight the day before serving.

## CRUST
2 tablespoons flaxseed meal
3 tablespoons water
1 cup pistachios, pulsed until crumbly (plus additional crushed pistachios for garnish)
3 tablespoons fine yellow cornmeal
2 scant tablespoons sugar
½ teaspoon salt
3 tablespoons olive oil

## FILLING
2½ cups nondairy semi-sweet chocolate chips
1⅓ cups coconut milk
1 teaspoon vanilla extract
⅛ teaspoon ground cumin
¼ teaspoon sea salt

**YIELD: 8 SERVINGS**

- Preheat oven to 400°F.
- In a small bowl, combine the flaxseed meal with the water and let rest until gelled, for about 5 minutes. In a separate small bowl, whisk together the pistachios, cornmeal, sugar, and salt until well combined. Evenly mix in the olive oil and flaxseed gel, using clean hands.
- Press crust into a standard-size pie pan, about ⅛ inch thick. Bake for 10 minutes. Remove and let cool completely.
- To make the filling, place the chocolate chips in a large heat-safe bowl.
- In a small saucepan, combine the coconut milk, vanilla extract, cumin, and salt and bring just to a boil over medium heat. Once bubbly, pour over chocolate chips and mix well. Spread the chocolate mixture into the piecrust and let cool at room temperature, for about 1 hour. Sprinkle with crushed pistachios and transfer into the refrigerator to cool completely until firm. Store in airtight container in refrigerator for up to 2 days.

# PEARBERRY TART

This fruity concoction is pretty and delish! I recommend red raspberries as they look so beautiful against the amber-colored pears. The tart is easy to prep, and it has a silky custard texture that will make you yearn for a second slice!

½ **recipe Flakey Classic Piecrust (page 146)**
⅓ **cup besan/chickpea flour**
3 **tablespoons cornstarch**
⅓ **cup sugar**
½ **teaspoon salt**
1 **cup red raspberries or other berry**
2 **medium pears, peeled, cored, and sliced**
⅓ **cup turbinado sugar**

**YIELD: 8 SERVINGS**

- Preheat oven to 400°F.
- Prepare the piecrust as directed and chill in refrigerator for 30 minutes. Roll out in between two sheets of parchment paper to about ¼ inch thick. Flip over onto an 8-inch tart shell and press dough into the pan, trimming any excess.
- In a medium bowl, whisk together the besan, cornstarch, sugar, and salt. Rinse the berries and dredge them in the flour mixture to evenly coat. Remove and set aside. Toss the sliced pears into the mixture as well and then rustically (no fancy pattern needed) arrange the pears and berries into the tart shell. Top with an even layer of turbinado sugar. Bake for 35 to 40 minutes, or until crust is golden brown on edges. Store in airtight container in refrigerator for up to 2 days.

# ALMOND APPLE TART

This elegant dessert, which features the fragrant combination of almonds and apples, comes together effortlessly if you already have some puff pastry frozen. You'll have a fancy dessert ready to impress in no time flat. This tart also keeps well if refrigerated for up to 1 week; simply reheat at 350°F for 10 minutes and sprinkle with a touch of turbinado sugar before serving.

½ recipe Puff Pastry
  (page 147)
2 tablespoons turbinado
  sugar
1 large Granny Smith apple,
  peeled and thinly sliced
1 teaspoon lemon or lime
  juice
½ cup brown sugar, plus
  2 tablespoons for
  sprinkling on top
1 teaspoon vanilla extract
⅛ teaspoon salt
3 tablespoons cornstarch
2 tablespoons almond meal

**YIELD: 4 SERVINGS**

- Place a rectangle of chilled puff pastry dough in between two sheets of parchment paper and gently roll out into a rectangle about 5 x 8 inches. Transfer the dough to a baking sheet lined with parchment paper or a silicone mat. Crimp up the edges of the crust to form a lip, gently folding the top back onto itself. Sprinkle evenly with the 2 tablespoons turbinado sugar.
- In a medium bowl, toss the apples with the lemon juice, and then with the remaining ingredients, until the apples are well coated. Arrange the apples onto the tart shell in an even layer, overlapping each slice to form a pattern. Sprinkle with the 2 tablespoons brown sugar.
- Bake for 35 to 40 minutes, or until apples are tender and crust is golden brown. Store in airtight container for up to 2 days.

# CRANBERRY WHITE CHOCOLATE CITRUS TART

White chocolate and cranberry is a popular combination; the addition of orange here creates a nice tang. You can make your own dairy-free white chocolate for this tart (page 253) or seek out your favorite brand elsewhere.

## CRUST
1¾ cups almond meal
¼ cup brown sugar
3 tablespoons coconut oil, liquid
Dash salt

## TOPPING
1½ cups fresh cranberries
¼ cup sugar

## FILLING
2 cups raw cashews, soaked at least 3 hours and drained
¼ cup sugar
½ cup orange juice
1 teaspoon orange zest
5.5 ounces (150 g) nondairy white chocolate

**YIELD: 10 SERVINGS**

### For the Crust
- Preheat oven to 400°F.
- In a small bowl, mix together the almond meal and brown sugar. Stir in the melted coconut oil and salt until completely mixed. Use slightly greased hands or the bottom of a drinking glass and press the mixture into an 8-inch tart pan.
- Bake the crust for 10 minutes in your preheated oven. Remove from the oven and let cool completely.

### For the Topping
- Combine the cranberries and sugar in a small saucepan and cook over medium heat, stirring often, until sugar granules have dissolved completely. Increase temperature slightly to reduce until thickened, for about 5 minutes.

### For the Filling
- In a food processor, blend the cashews with the sugar, orange juice, and zest until very, very smooth, for about 5 minutes. Over a double boiler, melt the white chocolate and then blend with the rest of the ingredients.
- Quickly spread the cashew filling into the cooled tart crust and top with the cranberry mixture. Gently run a knife through the top of the filling to swirl through. Chill in the refrigerator until firm. Store in airtight container in refrigerator for up to 2 days.

# WHITE CHOCOLATE PEANUT BUTTER PRETZEL TARTLETS

Salty pretzels pair so wonderfully with the combined sweetness of white chocolate and peanut butter and are presented in a cute little tartlet package.

**1½ cups crushed gluten-free pretzels**
**6 tablespoons softened nondairy margarine**
**2 tablespoons sugar**
**1 cup nondairy white chocolate chips**
**½ cup smooth peanut butter**
**¼ cup canned coconut milk**
**1 cup nondairy milk**

**YIELD: 12 TARTS**

- Preheat oven to 350°F. Gather about twelve 2-inch tart pans and lightly spray with nonstick cooking oil.
- Combine the crushed pretzels, margarine, and sugar together until very well mixed. Make sure there are no lumps of margarine. When pressed, the mixture should hold its shape. You may need to add a touch more margarine if it feels too crumbly . . . but just about a tablespoon or so.
- Gently press the crumbs into the tart pans, making an even crust that is about ¼ inch thick. Handle with care.
- Bake for about 12 minutes, or until dark golden brown. Remove tart shells from oven and let cool on wire racks.
- Once the crusts are cool, begin making your filling.
- Place white chocolate chips into a medium bowl. In a small saucepan, combine the peanut butter, coconut milk, and nondairy milk and cook over medium heat, stirring constantly using a wire whisk.
- Once the mixture just begins to bubble and is very hot, pour over white chocolate chips, stirring quickly to melt. Spoon into the prepared tart shells, allowing to cool at room temperature for about an hour before transferring to the refrigerator to chill completely. Store in airtight container in refrigerator for up to 2 days.

# PEACHY KEEN COBBLER

This cobbler is a perfect way to use up a bunch of fruit, especially when you have a lotta hard peaches rolling around—which tends to happen to me quite often during the summertime (I overpurchase and don't want to wait for all of them to ripen!). Any stone fruit can be used; try this recipe with plums or apricots, too!

4 peaches (about 4½ cups) peeled and sliced
½ cup sugar
¼ teaspoon ground allspice
3 tablespoons cornstarch
⅓ cup potato starch
⅓ cup white rice flour
⅓ cup besan/chickpea flour
1 teaspoon xanthan gum
1 teaspoon baking powder
3 tablespoons sugar
6 tablespoons nondairy margarine
¼ cup + 2 tablespoons nondairy milk
1 teaspoon lemon juice

**YIELD: 8 SERVINGS**

- Preheat oven to 375°F and lightly grease a small stoneware or ceramic baking dish, about 5 x 9 inches.
- In a medium bowl, toss together the peaches, sugar, allspice, and cornstarch. Arrange in the greased baking dish in an even layer.
- In a separate bowl, whisk together the potato starch, white rice flour, besan, xanthan gum, baking powder, and sugar. Cut in the margarine and blend using a pastry blender until even crumbles form. Add in the nondairy milk and lemon juice and stir until smooth.
- Drop by heaping spoonfuls on top of the sliced peaches. Bake for 35 to 40 minutes, or until bubbly and the biscuit top is golden brown on edges. Store in airtight container for up to 1 day.

# CHERRY CLAFOUTIS

This recipe is such a perfect use for fresh cherries as this dessert truly accentuates the color and flavor of the short-seasoned fresh fruit. Cherries not in season? Good news: frozen cherries work, too! Thanks to Lydia, who tested for this cookbook, for the tip.

½ block extra-firm tofu, drained but not pressed (about 215 g)
1½ cups besan/chickpea flour
1½ cups nondairy milk
1 teaspoon baking powder
2 tablespoons tapioca flour
¾ cup sugar
¾ teaspoon sea salt
1 teaspoon vanilla extract
2 cups pitted cherries
¼ cup confectioner's sugar

**YIELD: 8 SERVINGS**

- Preheat oven to 350°F and grease an 8-inch cast-iron skillet or glass pie pan with enough margarine to coat.
- Place all the ingredients but the cherries and the confectioner's sugar into a blender and blend until the mixture is uniform and very smooth, scraping down sides as needed. Pour the batter into the prepared pan and then dot evenly with pitted cherries, placing them about ½ inch apart on top of the batter.
- Bake for 50 to 55 minutes, or until a knife inserted into the middle comes out clean. Let cool completely and dust with confectioner's sugar before serving. Store in airtight container for up to 2 days in refrigerator.

# APPLE CRISP

This simple and rustic dessert is as easy to whip up as it is delicious. Serve à la mode for an over-the-top treat. My favorite type of apple to use in this is Granny Smith, but any crisp variety will do.

**5 apples, peeled and sliced ½ to ¼ inch thick**
**¾ cup brown sugar**
**½ cup brown rice flour**
**¼ cup potato starch**
**1 teaspoon cinnamon**
**¾ cup certified gluten-free oats**
**⅓ cup nondairy margarine**

**YIELD: 6 SERVINGS**

- Preheat oven to 375°F. Lightly grease a ceramic baking dish or cake pan, about 8 x 8 inches. Arrange the sliced apples evenly to cover the bottom of the baking dish.
- In a medium bowl, whisk together the brown sugar, brown rice flour, potato starch, cinnamon, and oats. Cut in the margarine using a pastry blender until crumbly. Sprinkle liberally over the apples.
- Bake for 35 to 40 minutes, until golden brown and bubbly. Store in airtight container in refrigerator for up to 2 days.

# MILLE-FEUILLE

Elegant and classy, this French dessert will make your dinner guests do a double take. Even though it looks complicated, it's really quite easy once you have the puff pastry prepared. Just assemble and serve!

½ recipe Puff Pastry
  (page 147)
½ recipe Mascarpone
  (page 32)
1 cup confectioner's sugar
½ cup Strawberry Preserves
  (page 229)
¼ cup cacao nibs
½ cup melted chocolate
Strawberries for garnish

**YIELD: 8 SERVINGS**

- Preheat oven to 400°F. Line a large baking sheet with parchment or a silicone mat. Roll out the puff pastry into a rectangle about ¼ inch thick. Chill briefly in the freezer, for about 10 minutes, and then carefully cut into even-size rectangles, about 2.5 x 4 inches. Using a flat metal spatula, carefully transfer the puff pastry to the prepared baking sheet, about ½ inch apart. Bake for 15 to 20 minutes, until puffed and golden brown. Let cool completely and then assemble the dessert.
- Mix the Mascarpone with the confectioner's sugar and place into a pastry bag equipped with a star tip. Glaze the tops of each pastry rectangles with Strawberry Preserves and then pipe on circles of the Mascarpone mixture until the top of the rectangle is covered. Sprinkle with cacao nibs. Top with another strawberry preserve-glazed pastry rectangle and again, pipe another layer of mascarpone and sprinkle with cacao nibs. Top with a final rectangle of pastry glazed with strawberry preserves and then drizzle with melted chocolate. Top with a halved strawberry. Chill for 1 hour in refrigerator and then serve cold.

Clockwise:
Apple Crisp, page 177
Mini Maple Donuts, page 180
Belgian Waffles, page 181
Mille-Feuille, this page

# MINI MAPLE DONUTS

If anything can take me back to the donut shop as a kid, it's these guys. These basic cake donuts have a hint of maple—not too cloying. The glaze also goes well with a variety of other desserts, such as the Devil's Food Cake (page 38), Maple Cookies (page 93), or even the Classic Chocolate Chip Cookies (page 85).

## DONUTS
⅓ cup + 2 tablespoons sorghum flour
⅓ cup + 2 tablespoons potato starch
¼ cup tapioca flour
¼ cup brown rice flour
¾ teaspoon xanthan gum
½ teaspoon salt
1 teaspoon baking powder
3 tablespoons olive oil
⅓ cup + 1 tablespoon maple syrup
½ cup brown sugar
⅓ cup + 2 tablespoons nondairy milk
1 tablespoon apple cider vinegar

## GLAZE
1¼ cups confectioner's sugar
2 tablespoons nondairy milk
1 teaspoon light corn syrup
1 teaspoon maple syrup
1 teaspoon maple extract
Dash salt

YIELD: 24 DONUTS

- Preheat oven to 325°F and place your oven rack in the middle of the oven. Lightly grease a mini-size donut pan.
- Combine all the ingredients through the salt into a medium mixing bowl and whisk until well combined. Gradually add in the rest of the donut ingredients, in the order given, and mix well until no lumps remain. You should end up with a tacky batter.
- Fill the cups of the donut pan with batter. Bake for 25 minutes. Let cool completely and then glaze.
- To make the glaze, simply whisk together all ingredients until smooth. Cover cooled donuts completely with glaze and then place onto a wire rack to firm up. Let glaze harden completely before serving. Store in airtight container for up to 4 days.

I like to use corn syrup in my glazes as it truly re-creates that donut-shop texture; however, you may replace the corn syrup with 1 teaspoon maple syrup, which will cause the glaze texture to have a slight variation.

# BELGIAN WAFFLES

Of course, you don't need a Belgian waffle maker to enjoy these, any type will do, but they are definitely better bigger! Top with your favorite toppings . . . I'm partial to Cherry Vanilla Compote (page 228) or Sweetened Whipped Coconut Cream (page 33).

1 cup sorghum flour
½ cup superfine brown
   rice flour
¼ cup potato starch
¼ cup tapioca flour
1 teaspoon xanthan gum
4 tablespoons sugar
4 teaspoons baking powder
¾ teaspoon salt
2 tablespoons lemon juice
5 tablespoons olive oil
1 teaspoon vanilla extract
½ cup canned full-fat
   coconut milk
1½ cups water

YIELD: 7 WAFFLES

- In a medium bowl, whisk together the sorghum flour, superfine brown rice flour, potato starch, tapioca flour, xanthan gum, sugar, baking powder, and salt.
- Form a well in the center of the flour mixture and add the lemon juice, olive oil, vanilla extract, coconut milk, and water.
- Stir gently with a fork until all ingredients are combined, and then use a whisk to make the batter completely smooth.
- Heat your Belgian waffle maker and lightly mist with non-stick cooking spray. Pour about 1¼ cups batter (depending on your waffle maker's size) and close. Cook for about 2 minutes, or until waffle is golden brown and easily releases from the waffle iron.

# APPLE FRITTERS

Like pocket-size apple pies, these crunchy fritters are hard to resist! I love making these when I overpurchase during apple season as this is a great recipe to get friends and family to gobble up all those extra apples quickly! You'll need a deep fryer for these to achieve a perfect crunch and quick, even cooking throughout.

**3 apples, peeled**
**1 cup besan/chickpea flour,**
    **plus ½ cup for dredging**
**⅔ cup sugar**
**⅔ cup nondairy milk**
**½ teaspoon salt**
**½ teaspoon cinnamon**
**Oil for frying**
**Turbinado and**
    **confectioner's sugar**
    **for dusting**

**YIELD: 15 FRITTERS**

- Preheat deep fryer to 360°F. Slice apples into ¼- to ½-inch-thick circles and use a small circular cookie cutter or apple corer to remove the seeds to form rings.
- In a medium-size bowl, whisk together the besan, sugar, nondairy milk, salt, and cinnamon until smooth. Once the fryer is ready, dredge the apple slices in the extra besan and then dip into the batter to completely coat.
- Fry apples three to four at a time for 5 minutes, flipping over two-thirds of the way through cooking time. Transfer to a paper towel– or paper bag–lined baking sheet (they will be soft at first) and then sprinkle with turbinado and confectioner's sugar. Repeat until all batter/apple slices have been fried.
- Let cool for at least 10 minutes before serving. Serve the same day, best within 1 hour of preparing.

# STRANGE WAIT, STRAWBERRY TOASTER PASTRIES

As a kid, I was obsessed with boxed toaster pastries, but, as I grew older and wiser about food, I became quite unimpressed with their extremely long ingredient lists. These pastries are just as tasty without the unpronounceable ingredients. You'll also find a brown sugar variation below.

## FILLING

3 tablespoons strawberry jam
1½ teaspoons cornstarch mixed with 1½ teaspoons water
Dash salt

1 recipe Flakey Classic Piecrust (page 146)
1 tablespoon flaxseed meal
2½ tablespoons water

**YIELD: 6 PASTRIES**

- In a small bowl, combine the ingredients for the filling until smooth. Preheat oven to 350°F.
- Prepare the Flakey Classic Piecrust according to recipe directions and chill for about 15 minutes in the freezer. Roll out in between two sheets of parchment paper until the dough is about ¼ inch thick. Use a pizza wheel or large flat knife to cut the dough into twelve even rectangles, about 3 x 4 inches wide; use a metal spatula to help transfer six of the rectangles to a parchment or silicone mat covered cookie sheet. Place the rectangles about 1 inch apart.
- Combine the flaxseed meal and water and let rest until thickened, for about 5 minutes. Lightly brush the tops of the rectangles on the cookie sheet with the flaxseed gel. Place about 1½ tablespoons filling into the center of the six rectangles. Use a spatula to help transfer the remaining six rectangles to cover each mound of filling.
- Crimp the sides of the dough to seal using the tines of a fork. Brush the tops lightly with additional flaxseed gel and poke about seven holes in the tops of each pastry. Bake for 30 to 35 minutes, or until golden brown on edges. Let cool completely and toast in toaster oven before serving. Top with Royal Icing (page 78) or leave plain. Store in airtight container for up to 2 days.

### BROWN SUGAR CINNAMON VARIATION

¼ cup brown sugar
½ teaspoon cinnamon
2 tablespoons brown rice flour

Whisk together the ingredients and use in place of the strawberry filling in the recipe. Top with Vanilla Glaze (page 77) or Maple Glaze (page 180).

## Chapter 5

# FABULOUS FROZEN TREATS

*Chill out with* the cool treats on the following pages. Whether you're craving a sweet fix during the summertime, or you just need some fuel to help you veg out during a wintertime movie marathon, you'll be glad to have these recipes on hand (or in your freezer) when the craving strikes. You may be surprised that non-dairy milks, such as almond, cashew, and coconut, do a remarkable job of replicating that creamy dreamy texture we crave from traditional-style ice cream. When choosing alternative milks for your ice cream, just like traditional ice cream, the higher the fat content the better!

## Making Ice Cream Without a Machine

While it is possible to make ice cream without an ice cream machine, I do recommend sourcing an ice cream maker (from hand-crank to fully electric) if you make your own frequently, as I do. It is the best way to create unique flavors that are hard to come by in dairy-/egg-free versions at the supermarket or local gelataria.

I recommend using a machine only because of the amount of air that is able to be incorporated into the mix as it freezes, resulting in a lighter, airier texture, which is difficult to replicate without a machine. It is, however, easy to come pretty close. Most important, I recommend starting with a base that has a heavy fat content, such as the Vanilla Soft Serve (page 188) or Chocolate Hazelnut Ice Cream (page 190). This will help reduce the odds of ice crystals forming while freezing, producing a smoother, creamier treat. Also, dropping a touch of alcohol (such as vodka or bourbon) into the mix, or using a recipe that incorporates alcohol before freezing will also help reduce crystallization.

Follow the directions for preparing your chosen recipe, and then place the mixture into a stainless steel or glass bowl and chill completely in the refrigerator, up to 8 hours. Whisk thoroughly to stir and then pour the mixture into a nonstick pan (plastic works well), stirring with a whisk after adding. Cover lightly with plastic wrap. Let the mixture chill in the freezer for 30 minutes, and then whisk again. You can incorporate more air by using an electric hand mixer for mixing. Chill for another 30 minutes, and then whisk (or blend) again. Repeat until the ice cream is frozen through and creamy. Transfer to a flexible airtight container. Most ice creams will last in the freezer for about 3 months.

Matcha Cashew Ice Cream, page 191

# VANILLA SOFT SERVE

I absolutely adore flavors and add-ins of all kinds but, if I had to pick a favorite ice cream flavor, it wouldn't be anything fancy, just plain ol' vanilla. This ice cream is rich and dreamy and has a light vanilla flavor that lingers.

1 cup sugar
1 tablespoon agave
½ teaspoon xanthan gum
2 tablespoons vanilla extract
2 tablespoons coconut oil or nondairy margarine
1 cup nondairy milk (recommend almond or cashew)
1 cup canned full-fat coconut milk

• In a large bowl, whisk together the sugar, agave, xanthan gum, vanilla extract, coconut oil, and nondairy milk. Transfer to a blender and process until totally smooth. Whisk in the 1 cup coconut milk and process in an ice cream maker according to manufacturer's instructions or process according to the directions on page 186. Once blended, store in airtight, flexible container and freeze at least 6 hours before serving. Keeps for up to 3 months frozen.

YIELD: 1 PINT

# CHOCOLATE ESPRESSO ICE CREAM

This distinctive dessert is just like an indulgent drink at a coffee shop—so dark and creamy, it will have you requesting a doppio!

⅔ cup nondairy sour cream or plain yogurt
1 cup confectioner's sugar
½ cup cocoa powder
2 teaspoons espresso powder
1 (13.5-ounce) can full-fat coconut milk
¼ teaspoon salt

• In a large bowl, whisk together all the ingredients until completely smooth and absolutely no lumps remain. Process in an ice cream maker according to manufacturer's instructions, or process according to the directions on page 186. Transfer to a flexible airtight container and freeze at least 6 hours before serving. Keeps for up to 3 months frozen.

YIELD: 1 QUART

# BUTTER PECAN ICE CREAM

When I think of Butter Pecan Ice Cream, I think of my father. I'm not sure if it was his favorite flavor, but we always seemed to have a carton of it in the freezer when I was growing up, which undoubtedly helped make it one of *my* favorite flavors of ice cream.

1 cup pecans
1 cup brown sugar
1 (13.5-ounce) can full-fat
    coconut milk
1 tablespoon nondairy
    margarine
¼ teaspoon xanthan gum
½ teaspoon salt
1 teaspoon vanilla extract
2 cups almond milk
1 tablespoon cornstarch
1 tablespoon water

YIELD: 1 QUART

- Preheat oven to 400°F. Spread the pecans evenly onto a metal baking sheet and toast for 7 minutes, or until fragrant. Let cool, chop, and set aside.
- In a 2-quart saucepan, whisk together the brown sugar, coconut milk, margarine, xanthan gum, salt, and vanilla extract. Heat the mixture over medium-high heat until the sugar is dissolved and the margarine is melted. Add the almond milk. In a small bowl, whisk together the cornstarch and water to mix well. Stir the cornstarch slurry into the saucepan and continue to heat over medium heat. Stir constantly until the mixture coats the back of a spoon. Remove from heat and transfer to a metal bowl. Place in refrigerator and chill the mixture until cold.
- Process in an ice cream maker according to manufacturer's instructions, or process according to the directions on page 186. Once the ice cream is finished processing in the ice cream maker, fold in the toasted pecans. Transfer to a flexible airtight container and freeze for 6 hours. Store in the freezer for up to 2 months.

# CHOCOLATE HAZELNUT ICE CREAM

Use store-bought or homemade chocolate hazelnut butter for this recipe. There are a few varieties of dairy-free chocolate hazelnut butter out there, but I like Justin's brand the best.

½ cup nondairy chocolate hazelnut butter, such as Justin's brand
1 cup nondairy milk
2 tablespoons coconut oil
½ teaspoon xanthan gum
⅛ teaspoon salt
½ cup turbinado sugar
½ cup plain nondairy yogurt

YIELD: 1 PINT

• Place all the ingredients into a blender and blend until smooth, scraping the sides of the blender as needed. Process in your ice cream maker according to manufacturer's instructions or follow the directions on page 186. Transfer to an airtight flexible container and store in freezer for at least 6 hours. Keeps for up to 3 months frozen.

# BUTTERY BROWN SUGAR ICE CREAM

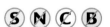

This ice cream proves you can have all of the indulgence of a buttery sweet flavor—without any of the dairy.

¼ cup nondairy margarine
1 cup brown sugar (light or dark)
½ teaspoon xanthan gum
1¾ cups canned full-fat coconut milk
½ teaspoon vanilla extract
⅔ cup nondairy milk

YIELD: 1 QUART

• Heat the margarine, brown sugar, xanthan gum, coconut milk, and vanilla extract just until sugar is dissolved and margarine is melted over medium heat. Stir in the nondairy milk and blend in blender. Chill for about 15 minutes, and then transfer into an ice cream maker. Following the manufacturer's instructions, process the ice cream until completely frozen, or process according to the directions on page 186. Transfer to a flexible airtight container and chill in freezer for at least 6 hours. Store in the freezer for up to 3 months.

# STRAWBERRY ICE CREAM

Forget the artificially flavored stuff, the only way to go with strawberry ice cream is with real strawberries! This is as authentic as you can get with the help of silken tofu and coconut milk to give it extra creaminess.

**2 cups whole strawberries, stems removed**
**1 block (12.3 ounces) firm silken tofu**
**1 (13.5-ounce) can full-fat coconut milk**
**1 teaspoon vanilla extract**
**¾ cup sugar**
**1 teaspoon coconut oil**
**1 cup strawberries, chopped into ½-inch pieces**

**YIELD: 1 QUART**

- Place the 2 cups strawberries into a blender along with the silken tofu, coconut milk, vanilla extract, sugar, and coconut oil. Blend until smooth and then transfer into the bowl of an ice cream maker and process according to manufacturer's instructions, or follow the method on page 186. Once the mixture is mostly frozen, mash the remaining 1 cup strawberries and mix into the ice cream. Continue to process until frozen and then transfer to an airtight flexible container. Freeze 6 hours before serving. Keeps for up to 3 months frozen.

# MATCHA CASHEW ICE CREAM

The magical cashew is the stand-in for traditional heavy whipping cream in this creamy confection. Matcha green tea powder adds a distinctive color and flavor, which matches the mellow texture of this ice cream.

**2 cups raw cashews**
**½ cup agave**
**½ cup nondairy milk**
**¼ teaspoon salt**
**1½ teaspoons matcha powder**
**1 small ripe banana**

**YIELD: 1 QUART**

- Place the cashews in a medium bowl and cover with water. Cap with a dinner plate and let the cashews soak for at least 3 hours, preferably 4.
- Drain the cashews and transfer into a food processor along with the remaining ingredients. Blend until very smooth, for about 8 minutes, scraping down the sides often. You can make this even creamier by transferring into a blender and blending until super smooth.
- Place in the bowl of an ice cream maker and process according to manufacturer's instructions, or follow directions on page 186. Transfer to a flexible airtight container and freeze 6 hours before serving. Keeps for up to 3 months frozen.

# MINT CHOCOLATE CHIP ICE CREAM

The brilliant green color of this dessert comes from the addition of fresh spinach, which I swear on my ice cream maker's life you won't taste. Make this even healthier by subbing cacao nibs in place of the mini chocolate chips.

2 cups packed fresh spinach
2 (13.5-ounce) cans full-fat coconut milk
½ cup sugar
½ cup coconut palm sugar
1 tablespoon agave
2 teaspoons peppermint extract
½ cup mini nondairy chocolate chips

YIELD: 1 QUART

- Place all ingredients up to the chocolate chips into a high-speed blender and blend until very smooth, scraping sides as needed. Pour into the bowl of an ice cream maker and process according to manufacturer's instructions, or follow the directions on page 186. Once frozen, fold in the chocolate chips and freeze for at least 6 hours. Store in an airtight flexible container in the freezer for up to 3 months.

# BLACK BEAN ICE CREAM

I first had bean-based ice cream at my son's grandmother's house, who is Korean. Skeptical at first, I soon fell in love with this addictive twist on the typically savory ingredient. Adzuki beans work well here, too, although they can be harder to source.

1½ cups cooked black beans, rinsed
1 (13.5-ounce) can full-fat coconut milk
¾ cup sugar
1 tablespoon cocoa powder
Pinch of salt
⅛ teaspoon xanthan gum

YIELD: 1 QUART

- In a blender, puree all ingredients until very smooth. Process in your ice cream maker according to manufacturer's instructions, or follow the directions on page 186. Store in a flexible airtight container and freeze at least 6 hours before serving. Keeps for up to 3 months frozen.

# PUMPKIN PATCH ICE CREAM

The first time I tasted pumpkin flavored ice cream was right after a hayride with my childhood bestie while we were in middle school. It was such a great memory, with the crisp fall chill in the evening breeze and the smell of leaves crunching underneath our feet. Now, each time I taste pumpkin ice cream, I get transported right back to that day, autumnal bliss and all.

**1½ cups sugar**
**1 (13.5-ounce) can full-fat coconut milk**
**2 teaspoons vanilla extract**
**1 (15-ounce) can pumpkin puree**
**1½ teaspoons cinnamon**
**⅛ teaspoon ground nutmeg**
**⅛ teaspoon cloves**
**½ teaspoon salt**

**YIELD: 1 QUART**

- Over medium heat, in a 2-quart saucepan, warm the sugar and coconut milk just until the sugar has completely dissolved. Whisk in the vanilla extract, pumpkin puree, spices, and salt. Process in an ice cream maker according to manufacturer's instructions, or follow the directions on page 186. Transfer to a flexible airtight container and freeze at least 6 hours before serving. Store in freezer for up to 3 months.

# CHOCOLATE EARL GREY GELATO ⓢ ⓝ ⓒ ⓑ

This popular flavor combination gets its time to shine in this recipe. The floral notes of Earl Grey are subtle, but unforgettable.

**7 Earl Grey teabags**
**¾ cup very hot water**
**1 cup nondairy chocolate chips**
**¾ cup sugar**
**1 (13.5-ounce) can full-fat coconut milk**
**1 tablespoon extra-dark cocoa powder**
**Dash salt**
**¼ teaspoon xanthan gum, optional, for creaminess**
**½ cup nondairy milk**

**YIELD: 1 QUART**

- Steep the tea bags in the hot water for at least 15 minutes. Squeeze and remove the tea bags and set tea aside.
- Place the chocolate chips in a large heat-safe bowl.
- Combine the sugar, coconut milk, cocoa powder, salt, and xanthan gum, if using, in a small saucepan over medium heat. Heat just until hot (do not let boil) and pour over chocolate chips to melt. Add the nondairy milk and prepared tea and stir well to combine. Chill the mixture in the refrigerator for 1 hour.
- Place into an ice cream maker and let run just until thickened to a soft serve ice cream consistency, or follow instructions on page 186. Transfer immediately to a flexible airtight container and chill at least 6 hours until firm. Keeps for up to 3 months frozen.

# BLACKBERRY CHEESECAKE GELATO Ⓝ Ⓒ Ⓑ

I dare you to take just one bite of this creamy concoction; the flavor is highly addictive. The bright purple hue that comes from the blackberries takes this gelato over the top. If blackberries aren't available, feel free to replace with another type of berry, frozen or fresh—all berries go great with cheesecake-flavored gelato! You can use Sweet Cashew Cream (page 32) in place of the nondairy cream cheese if you like.

2 cups blackberries
1 cup nondairy cream cheese
1 cup nondairy milk
¾ cup sugar
1½ teaspoons vanilla extract

YIELD: 1 QUART

- Place all ingredients into a blender and blend until smooth. Transfer to the bowl of an ice cream maker and process according to manufacturer's directions, or follow directions on page 186. Once frozen, store in a flexible airtight container for up to 2 months.

# BUTTERSCOTCH PUDDING POPS Ⓢ Ⓝ Ⓒ Ⓑ

These pudding pops make the perfect warm weather treat with their salty butterscotch base and creamy cool texture. You'll need popsicle molds for these, or you can use silicone ice cube trays for mini-pops, or you can even use small paper cups.

1 recipe Butterscotch Sauce
  (page 81)
1 (13.5-ounce) can full-fat
  coconut milk
2 tablespoons coconut
  palm sugar
⅛ teaspoon salt
3 tablespoons superfine
  brown rice flour

YIELD: 6 POPS

- In a 2-quart saucepan over medium heat, combine the Butterscotch Sauce, coconut milk, coconut palm sugar, and salt and whisk well until combined. Heat just until the mixture is hot and all coconut milk and sugar has dissolved. Whisk in the superfine brown rice flour and continue to cook over medium heat, stirring often, until thickened, for 4 to 5 minutes.
- Let cool briefly and then pour into popsicle molds, placing wooden sticks directly into the centers. Freeze overnight before enjoying. Keeps for up to 1 month frozen.

This recipe also makes a delicious Butterscotch Pudding—just don't freeze it! Instead, pour the pudding into serving dishes and refrigerate until set, for about 3 hours.

# CLASSIC ICE CREAM SANDWICHES

This recipe produces a cookie that stands up well to freezing and stays soft once frozen, in a classic ice cream sandwich fashion. The base flavor is chocolate—pair the wafers with your favorite ice cream!

¾ cup cold nondairy
    margarine
1 cup sugar
1 teaspoon vanilla extract
1 cup sorghum flour
¾ cup cocoa powder
½ cup potato starch
1 teaspoon xanthan gum
¼ teaspoon baking soda
2 tablespoons nondairy milk
4 cups of your favorite
    nondairy ice cream

**YIELD: 8 SANDWICHES**

- In a large mixing bowl, cream together the margarine, sugar, and vanilla extract. In a separate, smaller mixing bowl mix the sorghum flour, cocoa powder, potato starch, xanthan gum, and baking soda until well combined.
- Gradually incorporate the flour mixture into the sugar mixture until crumbly. Once crumbly, add the nondairy milk until completely combined. If using an electric mixer, just let it ride on low as you add the nondairy milk. Your dough should get quite stiff at this point.
- Shape into a rectangular log, about 2 x 10 inches, using the help of parchment paper and a bench scraper/offset spatula to flatten and form the sides. Wrap loosely with parchment paper and chill in the freezer for 30 minutes, until very cold.
- Preheat oven to 350°F. Once the dough is well chilled, cut the log in half, making two even-sized bricks (about 2 x 5 inches each). Flip each brick on its side, and then slice evenly into rectangles about 2 x 3 inches and about ⅛ inch thick to emulate a cookie from a store-bought ice cream sandwich.
- As you slice the cookies, place each slab of thin dough gently onto parchment paper or a silpat mat.
- Bake in preheated oven for 14 to 16 minutes. Remove from oven and allow to cool completely at room temperature. Transfer to the freezer just before assembling and chill for at least 10 minutes. Meanwhile, soften your chosen ice cream for about 10 minutes, or until easily scoopable.
- To assemble, take one cookie, and plop a few spoonfuls of your favorite ice cream on top. Smoosh down the ice cream with another cookie and run a spoon around the edge to ensure even distribution of ice cream.
- Return sandwiches to freezer and chill until firm. Once firm, neatly wrap them in waxed paper to store. Keeps for up to 3 months frozen.

# SORBETS AND ICES

# ROSEMARY APPLE SORBET

I can't get enough of this sorbet. The apple flavor is really enticing and enhanced elegantly with the addition of rosemary. Be sure to seek out fresh rosemary, rather than dried, as it will absolutely make a difference.

**2½ cups apple cider (no sugar added)**
**⅓ cup sugar**
**1 sprig fresh rosemary**

**YIELD: 1 QUART**

• In a small saucepan over medium heat, combine the apple cider, sugar, and rosemary and cook for about 7 minutes, stirring often, until sugar is dissolved and the rosemary has added a hint of fragrance to the cider. Remove syrup from heat and let cool completely, either in the refrigerator, or at room temperature. Process in ice cream maker according to manufacturer's instructions or by following directions on page 186. Once frozen, store in an airtight container in the freezer for up to 2 months.

# STRAWBERRIES AND CHAMPAGNE SORBET

I don't actually recommend that you use Champagne to make this delightful sorbet, but you certainly can if you roll hard like that! I prefer Prosecco, for its subtle notes and its more modest price tag.

**1 pear, peeled and cubed (about 1 cup)**
**2 cups strawberries, greens removed**
**1 cup Prosecco, Spumante, or other sparkling white wine**
**¾ cup sugar**

**YIELD: 1 QUART**

• In a food processor, pulse together the pear and strawberries until well chopped. In a separate bowl, gradually mix the Prosecco with the sugar and stir gently to dissolve. Let rest for about 5 minutes and then stir gently again. Drizzle about ½ cup of the Prosecco mixture into the food processor and blend until quite smooth, for about 1 minute, scraping down the bowl as needed.

• Add in the rest of the Prosecco mixture and blend until very well combined. Transfer to the bowl of an ice cream maker and process according to manufacturer's instructions or by following directions on page 186.

• Store in an airtight container for up to 2 months in the freezer.

# DRAGONFRUIT SORBET

Although I consider most all of nature's creations beautiful, I am always awestruck each time I cut into a dragonfruit. These bright fuchsia fruits open to a Dalmatian inside and have a neutral flavor similar to grapes. They make one heck of a gorgeous sorbet, too! Check for ripeness by gently pressing into the fruit's thick peel. If it gives to a little pressure under the thumb, then it's ripe.

**2 large dragonfruits**
**1 cup sugar**
**1 cup water**
**¼ teaspoon vanilla extract**

**YIELD: 1 QUART**

- Peel the dragonfruit by cutting the top stem section off just enough to reveal the white fruit. Gently peel the fruit as you would a banana to remove the skin cleanly and easily.
- Cube the fruit and place into a food processor. Pulse until the consistency of a slushy.
- In a small saucepan over medium heat, cook the sugar and water together just until the sugar has completely dissolved, for 1 to 2 minutes.
- Transfer the pureed dragonfruit into a bowl and mix in the sugar syrup and vanilla. Chill the mixture in the freezer for 30 minutes, stir, chill for 10 more minutes, then process in an ice cream maker until it is bright white and the consistency of sorbet. This can also be made following the directions on page 186, but an ice cream maker is preferred if available. Store in flexible airtight container in freezer for up to 3 months.

# GINGER PEACH SHERBET

Warm ginger combines so beautifully with this cool peach sherbet to bring a dessert that would be welcome at the end of any dinner party.

4 large ripe peaches
   (not too soft)
1 teaspoon fresh grated
   ginger
Dash salt
1 cup sugar
½ cup canned full-fat
   coconut cream (thickest
   part from a can of milk)
½ cup nondairy milk

YIELD: 1 QUART

- Fill a 2-quart pot about halfway with water and bring to a boil over medium-high heat. Carefully place peaches into the boiling water and cook for 1½ minutes. Drain immediately and gently run the peaches under cold water. Carefully remove the skins and pits and discard.
- Place the blanched peaches, ginger, salt, sugar, coconut cream, and nondairy milk into a food processor or blender and blend until smooth. Chill in the refrigerator until cold and then transfer to an ice cream maker and process according to manufacturer's instructions, or follow the directions on page 186. Transfer to a flexible airtight freezable container and freeze for at least 4 hours before serving. Keeps for up to 3 months frozen.

# STRAWBERRY BALSAMIC SORBETTO

An absolutely delightful dessert, this tastes just like fresh-picked strawberries. The balsamic complements the berries well and counteracts the sweetness of the simple syrup.

¾ cup Simple Syrup
   (page 28)
1 tablespoon white or red
   balsamic vinegar
2 cups fresh strawberries,
   greens removed

YIELD: 2 CUPS

- In a blender, puree all the ingredients until smooth. Place in metal baking dish, about 8 inches round, and cover with plastic wrap. Freeze for 3 hours, or until solid, but still soft. Store in airtight container in freezer for up to 2 months.

# LIMONCELLO SEMIFREDDO

A bright and boozy treat that's for adults only. This creamy, fluffy, semifreddo is best made in a high-speed blender, such as a Vitamix, for extra airiness.

**2 cups raw cashews**
**½ cup sugar**
**1 cup coconut cream (from the tops of 2 chilled cans of full-fat coconut milk)**
**⅔ cup Limoncello**
**Fresh lemon zest, for garnish (optional)**

**YIELD: 6 SERVINGS**

- Place the cashews into a medium bowl and cover with water. Let the cashews soak for least 4 hours, but no longer than 6. Drain and place into a high-speed blender.
- Add the rest of the ingredients and blend on low just to combine. Increase speed to high and let blend until completely smooth, for about 1 minute.
- Pour the mixture into silicone baking cups or ice cream molds and freeze for at least 6 hours and up to overnight. For an extra-special touch, serve garnished with lemon zest. Keeps for up to 3 months frozen.

# ALMOND CHAMOMILE GRANITA

Such a soothing treat for a hot summer day, this light-tasting granita is a great choice when ice cream seems too heavy. The chamomile adds a floral note that's perfectly offset with the almond milk.

2 chamomile tea bags
   (or 2 teaspoons chamomile
   tea in tea strainer)
1 cup very hot, but not
   boiling, water
½ cup Simple Syrup
   (page 28)
1 teaspoon almond extract
½ cup almond milk

YIELD: ABOUT 3 CUPS

• In a medium bowl, steep the tea and the hot water for 5 minutes, until the water is fragrant and golden. Remove tea bags and let cool to room temperature. Mix with the syrup, almond extract, and almond milk. Place in metal baking dish, about 8 x 8 inches, on flat surface in freezer. Chill mixture until frozen solid and then scrape into granules using a fork. Serve in chilled dishes. Keeps for up to 3 months frozen if stored in airtight container.

# MOJITO GRANITA

I love mojitos in the summertime. I get giddy when I see the fresh mint peek over our fence in the springtime, letting me know it's almost time to stock up on lime and seltzer. This granita will satisfy your craving for the summertime libation any time of year.

¾ cup Simple Syrup
   (page 28)
Juice of 3 limes, about
   6 tablespoons
2 tablespoons rum
1 cup cold sparkling water
½ teaspoon mint extract

YIELD: 3 CUPS

• Combine all the ingredients in a medium bowl, and then pour into a nonstick plastic or metal dish. Freeze for 3 hours. Once frozen, gently scrape the mixture into granules using the tines of a fork. Serve with a fresh sprig of mint or a lime twist. Store in airtight container in the freezer. Keeps for up to 3 months frozen.

# MANDARIN ICE

This delightful frozen treat is a refreshing way to get your vitamin C! I like using clementines, for extra sweetness, but tangerines or other oranges work nicely, too.

1½ cups mandarin juice,
   about 8 clementines'
   worth
2 teaspoons rum or
   vanilla extract
1 tablespoon agave

YIELD: 1 QUART

• Place all the ingredients into a bowl and whisk together well to combine. Pour into a metal cake pan (about 9 inches round) and place into the freezer. Freeze for 4 hours, or until frozen solid. Gently but quickly scrape the mixture into ice with a fork—don't overdo it or it may turn to a slushy—and then transfer into a sealable airtight container. Keeps for up to 3 months frozen.

# PINEAPPLE ICE POPS

These tropical treats are actually quite popular in Mexico and are referred to as *paleta de pina*. Paleta have countless flavor variations, but I love these pineapple pops because of the natural candy-like flavor of the pineapple.

You'll need popsicle molds or silicone ice cube trays for mini-pops or simply use small paper cups.

**2 cups diced pineapple, drained**

**½ cup Simple Syrup (page 28)**

**½ teaspoon rum or vanilla extract**

**2 tablespoons full-fat coconut milk**

**YIELD: ABOUT 4 POPS**

- Place all ingredients into a blender or food processor and blend until mostly pureed. Pour into popsicle molds, place wooden sticks into the center, and freeze overnight. Keeps for up to 3 months frozen.

Use agave in place of the simple syrup if desired, but expect a darker color to your pops.

## Chapter 6

# TEMPTING PUDDINGS, CUSTARDS, JELLIES, AND FRUITS

*This chapter covers* everything you need to know for perfect puddings, fillings, fruits, and more. These are some of my favorite desserts to make because of the quickness and ease, as well as their uses in other desserts as fillings, toppings, and garnishes.

# PUDDINGS AND CUSTARDS

# CRÈME BRÛLÉE

If you thought that getting just the right texture for classic crème brûlée would be impossible without eggs and cream, this recipe will prove just the opposite! If you don't have a culinary torch (why not?! . . . they're so much fun), then you can also place these under a broiler set on high for 5 minutes; just watch carefully so that you don't burn the sugar tops.

1 (13.5-ounce) can full-fat
    coconut milk
1½ cups nondairy milk
1 cup water
1¾ cups sugar
3 tablespoons nondairy
    margarine
¾ cup cornstarch mixed with
    ½ cup water
3 tablespoons besan/
    chickpea flour
1 teaspoon vanilla extract
¾ teaspoon sea salt
2 tablespoons sugar for
    topping

**YIELD: 4 SERVINGS**

- Prepare four ramekins by very lightly greasing them with coconut oil or margarine.
- In a 2-quart saucepan, combine the coconut milk, nondairy milk, water, sugar, and margarine and cook over medium heat for about 5 minutes, or until the mixture is hot.
- In a small bowl, mix together the cornstarch slurry, besan, and vanilla extract until very smooth. Add the cornstarch mixture into the coconut milk mixture along with the salt and stir constantly with a whisk over medium heat to let it thicken, which should happen after about 5 minutes.
- Transfer to the prepared ramekins and let cool completely at room temperature until firm. Sprinkle each cup with about ½ tablespoon sugar, then brûlée the tops using a blowtorch. Store in airtight container for up to 1 week in refrigerator.

# CHOCOLATE PUDDING

When I was a little girl, one of my favorite treats my mother used to make was chocolate pudding. I loved how involved it all seemed, with her standing over the stove, meditatively whisking away. Even if she used a boxed mix, it always tasted like it was made with love. This pudding brings back that nostalgia with its thick and creamy texture and an unforgettably chocolate flavor.

½ cup cocoa powder
½ cup sugar
2 teaspoons vanilla extract
¼ teaspoon salt
1 cup nondairy milk
3 tablespoons cornstarch
3 tablespoons water

**YIELD: 2 TO 4 SERVINGS**

- In a 2-quart saucepan, whisk together the cocoa powder, sugar, vanilla extract, salt, and about ⅓ cup of the nondairy milk. Mix until very smooth with no lumps remaining, and then add in the additional nondairy milk.
- Warm over medium heat. In a small bowl, whisk together the cornstarch and water until no lumps remain. Stir in the cornstarch slurry and keep stirring continuously, over medium heat, until thickened, for about 5 minutes. Transfer to two medium or four small dishes and chill before serving. Store in airtight container for up to 1 week in refrigerator.

# PISTACHIO PUDDING

This slightly salty and oh-so-sweet treat is easy to bring together and a sure winner for the pistachio lover in your life. I especially love this rich pudding served in small amounts as a dessert or aperitif.

1 cup roasted and salted
   pistachios, shelled
½ cup granulated sugar
⅓ cup nondairy milk, plus
   1½ cups nondairy milk
¼ cup additional granulated
   sugar
5 tablespoons cornstarch
4 tablespoons water

**YIELD: 2 TO 4 SERVINGS**

- In a food processor, pulse the pistachios until crumbly. Add in sugar and blend until powdery—with just a few larger chunks remaining. Add the ⅓ cup nondairy milk and puree until very well combined.
- Transfer pistachio mixture to a 2-quart pot and whisk in the additional nondairy milk and sugar.
- In a small bowl, use a fork to combine the cornstarch and water until no lumps remain. Add this slurry to the pistachio mixture.
- Heat over medium heat, stirring frequently until thickened, for 5 to 7 minutes. Pour into two to four ramekins or serving dishes and let cool completely. Serve chilled with whipped topping! Store in airtight container for up to 1 week in refrigerator.

# VANILLA PLUM RICE PUDDING

A fragrant take on traditional rice pudding, I like to use basmati for its gorgeous floral notes in addition to the vanilla and plum.

¾ cup basmati or long-grain rice

1½ cups cold water

3 plums, unpeeled, stone removed, and diced

3 teaspoons vanilla extract

½ teaspoon salt

1 cup nondairy milk

½ cup sugar

2 tablespoons sweet white rice flour

¼ cup water

**YIELD: 6 SERVINGS**

- In a 2- or 3-quart saucepan with a tight-fitting lid, stir together the rice and the cold water. Bring to a boil over medium-high heat. Immediately reduce to a simmer and cover. Do not stir.
- Let simmer for about 20 minutes, or until rice can be fluffed easily with a fork. Increase heat to medium and stir in the plums, vanilla extract, salt, nondairy milk, and sugar. In a smaller bowl, use a fork to stir together the sweet white rice flour and water. Stir the slurry into the rice mixture and cook for about 5 to 7 minutes, stirring constantly, until thick. Serve warm or cold. Store in airtight container for up to 1 week in refrigerator.

# TAPIOCA PUDDING

Tapioca pudding is one of those desserts that most people either love or hate, and I truly do adore it! Having grown up with only the instant puddings, I find this homemade version is so much better. It may change your mind if you're not a fan already. Seek out tapioca pearls in the baking section of most grocery stores, or find an endless variety of shapes and colors in Asian markets.

½ cup small tapioca pearls (not instant)

1 cup canned full-fat coconut milk

2 cups nondairy milk

½ teaspoon salt

½ cup sugar

1 teaspoon vanilla

**YIELD: 6 SERVINGS**

- In a 2-quart pot, whisk together all the ingredients until smooth. Over medium-high heat, bring to a boil, stirring constantly. Once boiling, reduce heat to low and simmer for 15 minutes, stirring very often, until pudding is thickened and pearls are no longer white and firm but instead clear and gelatinous.
- Place into serving dishes or a flexible airtight container and chill until completely cold. Serve cold. Store in airtight container for up to 1 week in refrigerator.

# FALL HARVEST QUINOA PUDDING

Fruits and fall-time spices combine to make one comforting pudding, and the quinoa gives it a dense, creamy, and chewy texture.

1 tablespoon coconut oil
1 cup chopped pecan pieces
1 apple, chopped into small
    pieces
½ cup dried dates, chopped
½ teaspoon ground nutmeg
1 teaspoon ground cinnamon
¼ teaspoon cardamom
½ teaspoon salt
½ cup cold nondairy milk
2 teaspoons cornstarch
1 teaspoon vanilla extract
2 cups cooked quinoa
1 cup brown sugar

**YIELD: 6 SERVINGS**

- Over medium heat, in a 2-quart saucepan, warm the coconut oil until melted. Add the pecans, apples, dates, nutmeg, cinnamon, cardamom, and salt. Continue to cook over medium heat, stirring as to not let the mixture burn. Cook for 3 to 5 minutes, or until apples soften and pecans become fragrant.
- In a small bowl, mix the nondairy milk with the cornstarch and vanilla extract. Whisk together until well combined and no lumps are visible.
- Add the cooked quinoa to the saucepan. Stir in the brown sugar and nondairy milk mixture. Cook over medium heat for about 2 minutes, or until thickened. Serve warm or chilled. Store in airtight container for up to 1 week in refrigerator.

Clockwise:
Fall Harvest Quinoa Pudding, this page
Pumpkin Flan, page 216
Tiramisu, page 217

# PUMPKIN FLAN

This is a traditional method of making pumpkin flan, where the pumpkin is allowed to shine on its own, rather than being masked by spices like cinnamon and cloves.

1 cup canned pumpkin or
    strained pumpkin puree
1 cup nondairy milk
½ cup + 1 tablespoon sugar
¼ teaspoon salt
Dash ground nutmeg
⅓ cup cornstarch
4 tablespoons cold water

**YIELD: 4 SERVINGS**

- Lightly grease four ramekins or teacups with margarine or cooking spray.
- In a 2-quart saucepan, whisk together the pumpkin, nondairy milk, sugar, salt, and nutmeg until smooth. Warm over medium heat.
- Combine the cornstarch with the cold water and stir until no lumps remain. Drizzle into the pumpkin mixture and continue to whisk, constantly, over medium heat until thickened, for about 7 minutes. You will notice a significant strain on your wrist as it becomes thickened.
- Pour/spoon into lightly greased ramekins and let cool. Transfer to refrigerator and chill completely until cold. Invert onto a small flat plate, or leave in cups for serving. Top with Caramel Sauce (page 81). Store in airtight container for up to 1 week in refrigerator.

# CREAMSICLE CUSTARD

This pudding's sunny orange flavor will brighten your day. You can even freeze this pudding in popsicle molds to make creamsicles!

4 tablespoons cornstarch
4 tablespoons cold water
2 cups nondairy milk
½ cup freshly squeezed
    orange juice
1 cup sugar
1 teaspoon orange zest
½ teaspoon salt

**YIELD: 4 SERVINGS**

- In small bowl whisk together the cornstarch and cold water and mix well until dissolved. In a small saucepan, combine the nondairy milk, orange juice, and sugar. Stir in the zest and salt. Warm up slightly over medium-low heat, and gradually add in the cornstarch slurry while stirring frequently with a whisk until the mixture reaches a slow boil.
- Reduce heat to low and continue to stir until the mixture becomes thick, for about 10 minutes cooking time total. Divide between four serving dishes and let sit at room temperature until warm. Transfer the dishes to the refrigerator and chill for at least 3 hours, or until it is completely set. Serve chilled. Store in airtight container for up to 1 week in refrigerator.

# TIRAMISU

Tiramisu is perhaps one of the most popular desserts at Italian restaurants. I always love Tiramisu for its intoxicating fragrance and delightfully melt-in-your-mouth texture. After going gluten-free, I was convinced this dessert would be off limits for good, but no more! Allergy-friendly fancy dessert, at your service.

10 to 12 Ladyfingers
    (page 131)
¼ recipe Devilishly Dark
    Chocolate Sauce
    (page 80)

FILLING
1 recipe Mascarpone
    (page 32)
1½ cups confectioner's sugar
⅛ teaspoon salt
12 ounces firm silken tofu
3 ounces (about 3
    tablespoons) nondairy
    cream cheese
3 tablespoons cornstarch
4 tablespoons cold water

SAUCE
1 tablespoon cocoa powder,
    plus more for dusting
1 tablespoon agave
2 tablespoons very strong
    coffee or espresso

YIELD: 10 SERVINGS

### For the Filling

- Place the Mascarpone, confectioner's sugar, salt, tofu, and nondairy cream cheese into a food processor and blend until very smooth, for about 2 minutes. Transfer the mixture into a 2-quart saucepan over medium heat.
- Whisk together the cornstarch and cold water until no lumps remain. Drizzle the cornstarch slurry into the rest of the ingredients and whisk together, continuing to cook over medium heat. Keep stirring continuously until the mixture thickens, for about 5 minutes. Do not walk away from the mixture or it will burn!
- Let cool briefly.

### For the Sauce

- Prepare the sauce by whisking together the cocoa powder, agave, and coffee in a small bowl until smooth.

### To assemble the Tiramisu

- In a small, square baking pan, arrange five or six ladyfinger cookies to fit into the pan. Spread the Cocoa Espresso Sauce into a shallow flat dish, big enough for the cookies to lay flat. One by one, dip each side of the cookie into the sauce, briefly, and carefully replace. Repeat until all the cookies have been lightly dipped.
- Divide the Tiramisu filling in half and spread half of the filling on top of the ladyfingers and repeat with one more layer of each. Dust the top with cocoa powder and then drizzle with the Devilishy Dark Chocolate Sauce right before serving. Store in airtight container for up to 3 days in refrigerator.

# BROWNIE BATTER MOUSSE

Tiny bites of chocolate-covered walnuts—that taste a heck of a lot like miniature brownies—speckle this silky mousse, delivering a double dose of chocolate flavor.

6 ounces chopped semi-
    sweet chocolate
2 tablespoons nondairy milk
1 tablespoon maple syrup
1 cup roughly chopped
    walnuts
2 (350 g) packages extra-
    firm silken tofu
1 cup sugar
¾ cup cocoa powder
½ teaspoon salt
1 teaspoon vanilla extract

**YIELD: 6 SERVINGS**

- Melt the chocolate in a double boiler over low heat until smooth. Stir in the nondairy milk and maple syrup and remove from the heat. Add the walnuts and coat liberally with a thick chocolate layer.
- Line a cookie sheet with a silicone mat or waxed paper. Spread the chocolate-covered walnuts in an even layer on the prepared cookie sheet. Chill the walnuts in your freezer until you are finished making the mousse.
- To make the mousse, simply blend the tofu, sugar, cocoa powder, salt, and vanilla extract in a food processor or blender until extremely smooth, for about 2 minutes, scraping down the sides as needed.
- Remove the chocolate-covered walnuts from the freezer when they are firm and stir them into the mousse. Spoon into individual dishes and serve very cold. Store in airtight container for up to 1 week in refrigerator.

# BUTTERNUT POTS DE CRÈME

Tender butternut squash is the base for this incredibly rich chocolate dessert. This makes a fabulous fall-time indulgence. The Pots de Crème can be made up to two days in advance.

2 cups cubed, roasted
    butternut squash
½ cup coconut sugar or
    packed brown sugar
¼ cup cocoa powder
¼ cup sorghum flour
1 teaspoon vanilla extract
½ teaspoon salt
Smoked salt for topping

**YIELD: 2 SERVINGS**

- Preheat oven to 350°F and lightly grease two 4-inch ramekins.
- Puree the squash in food processor until smooth. Add in the sugar, cocoa powder, sorghum flour, vanilla extract, and salt. Blend until all ingredients are well combined, scraping the sides as needed.
- Spoon the mixture into the two ramekins and sprinkle smoked salt onto the custards. Bake for 45 to 50 minutes, or until the sides of the pudding begin to pull away from the ramekins. Serve hot for a softer pudding or serve chilled for a firm dessert. Store in airtight container for up to 1 week in refrigerator.

# CHOCOLATE SOUP

Somewhere in between pudding and chocolate sauce, this unusual dessert is such a fun choice for dinner parties. Serve this extra-rich dish in very small bowls.

1 cup canned coconut milk, lite or full-fat
¾ cup nondairy milk (unsweetened)
2 teaspoons vanilla extract
⅓ cup sugar
⅛ teaspoon salt
1 tablespoon cocoa powder
½ cup nondairy chocolate, chopped
1 tablespoon cornstarch mixed with 2 tablespoons water

YIELD: 4 SERVINGS

- In a small saucepan, whisk together the coconut milk, nondairy milk, vanilla extract, sugar, salt, and cocoa powder. Heat over medium heat until very hot, but not yet boiling, for about 5 minutes. Stir in the chocolate, and heat just until melted, stirring continuously, making sure not to let the mixture come to a boil. Whisk in the cornstarch slurry and heat for about 3 minutes, stirring constantly, until the mixture has thickened and it coats the back of a spoon. Serve hot in individual bowls garnished with vegan marshmallows or Sweetened Whipped Coconut Cream (page 33) and cacao nibs (or mini chocolate chips). Store in airtight container for up to 2 days in refrigerator. Reheat simply by warming over medium-low heat in small saucepan until desired temperature is reached.

# BREAD PUDDING

This pudding lends itself perfectly to mix-ins of all sorts. Try pineapple chunks mixed in and then top with toasted coconut for a tropical twist. Or, try mixing in chunks of a banana and ½ cup chocolate chips.

8 slices gluten-free bread
2 tablespoons melted nondairy margarine
¾ cup besan/chickpea flour
1½ cups nondairy milk
⅔ cup light brown sugar
1 teaspoon cinnamon
1 teaspoon vanilla extract
¼ cup raisins, or other dried fruit (optional)

YIELD: 8 SERVINGS

- Preheat oven to 350°F and lightly grease an 8 x 8-inch baking pan.
- Cube the bread into bite-size pieces and arrange them evenly into the pan. Drizzle the bread with the melted margarine.
- In a small bowl, whisk together the besan, nondairy milk, brown sugar, cinnamon, and vanilla extract until no lumps remain in the batter.
- Pour the mixture evenly over the bread until it is fully covered. Press down on the bread pieces gently to fully submerge the bread in the batter. Sprinkle with raisins, if using.
- Bake for 35 to 40 minutes, or until golden brown on top and cooked through the center. Store in airtight container for up to 1 week in refrigerator. Reheat at 350°F for 10 minutes before serving.

# CHOCOLATE BERRY PARFAITS

These luscious parfaits are the perfect blend of tart and sweet, with just a touch of crunch from the cacao nibs. This makes a lovely treat for Valentine's Day, or just about any day!

**1 cup red raspberries**
**2 cups strawberries, sliced**
**1 cup nondairy chocolate chips**
**12.3 ounces (349 g) extra-firm silken tofu**
**1 tablespoon agave**
**1 teaspoon vanilla extract**
**½ cup cacao nibs**
**½ cup Sweet Cashew Cream (page 32)**

**YIELD: 4 PARFAITS**

- Toss the raspberries and strawberries together into a small bowl.
- Over a double boiler, melt your chocolate chips until very smooth. In a food processor, blend the silken tofu with the agave and vanilla extract. While the food processor is spinning, drizzle in your melted chocolate until all is combined.
- Assemble parfaits by layering in four fancy glasses the berries, cacao nibs, pudding, more berries, and more pudding, then top each glass with a dollop of Sweet Cashew Cream page 32.
- Serve chilled. Store in airtight container for up to 1 week in refrigerator.

*Caramel Roasted Pears, page 223*

# JELLIES, FRUITS, AND SAUCES

# BELLINI GELEE

This boozy dessert has all the crisp sweet flavor of the adult drink! Agar is used as a gelatin substitute in this gelled dessert. Be sure to dissolve the powder all the way or it won't set correctly.

1 cup peaches, blanched
   and pureed, or 1 cup
   peach nectar
1 cup sugar
3 cups Prosecco or
   Pinot Grigio
1 cup water
4 teaspoons agar powder

YIELD: 4 SERVINGS

- Gather four sturdy wine glasses or medium silicone molds.
- Whisk together the pureed peaches, sugar, Prosecco, water, and agar in a 2- or 3-quart heavy saucepan. Bring to a boil, and then immediately reduce heat to low. Stir regularly and let simmer for 5 to 6 minutes.
- Let cool slightly, for about 10 minutes, before pouring into wine or champagne glasses or silicone molds.
- If you are using the silicone mold, be sure to place a larger, sturdier pan underneath the mold before you pour your liquid in, ensuring a smooth transport to the fridge.
- Let the mixture chill in the refrigerator until firm, for at least 2 hours. Store in airtight container for up to 1 week in refrigerator.

# CRANBERRY FAUX-GURT

The tart cranberries give this delectable treat an authentic yogurt flavor without the waiting. Top with fresh fruit and granola for an irresistible treat.

1 cup fresh cranberries
½ cup sugar or agave
1 tablespoon water
1 cup Sweet Cashew Cream
   (page 32)
½ cup coconut cream
   (from the top of a can
   of coconut milk)

YIELD: 2 SERVINGS

- In a small saucepan, over medium-low heat, cook the cranberries, sugar, and water until cranberries are very soft, for about 10 minutes. Let cool briefly and then blend in a blender along with the cashew cream and coconut cream until fluffy. Pour into jar and chill; mixture will thicken slightly upon chilling. Store in airtight container for up to 1 week in refrigerator.

# CARAMEL ROASTED PEARS

One of my first memories of being with my husband was when he confidently executed some incredibly gorgeous roasted pairs as a finale to a killer dinner he had prepared for us. I have to admit, his skills in the kitchen went a long way at winning my affection, and he taught me a thing or two about roasting a pear. This is a simple recipe, but full of complex flavor.

**4 red pears, peeled but stems left intact**

**⅓ cup agave**

**⅓ cup brown sugar or coconut sugar**

**2 tablespoons nondairy margarine, melted**

**⅓ cup canned coconut milk**

**YIELD: 4 SERVINGS**

- Preheat oven to 400°F. Carefully slice the bottoms of the pears straight across just to remove the nodule on the bottom, so that they easily stand in a small stoneware or metal baking dish.
- In a small bowl, mix together the agave, brown sugar, margarine, and coconut milk. Drizzle generously over the pears, and then allow the rest to fall to the bottom of baking dish. Bake in a preheated oven for 25 to 30 minutes, stopping to baste with the caramel sauce every 5 minutes or so, until the pears are tender and lightly golden brown.
- Carefully transfer using a flat metal spatula to a saucer or lipped dish with the sauce drizzled onto the pears. Serve immediately. Store leftovers in an airtight container in the refrigerator for up to 2 days.

# THAI MANGO STICKY RICE

One of my favorite parts about visiting a Thai restaurant is enjoying the Mango Sticky Rice when mangoes are in season. Luckily, this addictive treat can be made at home! When making this recipe, it's important to seek out "glutinous" rice, usually sold as "short grain" or "sticky" rice, which refers to the glue-like stickiness of the rice, not gluten.

1 cup short-grain glutinous
    rice
1½ cups canned full-fat
    coconut milk
1 cup water
3 tablespoons sugar
Dash salt
1 mango, peeled and sliced
    into strips

### SAUCE
½ cup canned full-fat
    coconut milk
1½ tablespoons sugar
1 teaspoon cornstarch
2 teaspoons water
Dash salt

**YIELD: 2 SERVINGS**

- Soak 1 cup rice in 3 cups of water for 1 hour. Drain and rinse the rice and place into a saucepan with a tight-fitting lid. Stir in coconut milk, water, sugar, and salt, and bring to a boil over medium-high heat. Once it hits a boil, immediately reduce the temperature to low, stir, cover, and simmer for about 20 minutes, or until all liquid is absorbed and rice is tender.
- To make the sauce, in a small saucepan, combine the coconut milk with the sugar. In a small bowl, whisk together the cornstarch and water until smooth. Whisk the cornstarch slurry and the salt into the coconut milk mixture and cook over medium heat, stirring constantly, until thickened.
- Plate by placing a small mound of cooked rice in a bowl, along with the sliced mangos, and top with the coconut sauce. Serve immediately.

# BROILED PERSIMMONS

If you've never had persimmons, you're in for a treat. This simple dish showcases the soft texture and almost peachy flavor of the fruit. Seek out persimmons between the months of October and February. Ripe persimmons will have bright orange, shiny skin and will be soft to the touch. You don't want to try and eat an unripe persimmon, as it will taste extremely chalky and unpleasant. A good test for ripeness lies in the calyx, or center tuft on top of the fruit: it will stay intact until ripened; once ripe, it can be easily removed from the fruit. To speed ripening, place in a paper bag in a dry place.

**3 ripe persimmons,**
   **any variety**
**2 tablespoons agave**
**1 teaspoon vanilla extract**
**½ teaspoon lemon juice**

**YIELD: 6 SERVINGS**

- Preheat oven to broil.
- Slice the persimmons in half horizontally and place each, middle side up, so that they fit snugly into a ceramic or metal baking dish. In a small bowl, whisk together the agave, vanilla extract, and lemon juice and then brush the mixture liberally onto the tops of the persimmon halves.
- Broil for 8 to 10 minutes, rotating the pan at least once while cooking to evenly brown the fruits. Keep an eye on them so they do not burn, and broil just until browned evenly. Serve with Vanilla Soft Serve (page 188) or Mascarpone (page 32). Serve immediately.

# BAKED APPLES

A warm and welcome treat come autumn, these are quick to make and fun to eat. I like to peel the apples so that I leave a stripe of peel for color. This works especially nicely with red apples, but green is pretty, too.

**6 firm, tart apples such as Gala, Granny Smith, or Honeycrisp**

**FILLING**
⅔ **cup crushed walnuts (pulsed in food processor until crumbly)**
⅔ **cup certified gluten-free oats**
**2 tablespoons coconut oil**
2½ **tablespoons coconut palm sugar**
¼ **teaspoon cardamom**
½ **teaspoon cinnamon**
**Dash sea salt**
½ **cup golden raisins**

**YIELD: 6 SERVINGS**

- Core the apples making sure to leave the bottom intact. The easiest way to do this is to start with an apple corer and then use a small paring knife or vegetable peeler to scoop out a larger cavity to hold the filling.
- Next, peel the apples. Peel them only halfway, making a swirled design from the remaining skin.
- In a small bowl, combine the filling ingredients with a spoon until very well mixed. Stuff the apples with the filling, dividing evenly among the six apples.
- Preheat oven to 375°F and place the apples individually into a large-size muffin pan. Add 1 tablespoon water to the bottom of each muffin tin and then cover loosely with aluminum foil. Bake the apples for 35 to 40 minutes, or until apples are tender—don't overcook, or they will fall apart.
- Let cool briefly and then serve.

# CHERRY VANILLA COMPOTE

This recipe makes a delightful condiment and can be used in both sweet and savory combinations. I love the Chocolate Soup (page 219) with a dollop of this compote in the center, along with a touch of Sweetened Whipped Coconut Cream (page 33).

2½ cups cherries, pitted
¼ cup coconut palm sugar
1 vanilla bean or 2 teaspoons
   vanilla extract
1 tablespoon brandy or rum

**YIELD: 2 CUPS**

• In a heavy 2-quart saucepan, combine all the ingredients and, over medium heat, bring to a boil, while stirring often. Reduce the heat to medium low and cook for about 10 minutes, until cherries are soft.

• Strain the cherries, reserving the liquid. Pour the liquid back into the saucepan and simmer over medium-low heat until sauce is thickened, stirring occasionally, for about 15 to 20 minutes. Place cherries back into the syrup and serve warm. Store in airtight container for up to 1 week in refrigerator.

# BLUEBERRY LAVENDER JAM

I learned about this flavor combination through one of the many awesome Food Swaps that happen in my town of Philly. I wanted to re-create a version just so I'd never forget its intriguing fragrance and delightful flavor. I especially love this stirred into some plain nondairy yogurt or chia pudding, and it even works well as a cheesecake topping.

1½ cups sugar
2 tablespoons fresh or
   dried lavender buds
¼ cup water
6 cups blueberries

**YIELD: 2½ CUPS**

• In a small saucepan, whisk together ½ cup of the sugar, lavender buds, and water. Simmer for 2 minutes, until fragrant, and then strain to remove the lavender buds. Transfer the scented sugar syrup along with the blueberries and remaining sugar into a 2-quart saucepan.

• Using a potato masher, gently smash the blueberries and cook over medium heat for 15 minutes. Let cool completely before transferring to jars. Store in sealed jars in refrigerator for up to 1 month.

The syrup used to make the preserves also makes a delicious addition to lemonade. Use the syrup in place of sugar and add lemon juice and water to taste. Store in airtight container for up to 1 week in refrigerator.

# STRAWBERRY PRESERVES

I find myself using this type of preserve more than any other to add a touch of sweetness or flavor to many desserts. The amount of sugar in this recipe is essential in making the correct consistency; otherwise you may end up with a runny end result.

**1 pound strawberries**
**2 cups sugar**
**2 tablespoons lemon juice**

**YIELD: 2½ CUPS**

- Slice the strawberries and reserve the greens for another use, such as smoothies or salad greens.
- Place the fruit into a stockpot and combine with the sugar and lemon juice and heat over low heat just until the sugar is dissolved. Increase temperature to medium-high heat and bring the mixture to a boil, stirring constantly. Heat until the mixture registers 220°F on a candy thermometer.
- Transfer into sterile jars (a wash and dry on high heat through the dishwasher does the trick) and let cool to room temperature. Transfer to freezer, or, if you plan to eat right away, store in refrigerator in a sealed airtight jar for up to 2 weeks.

This jam as well as the Blueberry Lavender Jam (page 228) and Cherry Vanilla Compote (page 228) can certainly be processed in a water bath rather than transferred into a freezer. I don't have quite enough room in this book to go into canning and preserving, but please see my Recommendations section for a list of my favorite books on the topic.

# QUICK AND EASY APPLESAUCE

Applesauce is so easy to make, you really should give it a whirl if you never have. You may wonder why it has taken so long to DIY!

**10 medium Granny Smith apples, peeled, cored, and sliced (about 11 cups)**
**¼ cup sugar (optional)**
**½ cup apple cider (or water)**
**2 teaspoons lemon juice**

**YIELD: 6 CUPS**

- In the bowl of a large slow cooker, toss together the apples and sugar. Mix together the apple cider and lemon juice and drizzle over the apples. Cover and cook on high for 3 hours, until very soft, stirring occasionally. Alternatively, cook for 6 hours on low temperature until very soft and completely transformed to applesauce. Store in airtight container for up to 1 week in refrigerator.

*Chapter 7*

# CHOICE CHOCOLATES AND DANDY CANDIES

*Any candy craving* can easily be satisfied at home once you get the knack for candy making—all it takes is a little patience and practice for results that far surpass store-bought. Plus, you can customize it! I've been making candy since I was tall enough to use the stove; so if you've never made candy before, don't be intimidated—even a child can do it! In this chapter you'll find recipes for everything from hard candies to chocolate treats to gooey chewy caramels.

# CANDY MAKING BASICS

The best piece of advice I can give for making candy is to have all ingredients out and ready to go before beginning, and make sure you read the candy recipe instructions at least three times before beginning, until you have a clear grasp of how the recipe will work. The tricky thing about candy making is that it all happens so quickly once the sugar comes to the correct temperature, so you need to be prepared!

In the following recipes, be sure to follow the steps precisely. I recommend a (calibrated) candy thermometer for recipes requiring one, but, if you don't have one, you can always use the Cold Water Method. This is actually how I learned to make candy, so again, a very easy method that just takes a little practice to master.

## COLD WATER METHOD

Place cup of ice-cold water next to your saucepan containing your candy mixture. Test for the candy doneness by dropping about a teaspoon or so of the hot syrup from a spoon into the cold water. Follow the temperature guidelines below, which outline the properties of the candy at each stage of doneness

### Soft-Ball Stage
235°F–240°F
A soft, flexible ball that will flatten when removed from water.

### Firm-Ball Stage
245°F–250°F
A firm ball that will hold its shape when removed from the water but is malleable.

### Hard-Ball Stage
250°F–265°F
A firm ball that is a little more difficult to change the shape, but possible.

### Soft-Crack Stage
270°F–290°F
Flexible threads will form when dropped into ice-cold water.

### Hard-Crack Stage
300°F–310°F
This is the hottest stage of most candy recipes, so be sure to let the dropped syrup cool completely in the water before touching it in this stage. When sugar is dropped into the cold water, brittle hard threads will form.

## WASH DOWN

When cooking sugar into candy, be sure to wash down the sugar crystals from the sides of the pan as you go. You can do this simply with a silicone brush dipped in a running stream of water. Just brush lightly over the crystals, as many times as needed, until all crystals are dissolved. This is important as a single sugar crystal can cause recrystallization, ruining the whole batch of candy. Always have a silicone or bristle brush handy to wash down the sides of your saucepan.

## SAUCEPAN

When making candy it is important that you use a good-quality saucepan for best heat distribution. Too thin of a saucepan can cause scorching and other unpleasantries. You don't need to spend a lot of money, though; one of my favorite candy-making pots is an old Revere Ware copper-bottomed 3-quart pan that I learned to make candy with as a kid. It still serves me well today. I recommend a 2- or 3-quart pan for all the recipes listed, unless otherwise specified. Also, make sure that the sides of the pan are straight, so that you can get an accurate read on your thermometer.

# CHOCOLATE BASICS

## CHOOSING QUALITY CHOCOLATE

When you're out perusing the specialty food stores or hobby shops, you may notice that there are basically two different types of chocolate to choose from: couverture and baking chips, such as Ghirardelli. Couverture is very high quality chocolate that contains extra cocoa butter. You may be unable to find good-quality couverture at a supermarket but seek it out at specialty groceries, craft stores,

or even online. Amazon has a good selection of dairy-free couverture at excellent prices.

The main difference between couverture and baking chips is the final outcome of the chocolate. Couverture results in a snappy, shiny texture (like chocolates from chocolatiers and patisseries), and chocolate chips—when used to coat—oftentimes have a softer texture that's best if kept chilled in the refrigerator. And, it's never shiny. There are benefits to using both, and I'll let you decide what type of chocolate you choose when making chocolates and other confections. I spent years making my own "artisan" chocolates simply using chocolate chips before I ever learned of tempering, and they tasted great! But, quality counts, so regardless of whether or not you decide to temper, be sure to seek out the best-tasting, highest-quality chocolate you can afford when chocolate making (we'll talk about tempering below).

For couverture, most chocolate over 55 percent is dairy-free, making it suitable for vegans. I like Guittard and Barry-Callebaut brands. Coppeneur Germany is a great brand for soy-free.

> Technically, there is a variety of melting or dipping chocolate available, too—sometimes sold as "Candy Melts." These are often made with weird additives and dairy, so it's best to avoid them anyway, but they are also not made with cocoa butter and therefore are not true chocolate.

## TEMPERING CHOCOLATE 101

While it is simple to coat candies and other confections in melted chocolate chips, resulting in an even, soft layer of chocolate, tempering is the process that gives hardened chocolate the typical snap and shine of professional chocolates. Tempering chocolate may seem daunting, especially if you've never even heard of it, but I assure you, just like anything, with a little practice, you'll soon have perfect results. You must gather a few required ingredients and tools before attempting to temper chocolate:

1. High-quality couverture chocolate
2. A double boiler/bain marie or stainless steel bowl and saucepan to act as a double boiler
3. A chocolate thermometer. Be sure to seek out a thermometer made for chocolate, or one that reaches a temperature of at least 80°F accurately and measures in small increments.
4. Patience and persistence
5. Chocolate molds (and chocolate gloves)

When you first begin tempering, you may feel nervous; rest assured, you can always let the chocolate cool and then start all over again if you've messed up. Plus, once you finally nail tempering, you will have a remarkable sense of satisfaction. The gorgeous sheen and tight snap from tempered chocolate is well worth the additional effort, which is mostly wait time.

To temper, follow these instructions, making sure never to allow any water near or around the chocolate. If water hits the chocolate, it will be ruined—even the teensiest amount—and you won't be able to ever temper it. I also recommend using a stainless steel bowl to temper rather than stoneware or glass, as the latter tends to retain heat longer, which can be problematic for tempering.

Also, keep in mind that different couverture brands and percentages of cocoa can and will have different tempering temperatures. The directions below outline a general guideline for dark chocolate, about 61 to 66 percent cocoa content.

1. Over medium-low heat, warm about 1 to 2 inches of water in a double boiler. Place the required amount of couverture (chopped or in coins, don't grate it) into the bowl of the double boiler while the water is still cool, making sure not to get any water whatsoever on the couverture. Melt the chocolate completely, stirring occasionally and heat to 115–120°F.

2. Remove from heat and let cool to about 82°F, stirring occasionally. Once at that temperature, drop about 1 teaspoon of already tempered solid chocolate (about 3 coins from the bag of chocolate you are using) into the melted couverture. Stir a lot. This is called "seeding."

3. Place the double boiler bowl back onto medium-low and heat while stirring, until the temperature of the chocolate is increased to 88–91°F; once in this range, remove from heat. Do not let it get above 91°F or it won't temper. Keep a close eye on the chocolate during this step as it reheats quickly.

4. Voilà! You have tempered chocolate. If there is any remaining "seed" chocolate, remove it before dipping, coating, or molding. Once your chocolate is tempered it should set quickly (about 20 minutes) at room temperature and will appear shiny and "snappy" when bitten into. Use in molds or to coat candies, such as the Buttery Fingers (page 240) or to coat the Salted Espresso Truffles (page 259). Don't place the chocolate in the refrigerator, or it will cause "bloom," which is white streaks in chocolate that form from cocoa butter separating.

# CLASSIC CANDIES

# LOLLIPOPS OR HARD CANDY

Have you ever thought to make your own lollipops? If not, now's the time! They are easy as can be and you can completely control the flavor. One trip to a craft or candy supply store and you'll have what it takes to make enough lollies to last a year! Seek out white plastic molds as they are made specifically for molding hard candies and releasing without breakage.

**1 cup sugar**
**½ cup water**
**⅛ teaspoon cream of tartar**
**1 to 2 drops food coloring**
   **(optional)**
**½ teaspoon flavored oil or**
   **extract, such as lemon**
   **or cherry**

**YIELD: 20 CANDIES**

- Place the plastic (white) hard candy molds onto a flat surface and place in the lollipop sticks, if you're using them. Have the molds nearby for when your sugar is ready to go.
- Over medium heat, in a 2- or 3-quart saucepan, combine the sugar, water, and cream of tartar and heat until boiling, stirring often as it cooks. Be sure to brush down the sides of the pan with a wet pastry brush once the sugar crystals mostly are dissolved. Once the mixture is boiling, stop stirring.
- Clip on a candy thermometer. Let mixture cook until the candy thermometer reaches 300°F (or Hard Crack Stage using the Cold Water Method) or until it turns from clear to a very light caramel hue.
- Working quickly, immediately stir the food coloring and flavoring into the pot. Pour the mixture into candy molds. Rap the mold lightly on flat surface to remove any air bubbles from the candy, and let the candies set until totally hardened. Pop out and place onto waxed paper. Store in airtight container for up to 1 month.

Silicone molds are the best to use, in my opinion, when making hard candies. But, white plastic molds can be used, too. I find the plastic lollipop molds release easiest when candy is still very warm, but firm.

# ENGLISH TOFFEE

This crunchy toffee is coated with decadent dark chocolate and topped with toasted nuts. If you have a nut allergy, replace with toasted sunflower or hemp seeds, which will be just as delicious, or leave them off altogether. In the unlikely event you find yourself with leftover candy, this recipe makes a fabulous mix-in to ice cream when crushed and stirred in after the ice cream has churned. Or, try it instead of chocolate chips in the Classic Chocolate Chip Cookies (page 85).

**1½ cups nondairy margarine**
**1½ cups sugar**
**¼ teaspoon salt**
**2 cups nondairy chocolate
   chips**
**1 cup nuts (such as almonds
   or pecans), toasted and
   chopped**

**YIELD: 8 SERVINGS**

- Prepare a cookie sheet or jelly roll pan with enough parchment paper or a silicone mat to cover.
- Combine the magarine, sugar, and salt in a 2-quart saucepan and melt gently over medium heat, stirring often.
- Continue stirring as the mixture hits a boil, and keep cooking until the candy mixture reaches 300°F on your candy thermometer (for about 30 minutes or Hard Crack Stage if you're using the Cold Water Method). Immediately pour liquid candy mixture onto the prepared surface and spread until about ¼ inch thick. Let cool for about 3 minutes, or until slightly firm, and then carefully place the chocolate chips into an even layer on top of the hot toffee. Allow the chips to rest for about 2 minutes, and then use a silicone spatula to smooth the chocolate over the top of the toffee.
- Sprinkle with nuts and allow to cool completely. Break into bite-size pieces. Store in airtight container for up to 1 month.

# BUTTERY FINGERS

These irresistible candies taste just like the commercial brand, with addictively crunchy peanut butter candy layers encased in creamy chocolate. Of course, these are just as nice without the chocolate on the outside . . . especially when crumbled up and sprinkled on ice cream.

**1 cup sugar**
**⅓ cup corn syrup**
**⅓ cup water, room
 temperature**
**1 cup creamy peanut butter**
**1 teaspoon vanilla extract**
**2 cups couverture, tempered
 (see page 234)**

**YIELD: 8 SERVINGS**

You can replace the corn syrup here with agave to make it corn-free, although the color of the candy will be darker and it may have a slightly different taste than traditional Butterfinger candy.

- Line a 9 x 13-inch baking sheet with parchment paper or have ready a silicone baking mat the same size.
- In a 2-quart saucepan combine the sugar, corn syrup, and water. Bring to a boil over medium heat, stirring often with a clean wooden spoon and washing down sides with a silicone brush. Once boiling, reduce stirring to occasionally until mixture reads 290°F on a candy thermometer (or the Soft Crack Stage if using the Cold Water Method).
- Remove from heat immediately and quickly stir in the peanut butter and vanilla extract and spread about ½ inch thick onto the baking sheet or silicone baking mat. Score lightly using a sharp knife and break into 1 x 2 inch-bars.
- Cover with tempered couverture and let the candy set until the chocolate becomes firm, for about 1 to 2 hours. Store in an airtight container for up to 1 month.

Clockwise:
Honeycomb Candy, page 242
Pinwheel Candy, page 250
Buttery Fingers, this page

# HONEYCOMB CANDY

Whether you call it Hokey Pokey, Puff Candy, Sea Foam, Sponge Candy, or another one of its many different and amusing names, this is an especially kid-friendly candy—and a fun project for a rainy afternoon. Let the kids watch as you add in the baking soda as a super-fun surprise awaits! You'll need a large stockpot suitable for candy cooking; the candy gets BIG when you add baking soda, so make sure it's quite roomy.

¼ cup water
¼ cup agave or maple syrup
1 cup sugar
¼ cup brown sugar
   (dark or light)
2 teaspoons baking soda
2 cups nondairy couverture
   or nondairy chocolate
   chips, melted (see page
   233)

**YIELD: 10 SERVINGS**

- Place a silicone mat onto a cookie sheet and set on a flat surface.
- In a stockpot thoroughly combine the water, agave, and sugars. There is no need to stir the candy while it cooks, but a nice and thorough mixing at the beginning is a good thing to do. Clip on your candy thermometer and cook over medium heat until the thermometer reaches about 285°F to 290°F, (or Soft Crack Stage using the Cold Water Method) or until the syrup darkens in color.
- Be sure to wash down the sides of the pot with a wet silicone brush at the beginning of the cooking stages, so as to not incorporate any sugar crystals into the already dissolved, cooked mixture.
- When the mixture has reached 285°F, remove from heat and quickly and carefully stir in the baking soda. It will foam up about four times its size! Stir quickly and evenly and then pour out onto the silicone mat, allowing it to freeform into a nice solid blob. Do not try to spread the mixture; just let it rest until it has cooled. Cut into bite-size squares and then cover with the chocolate. Store in airtight container for up to 1 month. If you do not wish to cover these candies, they need to be stored immediately in an airtight, dry plastic bag with all air removed (using a straw, etc.)—uncovered, the honeycomb candy will only keep a short while before changing texture.

# CARAMELS

Is there anything more sinfully delicious than a chewy caramel? These sticky sweet candies will make you do flips over their authentic taste, with no need for heavy cream or butter.

**1 cup sugar**
**1 cup canned full-fat**
**coconut milk**
**½ cup light corn syrup**
**or agave**
**¼ cup nondairy margarine**
**or coconut oil**
**1 teaspoon vanilla extract**

**YIELD: 20 CANDIES**

- Grease a baking dish or pan (or use a nonstick silicone pan). The smaller the base of the pan, the thicker your pieces of caramel will be.
- Place all ingredients, except for the margarine and vanilla extract, into a heavy 2- or 3-quart saucepan (make sure that the sides of your pan are at least 6 inches high because the caramel mixture will bubble up).
- Over medium heat, stirring constantly with a wooden spoon, dissolve the sugar completely. Next, add the margarine and stir just until boiling. Once boiling, stop stirring.
- Let the mixture continue to boil, without stirring, until it reaches 245° to 250°F on your candy thermometer (or Firm Ball Stage if you're using the Cold Water Method), which takes about 15 to 20 minutes.
- When the mixture is at the right temperature, immediately remove from heat and stir in the vanilla extract. Quickly pour into your prepared dish.
- Let cool at room temperature for a few minutes and then slip into your fridge for about an hour. Once firm, cut the caramel into squares. You can freeze the candy just for a few minutes right before cutting to make it slightly less sticky to handle.
- Wrap the candies in waxed paper and store in fridge or in cool, dry place for up to 1 month.

For an extra-special treat, try covering the firm caramels with chocolate, either couverture that has been tempered (see page 234) or melted chocolate chips. Be sure the caramels are room temperature or colder before attempting to coat with chocolate, and once dipped, place on parchment or waxed paper. Let the chocolate reharden at room temperature for about 1 to 2 hours.

# HAND-PULLED TAFFY

The first time I made taffy I will never forget it. My BFF and I got snowed in together for five days straight one week during grade school (best week ever!), and we decided to take advantage of our time by making a ton of candy. This was one of the recipes mastered on the first go. The teamwork certainly helped, and I encourage you to seek out a willing partner if you have one handy to help pull. Not only is it more fun, but it's a little easier on your upper body as well!

1 cup sugar
1 tablespoon cornstarch
½ cup light corn syrup
1 tablespoon nondairy
   margarine or coconut oil,
   plus more for your hands
   as you pull
6 tablespoons water
¼ teaspoon salt
1 teaspoon vegetable glycerin
   (optional—see note)
½ teaspoon orange oil,
   lemon oil, or other extract
   flavoring

**YIELD: 40 PIECES**

- Grease a small glass baking dish and gather a candy thermometer and waxed paper. Set aside a bit of margarine or coconut oil for greasing your hands as you pull.
- Whisk together the sugar, cornstarch, corn syrup, margarine, water, salt, and glycerin, if using, in a 1-quart saucepan until no lumps remain and heat over medium heat. Stir constantly until mixture comes to a boil.
- Cook, undisturbed, just until the mixture reaches 265 to 270°F on your candy thermometer (or Soft Crack Stage if using the Cold Water Method) and then immediately remove from the heat and add the flavoring.
- Pour the liquid taffy into the greased baking dish and allow to cool for about 10 minutes, or until easy to handle. Once you know you won't burn yourself, grease your (very clean) hands and grab the taffy and form into a log. Begin to stretch and pull at the taffy, creating ropes and then folding and repulling to add air into the candy. Continue pulling for about 15 minutes, until the color has lightened significantly and feels light and airy, like taffy. Cut into bite-size pieces and then wrap individually in waxed paper. Store in airtight container for up to 1 month.

The glycerin in this recipe can be sourced from candy-making supply stores and online. It's totally optional, but it does help ensure a creamy, smooth texture to your taffy.

# TURKISH DELIGHT

Turkish Delight may be the origin of the jelly bean, with its chewy fruity center being an inspiration for the candy-covered beans. Like many children, I was introduced to Turkish Delight from the enticing description in *The Lion, the Witch and the Wardrobe*. When I first tasted it, I admit I wasn't quite as impressed as Edmund, but close! This candy is easy to prepare as long as you have all your equipment and ingredients gathered and ready to go.

## MIX #1
**3 cups granulated sugar**
**½ cup agave**
**½ cup water**
**⅛ teaspoon cream of tartar**

## MIX #2
**1 cup cornstarch**
**1 cup confectioner's sugar**
**1 teaspoon cream of tartar**
**2½ cups water**
**2 drops food coloring, any color**
**⅛ teaspoon lemon or orange oil, or 1 teaspoon rosewater**

**½ cup confectioner's sugar for dusting**
**¼ cup cornstarch for dusting**

**YIELD: 30 PIECES**

- Grease an 8 x 8-inch baking dish. Have a sheet of cling wrap handy for covering the candy.
- In a 2- or 3-quart saucepan, combine all the ingredients for Mix #1 and bring to a boil over high heat. Once the mixture comes to a boil, reduce heat to medium and continue to cook, stirring often, until the mixture reaches 260°F (or Hard Ball Stage using the Cold Water Method). While the mixture is heating up to that temperature, move on to the next step.
- In a stockpot, whisk together the ingredients for Mix #2 (except for the food coloring and flavoring) until completely smooth and cook over medium-high heat until boiling. Once the mixture comes to a boil, cook for about 2 minutes, or until very thick. Remove from the heat.
- Once Mix #1 hits 260°F, quickly pour it into the stockpot containing Mix #2 and stir vigorously but carefully until well combined. Reduce heat to medium low and cook for 35 more minutes, stirring often with a silicone spatula until the mixture is thick and smooth, like whipped honey.
- Add the 2 drops of food coloring and ⅛ teaspoon flavoring. Pour into prepared baking dish and cover immediately with cling wrap. Let candy firm and cool down to room temperature, for about 30 minutes.
- Whisk together cornstarch and confectioner's sugar and gently coat the cooled candy square with the sugar mixture on each side. Use a sharp knife to cut the candy into bite-size squares. Store in airtight container for up to 1 month.

# SUGAR NESTS

Sugar Nests make a very fun addition to a dessert's presentation and are not as difficult as they appear. You do need to take caution when handling the hot syrup, making sure not to get any on you accidentally—as it gets *hot!* Otherwise, drizzle the sugar to your heart's content to make stunning shapes and designs. The bowls make a lovely presentation for ice cream when frozen for 10 minutes before scooping, or use as decorative additions to cakes.

**2 cups sugar**
**½ cup water**
**3 tablespoons agave**

**YIELD: 10 NESTS**

- Prepare your entire workspace by covering around the stove and on the floor with parchment, careful not to let any come too close to the burner, lest it catch fire. Keep a sheet of parchment handy for placing your finished nests.
- On one piece of parchment, flip over a large or standard-size muffin pan so you can use the bottom and outside of the cups as a mold and lightly grease the bottoms of the cups. I like almond oil, but a nonstick spray will work just fine. Secure your candy thermometer into a 2- or 3-quart saucepan. Have a large metal bowl of ice water next to you so you can be ready to dunk the pot of cooked syrup in the bowl to cool it down.
- Over medium heat, combine the sugar, water, and agave. Stirring occasionally, and brushing down the sides of the pan with a wet silicone brush to wash away any sugar crystals, cook the syrup until it reaches 310°F on your candy thermometer and turns dark amber in color (or Hard Crack Stage if using the Cold Water Method).
- Remove immediately from the heat and dunk the pot into the ice water bath. Stir briefly just until thickened and remove from the water. Using the tines of a whip-style whisk or a fork, very carefully drizzle thin strands of the hot syrup onto the greased upturned muffin tins, creating a lovely mess of strands. Set the hot sugar mixture aside on a trivet until you're ready to make the next batch of nests. Careful when working with this mixture as it is extremely hot. Use caution when handling and wear kitchen gloves if you have them.

*continued*

- Let the drizzled syrup rest for about 15 seconds or until only slightly warm to the touch. Use clean dry hands to gently remove the nests from the pan and bend and form the sugar into a nest shape, or other desired form, and place onto another clean dry sheet of parchment.
- Repeat with the remaining hot sugar mixture (the mixture will remain warm in the pot). Work fast! The syrup cools quickly and you want to catch it in its perfect state of malleability and coolness to the touch.
- Use immediately for garnish or store in an airtight container for up to 1 week.

# PEANUT BRITTLE

Be sure to seek out raw or "Spanish" peanuts when making this recipe, as the peanuts actually cook in the hot candy mixture. If you use roasted, the peanuts will be overcooked. This candy works well with other flavors mixed in. Try 1 teaspoon cinnamon or Sriracha sauce for a fun kick.

1 teaspoon baking soda
Optional: 1 teaspoon ground cinnamon, Sriracha sauce, or other flavoring
1¼ cups raw Spanish peanuts
1 cup sugar
½ cup light corn syrup or agave
¼ cup water
1 heaping tablespoon nondairy margarine or coconut oil
1 teaspoon vanilla extract

**YIELD: 8 SERVINGS**

- Grease a cookie sheet. In a small bowl mix together baking soda and cinnamon or other spice, if using. In separate container, measure out your peanuts.
- In a 2- or 3-quart saucepan, combine the sugar, corn syrup, water, and margarine. Over medium heat, stirring occasionally with a wooden spoon, bring the mixture to a boil. Once it has started boiling, add the Spanish peanuts.
- Bring back up to a boil and keep on medium heat until the candy mixture reaches 300°F on your candy thermometer (or Hard Crack Stage using the Cold Water Method).
- Remove from heat and add baking soda mixture and vanilla extract. If you are using additional flavoring, add it in now. Stir well and pour onto the greased cookie sheet. Wait a few minutes, until the candy is cool enough to handle, and pull gently to desired thickness.
- Let cool completely and then break into individual pieces. Store in airtight container for up to 1 month.

## ALLERGY NOTE

For a corn-free version, use agave rather than corn syrup.

# CANDY KETTLE CORN

Such a fun treat to serve at Halloween, or anytime! The sweet and salty combo of kettle corn is hard to resist, so be sure to double the recipe if making for a large crowd.

**5½ cups popped popcorn, salted to taste (about ½ cup unpopped kernels)**
**2 cups sugar**
**1 cup light corn syrup or agave**
**½ cup nondairy margarine**
**¼ cup apple cider**
**1 teaspoon vanilla extract**
**1 teaspoon apple cider vinegar**
**1 cup nondairy chocolate chips**
**⅔ cup sliced almonds, toasted**

**YIELD: 5½ CUPS**

- Make sure your popcorn is popped and set aside, ready to go in a large bowl. Have nearby a candy thermometer and a wooden spoon.
- Grease a 9 x 13-inch cookie sheet.
- In a heavy saucepan, at least 8 inches deep, combine the sugar, corn syrup, margarine, and apple cider. Over medium heat, bring the mixture to boil, stirring occasionally. Continue to cook over medium heat and stir regularly using a wooden spoon until your candy thermometer reads 300°F (or Hard Crack Stage if using the Cold Water Method). This takes a while. Patience totally pays off with these, so don't rush and pull the candy from the stove before it reaches hard crack stage. Be sure to wash down (page 233) the sides!
- Remove the candy mixture from the heat and quickly stir in the vanilla extract and vinegar. Pour HOT candy mixture over the popcorn and stir quickly until evenly coated. Let cool for about 5 to 7 minutes. Spread onto a greased cookie sheet and let cool completely.
- Using a double boiler, melt the chocolate until smooth. Drizzle melted chocolate over the candied popcorn and sprinkle with sliced almonds. Let chocolate harden and then break into bite-size pieces. Store in an airtight container in the fridge or a cool place where chocolate will not melt for up to 1 month.

To easily toast almonds, spread in an even layer on a cookie sheet and bake for 7 minutes at 375°F, or until fragrant.

# PINWHEEL CANDY

There is much speculation about the origins of this candy, ranging from German, to Irish, to Pennsylvania Dutch, to the product of ingenuity during the Great Depression when limited ingredients were all there were to work with, which may be why potatoes are a key ingredient here. Even though potatoes aren't normally thought of as dessert food, they really do work quite nicely in this recipe! I recommend using a Yukon Gold or similar variety; if you opt for russet, you may need a touch more nondairy milk to make smooth.

**1 large medium- to low-starch potato, peeled, mashed, and salted lightly**
**¼ cup nondairy milk**
**1 teaspoon vanilla extract**
**½ teaspoon salt**
**2 pounds (about 6 cups) confectioner's sugar (or enough to make stiff dough)**
**About 1 cup chocolate hazelnut butter (such as Justin's brand)**

**YIELD: 20 PIECES**

- In a large bowl, combine the mashed potatoes, nondairy milk, vanilla extract, and sea salt until smooth. Gradually incorporate the confectioner's sugar until a stiff dough forms. You may need a little more or a little less sugar depending on the moisture level of your mashed potatoes.
- Form the dough into a large patty and refrigerate for at least 2 hours. Place the chilled dough in between two sheets of plastic wrap and roll out into a rectangle about ½ inch thick. Slather generously with chocolate hazelnut butter until coated. Using the bottom piece of the plastic wrap, gently guide the dough into a roll longways as you would a jelly roll. Cover with plastic wrap and chill for an additional hour. Once chilled, cut into ½-inch-wide sections and wrap in waxed paper, twisting each side to close.
- Store in fridge in airtight container. Keeps for up to 1 week.

# AFTER DINNER MINTS

These mints are easy to whip up but impressive enough to brag about when serving to friends. Call them artisan and watch their eyes light up.

Note that you can feel free to sub in Sweet Cashew Cream (page 32) for the cream cheese, just add a little more confectioner's sugar until it reaches the correct consistency.

**8 ounces nondairy cream cheese**
**1 tablespoon nondairy margarine**
**2 drops pure peppermint extract/oil**
**Food coloring paste (use corn-free if needed)**
**3½ to 4 cups confectioner's sugar, plus extra for dusting (use corn-free if needed)**

**YIELD: 80 MINTS**

- Mix the cream cheese, margarine, peppermint oil, and food coloring with a whisk until smooth. Gradually add in the confectioner's sugar, about ½ cup at a time, until a stiff dough forms—much like Play-Doh.
- Pat into a disk and roll out in between two sheets of parchment paper. Cut with a very small cookie cutter (or use a knife/pizza cutter to cut into squares) into desired shapes and then place on cookie tray that will fit in your fridge. Chill for 1 hour, then transfer to a resealable plastic container to store for up to 1 month in refrigerator. These also freeze well and can be thawed in your refrigerator until eating.

# MARZIPAN

If there is one ingredient that I would eat my weight in—and not even fret that I can't use it in the recipe intended for—it's marzipan. Sold in tiny tubes at specialty stores or in the baking aisle of your neighborhood grocery, marzipan is easy to make at home, saving you both money and the effort of finding one that is dairy-, egg- and gluten-free, which can be difficult. Bonus: almonds, the main ingredient here, are tiny powerhouses rich in calcium, iron, potassium, magnesium, copper, and zinc!

1 tablespoon flaxseed meal
2 tablespoons water
3 cups blanched almond meal
1 cup confectioner's sugar,
    plus extra for rolling
Dash salt

**YIELD: 10 SERVINGS**

- In a small bowl, combine the flaxseed meal with the water and allow to rest until thickened, for about 5 minutes.
- In a food processor, blend the 3 cups almond meal until clumpy and the texture becomes somewhat like a paste, scraping down the sides and bottom of the bowl often. It should take 7 to 10 minutes' blending time to become clumpy.
- Add the confectioner's sugar and salt and pulse until once again crumbly, for about 30 seconds to 1 minute. Drizzle in about half of the prepared flaxseed meal while the food processor is blending and continue to add a little more until the mixture clumps together into a dough. Remove from food processor and form into a cylinder. Roll out gently onto a confectioner's sugar–covered surface and then wrap tightly to store. Use immediately or keep refrigerated for up to 2 weeks.

# SIMPLE WHITE CHOCOLATE

This confection is best used for baking or candy making, rather than straight snacking (although my kids love it), but it's perfect for the recipes in this book that call for white chocolate. Seek out the highest-quality food-grade cacao butter you can find for top-quality flavor.

**8 ounces food-grade cacao butter, chopped into ½-inch pieces**
**¼ cup soymilk powder**
**3 tablespoons agave**
**⅓ cup confectioner's sugar**
**⅛ teaspoon salt**
**1 teaspoon vanilla extract**

**YIELD: 8 OUNCES**

- In a double boiler, over medium-low heat, melt the cacao butter until completely liquefied. Whisk in the soymilk powder until completely dissolved. Stir in the agave, confectioner's sugar, salt, and vanilla extract and whisk again until very well blended with no lumps remaining. Pour straight into a plastic or silicone chocolate mold and refrigerate for 20 minutes until solid. Pop out of mold and use as desired. Store in airtight container for up to 1 month.

You can add flavored oils to the white chocolate, too, such as lemon or mint in small amounts—about 1 to 2 drops. If you opt for food coloring, go with paste rather than drops, otherwise the chocolate may seize with the additional liquid added. Add about 1/16 teaspoon of the desired color of paste along with the agave, confectioner's sugar, salt, and vanilla extract.

# CHOCOLATE ALMOND NUGGETS

As a child, one of my favorite candy combinations was simply chocolate with almonds. These bite-size morsels are a tribute to these two "made for each other" flavors.

**½ cup sliced almonds**
**1 cup nondairy chocolate**
**¼ cup almond meal**

**YIELD: 10 SERVINGS**

- Preheat oven to 375°F and spread the almonds onto a baking tray. Bake for 7 minutes, or until fragrant. Watch carefully so that they do not burn.
- Melt chocolate over a double boiler until totally smooth. Stir in the almond meal and toasted almonds. Drop by small spoonfuls onto waxed paper or a silicone mat. Let harden completely. Store in airtight container for up to 3 weeks.

# EASY HOLIDAY BARK

A surefire way to impress without any additional holiday stress! Add in your favorite candies from the holiday, or stick to the traditional version as I have below. Either way, you'll end up with a treat good enough to gift.

**2 cups nondairy dark**
    **chocolate, coins or chips**
**2 cups nondairy white**
    **chocolate, chunks or chips**
**1 cup crushed candy canes**
    **(check ingredients**
    **for gluten or animal**
    **products)**

**YIELD: 8 SERVINGS**

- Have an 8 x 8-inch silicone pan ready to go. You can also use a baking sheet lined with waxed paper or aluminum foil, but silicone is best.
- Over a double boiler, melt or temper (page 234) the dark chocolate and spread evenly into the silicone baking pan. Place the chocolate in the refrigerator to firm up.
- In the meantime, prepare the white chocolate by melting over a double boiler. Depending on what type of chocolate you are using, it could be totally liquid, or very thick. Once melted, spread or pour the white chocolate on top of the solidified dark chocolate. Sprinkle with crushed candy canes. Let harden and then score into pieces. Store in airtight container for up to 1 month.

# CHOCOLATE PEPPERMINT PATTIES ⓃⒸⒷ

This candy takes the classic peppermint patty one step further and infuses it with an extra-intense chocolate flavor. If you cannot locate the dark cocoa powder, regular cocoa powder will work well. You can use an equal amount of Sweet Cashew Cream (page 32) in place of the vegan cream cheese for a soy-free version.

2 cups confectioner's sugar
¼ cup dark cocoa powder
¼ cup + 2 tablespoons
   nondairy cream cheese
½ teaspoon sea salt
1 teaspoon peppermint
   extract
2 cups nondairy semi-sweet
   chocolate

**YIELD: 30 CANDIES**

• In a large mixing bowl (an electric mixer works best), combine the confectioner's sugar, cocoa powder, cream cheese, salt, and peppermint extract until very smooth. Divide into two equal disks and wrap in waxed paper. Chill in the refrigerator for at least 1 hour, or for 10 to 15 minutes in the freezer.

• Place one disk of chocolate dough between two sheets of parchment and roll until about ¼ inch thick. Use a 1½-inch round cookie cutter to cut out circles. Place circles of dough back into the fridge and let chill while you melt the chocolate.

• Over a double boiler on medium-low heat, melt the chocolate until shiny and smooth, or temper according to directions on page 234. Coat the disks of chilled dough by painting on the chocolate with a pastry brush. Gently place onto a waxed paper–lined wire rack to cool. Let set until chocolate is firm. Store in refrigerator in airtight container for up to 1 month.

# DOUBLE CHOCOLATE CARAMEL BARS

These candy bars are filled with an irresistible chocolate-caramel filling that just begs you to take one more bite. These full-size candy bars can be made into small chocolate caramels by using a smaller mold. Looking for a lighter flavor? Try these with white chocolate chips in the filling instead of the three additional tablespoons of dark chocolate.

1 cup plus 3 tablespoons
   nondairy couverture coins
   or chips
2 tablespoons nondairy
   margarine or coconut oil
2½ cups vegan marshmallows,
   such as Dandies or Sweet
   and Sara

**YIELD: ABOUT 4
CANDY BARS**

- Use the method on page 234 to temper the 1 cup of the chocolate. Coat the inside of four standard-size candy bar molds with three-quarters of the chocolate. Let the chocolate set completely for about 1 hour.
- In a small saucepan over medium-low heat, melt the margarine along with the 3 tablespoons chocolate coins. Add in the marshmallows and stir constantly until completely melted, for about 1 to 2 minutes.
- Let cool for about 5 minutes and then fill the chocolate molds with filling. Cover with the rest of the tempered chocolate and use a straight edge to flatten completely. Let candy bars set completely, for about 2 hours, or until they easily release from the molds. Store in cool, dry place, wrapped or unwrapped in airtight container for up to 1 week.

# CREAM EGGS

A childhood favorite of mine that has transformed into an adult obsession. These are so easy to make, you just need a good chocolate mold (clear plastic) and an afternoon with nothing going on. The food coloring isn't needed in this recipe but helps create the authentic "yolk" we've grown so accustomed to in a cream egg.

**1 egg-shaped plastic chocolate mold that fits twenty chocolate egg halves**
**2¼ cups couverture chocolate, divided**
**¼ cup light corn syrup**
**2 tablespoons nondairy margarine, softened**
**1 cup confectioner's sugar**
**1 teaspoon vanilla extract**
**1 to 2 drops yellow food coloring**

**YIELD: 10 CREAM EGGS**

- Over a double boiler, temper 2 cups of the chocolate according to the directions on page 234. Coat the insides of twenty plastic chocolate molds shaped like egg halves. You can also use a typical truffle-style mold and coat each cavity evenly with chocolate. Let chocolate harden completely and then make the filling.
- To make the filling, in a small bowl whisk together the corn syrup, margarine, confectioner's sugar, and vanilla extract until very smooth. Transfer one-quarter of the filling into a separate bowl and add in the yellow food coloring.
- Pop out the egg shapes from the mold.
- Fill ten of the chocolate egg cavities two-thirds of the way full with the white filling and then drop a central spot of yellow fondant into the center of the white to fill almost full, leaving a little room at the top so the fondant doesn't overflow. Temper ¼ cup of the remaining chocolate and pipe the chocolate onto just the edges of one of the eggs; use to glue each half of the eggs together, one filled and one hollow. Let chocolate harden completely. Store in cool dry place for up to 3 weeks.

# TRUFFLES AND FUDGE

# SALTED ESPRESSO TRUFFLES

The first chocolate truffle is speculated to have originated in France, but today, there are countless varieties from countless countries, making it one of the most popular chocolates in the world. I learned this technique of truffle making from René, the colorful owner of Rim Café in South Philadelphia. When he met me and learned of my panache for working with ganache, he gleefully told me that his secret to a perfect truffle was the ratio: 2 parts chocolate to 1 part cream. I have to agree that after implementing his technique—which was already quite close to my own, a perfect truffle was indeed formed. Thanks, René!

1 cup couverture chocolate or nondairy chocolate chips
½ cup canned full-fat coconut milk
⅛ teaspoon sea salt
1 teaspoon vanilla extract
½ teaspoon espresso powder
½ cup cocoa powder or almond meal, for dusting

**YIELD: 36 TRUFFLES**

- Over a double boiler, melt the couverture until completely smooth. Remove bowl from heat and place on a heat-safe surface.
- In a small saucepan, warm the coconut milk, salt, vanilla extract, and espresso powder just until it begins to simmer and is obviously hot to the touch, but do not let it come to a boil.
- Using a whisk, gently stir the warmed coconut milk mixture into the center of the melted couverture and blend gently and carefully in a circular fashion until completely mixed. Transfer mixture to a plastic bowl and cover with plastic wrap.
- Chill in refrigerator for about 1 to 2 hours, until firm.
- Using a small scoop or rounded spoon, and chocolate-dusted hands, roll the chocolate into 1-inch balls. Immediately roll the truffles into the cocoa powder. Chill before serving and store in airtight container in the refrigerator for up to 2 weeks.

Clockwise:
Salted Espresso Truffles, this page
Dark and Dreamy Fudge, page 263
Buckeyes, page 262

# STRAWBERRY PISTACHIO TRUFFLES

What a fantastic flavor combination strawberry and pistachio make along with chocolate. Feel free to use homemade Strawberry Preserves (page 229) or store-bought—both will taste equally as divine.

**2 cups nondairy semi-sweet chocolate chips**
**¼ cup + 2 tablespoons full-fat coconut milk**
**1 teaspoon vanilla extract**
**¼ cup strawberry preserves**
**1 cup pistachios, chopped finely**

**YIELD: 25 TRUFFLES**

- In a saucepan over medium-low heat, combine all of the ingredients except for the pistachios.
- Stir constantly until the chocolate is fully melted and the mixture is very well combined.
- Transfer to a bowl and chill just until it's easy to work into a ball, for about 2 hours. A quick trip to the freezer will help them out as well.
- Using a 1-inch ice cream scoop, form chocolate into balls and then roll into the chopped pistachios. Place onto a parchment-covered plate or tray and chill overnight in refrigerator or until firm. Store in airtight container in refrigerator for up to 1 month.

# CHERRY CORDIALS

These candies are simple to make but do require tempered couverture and chocolate molds to make them work, as untempered chocolate is too soft and no molds will cause messy cordials. For a quick refresher on how to temper chocolate, refer to page 234.

15 to 20 maraschino
    cherries, stems removed
    (see note)
¼ cup brandy
1 cup couverture, tempered
⅓ cup + 1 tablespoon
    confectioner's sugar
3 teaspoons cherry juice
    (from cherry jar)
¼ teaspoon vanilla or
    almond extract
A chocolate mold

**YIELD: 15 TO 20 CANDIES**

- Drain the liquid from the maraschino cherries, set it aside, and place the cherries on a paper towel. Transfer the cherries into a small bowl containing the brandy and allow to soak for 1 hour. Remove from brandy and place onto a dry paper towel. Let the cherries rest until they are fairly dry to the touch, for about 1 hour.
- Brush the tempered chocolate onto the insides of the chocolate mold to coat the sides evenly. Let chocolate completely harden. Place one cherry into each cavity.
- Mix together the confectioner's sugar, cherry juice, and vanilla extract and pour a small amount (just to fill) on top of the cherries. Top with tempered chocolate and let rest until chocolate has completely hardened. Store in airtight container for up to 1 week.

---

**ALLERGY NOTE**

Use vanilla extract instead of almond for a nut-free candy.

---

You can also omit the fondant filling and just dip the brandy soaked cherries straight into the tempered couverture. This works especially well if you leave the stems on the cherries. Just dip and place onto waxed paper to harden.

---

# BUCKEYES

You can use chocolate chips with these or couverture. Born and raised in Ohio, I tend to think the chocolate chip method is more authentic, but, admittedly, the couverture is definitely more glamorous and adds a nice shell to the outer layer. Be sure when dipping to leave a little bit of peanut butter exposed (about ½ inch in diameter) so that the candies resemble actual buckeyes!

1½ cups smooth peanut butter

1 cup nondairy margarine, softened to room temperature

2 teaspoons vanilla extract

¼ teaspoon salt

5¾ to 6 cups confectioner's sugar

3 cups nondairy chocolate chips or couverture

**YIELD: 30 BUCKEYES**

- Line a 9 x 13-inch cookie sheet with waxed paper.
- Mix together peanut butter and margarine until super smooth.
- Stir in vanilla extract and salt.
- Using electric mixer, slowly incorporate the confectioner's sugar until little crumbles form. The mixture should go from very creamy to looking like pulverized very crumbly dry cookie dough.
- Take a pinch or two of the powder/dough and, using your hands, work to form into 1-inch balls. If they appear uneven, keep working them in your hands until smooth and spherical.
- Place each onto a cookie sheet and insert a toothpick into the center. Gently pat around the toothpick to kind of "seal" it into the peanut butter ball.
- Chill in freezer for about 40 minutes, or until very firm. This prevents the toothpicks from sliding out while dipping.
- Using a double boiler, melt your chocolate until smooth or follow the directions for tempering on page 234. Remove the peanut butter balls from the freezer and carefully swirl the ball into the chocolate, taking care not to let the toothpick slide out. Place onto wax paper and repeat until all are covered.
- Let stand at room temperature until chocolate has firmed up. Remove toothpicks and seal over the tiny hole in the middle using the back of a spoon or clean fingertips. Store in airtight container for up to 1 month.

# DARK AND DREAMY FUDGE

Super rich and extra dreamy, this fudge is best enjoyed in small pieces so that you can savor the intense flavor. My mom always made her fudge with walnuts, and I really enjoy it this way, too. If you like some crunch in your fudge, simply add 1 cup of toasted walnut pieces into the fudge before spreading into a prepared pan, or sprinkle on top.

½ cup sugar
1 teaspoon vanilla extract
2 tablespoons nondairy milk
2 tablespoons nondairy margarine
10 ounces Ricemellow (vegan marshmallow) Cream
3 cups nondairy chocolate chips

**YIELD: 64 PIECES**

- Prepare an 8 x 8-inch pan by lightly greasing with nondairy margarine.
- In a 2-quart saucepan, combine the sugar, vanilla extract, nondairy milk, and margarine and bring to a boil over medium heat. Cook for 1 minute, stirring often. Stir in the Ricemellow Cream and heat just until warm and all of it has evenly combined with the sugar mixture, for about 4 minutes.
- Quickly stir in the chocolate chips until they have completely melted and pour the mixture into the prepared pan. Let cool completely and then chill in the refrigerator for at least 2 hours before cutting. Store in an airtight container in the refrigerator for up to 1 month.

# PEANUT BUTTER FUDGE

This easy and delicious fudge is a variation on a recipe my mother used to make whenever I'd ask for "candy." She called it peanut butter candy, but to me it tastes more like decadent peanut butter fudge. It's a perfect choice for when you're craving candy, but don't have a candy thermometer handy. Working quickly is an important part of making this fudge, so be sure to have all your ingredients and equipment ready before you begin.

½ cup nondairy margarine
2 cups brown sugar
½ cup nondairy milk
1 cup creamy peanut butter
1½ teaspoons vanilla extract
3 cups confectioner's sugar
1½ cups nondairy chocolate chips

**YIELD: 20 PIECES**

- Lightly grease a standard-size loaf pan or small square cake pan.
- In a 2-quart saucepan, over medium heat, warm the margarine until melted. Add the brown sugar and nondairy milk and cook over medium heat until mixture comes to a hard boil (for about 2 to 3 minutes).
- Once it comes to a hard boil, set your timer for exactly 2 minutes. Continue to cook over medium heat, stirring the entire time it is cooking, washing down sugar crystals as needed.
- After 2 minutes, remove from the heat and quickly stir in your peanut butter and vanilla extract, and promptly add the confectioner's sugar, mixing briefly just until all the sugar has been incorporated.
- Spread the thick candy into prepared pan and wait for it to set up slightly.
- Once the fudge has cooled slightly, melt chocolate chips over a double boiler and drizzle all over the fudge. Let chocolate reharden and then serve! Store in airtight container for up to 2 weeks.

# FRUIT-BASED CANDIES

## SUGAR PLUMS  Ⓢ Ⓒ Ⓑ

These little gems have become well known from their very important cameo in the classic Christmas tale, and, even though they may conjure up images of sugar-covered plums in your mind, they actually have never contained any plums at all. "Plum" used to be a popular way to describe any dried fruit, but sugar plums usually contained a mixture of dates, apricots, or figs to achieve their sweetness.

**1 cup raw almonds**
**1 teaspoon lemon or**
    **orange zest**
**½ cup chopped dried figs**
**½ cup chopped dried dates**
**½ teaspoon cinnamon**
**¼ teaspoon nutmeg**
**Dash ground cloves**
**2 tablespoons agave**
**½ cup confectioner's sugar**
    **for dusting**

**YIELD: 24 SUGAR PLUMS**

- Preheat oven to 400°F and spread the almonds in an even layer on a cookie sheet. Bake for 7 minutes, or until fragrant.
- Place almonds, zest, figs, dates, cinnamon, nutmeg, and cloves into a food processor and pulse until crumbly. Add in the agave, 1 tablespoon at a time, and pulse again, until the mixture comes together easily. Pinch into 1-inch balls and roll in the confectioner's sugar. Store in airtight container for up to 1 week.

### ALLERGY NOTE

For a nut-free variation, try these with toasted sunflower seeds, hemp seeds, or even flaked coconut in place of the almonds.

# CANDIED ORANGE PEELS

Candied orange peels are so nice to have for decorative purposes or to add a little zing to a dessert, like in my Florentines (page 97). This recipe also works nicely with lemon or lime peels, which add a nice color variation to the mix.

**4 navel oranges**
**1½ cups sugar**
**¾ cup water**
**Dash salt**

**YIELD: 3 CUPS**

- Remove the peels from the oranges by slicing through the peel and quartering it, without puncturing the fruit. Gently cut off the top and bottom of the orange and then carefully peel the orange peel, leaving behind the pith and fruit. Reserve pith and fruit for another use (these make fantastic juicing oranges).
- Lay one section of peel flat onto a cutting area, light-side-up. Slice the peel into thin, even strips, about ¼ inch wide.
- Place the peels into a medium saucepan and cover with 1 inch of water and salt very lightly. Boil for 20 minutes, and then drain. Briefly place onto clean kitchen towel to dry.
- Drain the saucepan and then wipe dry. Place the drained peels, sugar, water, and salt into the pot and cook over medium heat. Cook until the mixture reaches 235°F on a candy thermometer (or Soft Ball Stage if using the Cold Water Method). Spread in an even layer onto a waxed paper–covered cookie sheet or silicone mat. Let harden for 2 hours, and for up to 12 hours before transferring to airtight container. Store for up to 1 month.

# SOUR FRUIT JELLIES

These jelly candies are a touch softer than traditional gumdrops. They actually taste more like fruit snacks made for children's lunches.

¾ cup white grape juice
⅓ cup fruit pectin
½ teaspoon baking soda
1 cup sugar
1 cup agave
1 to 2 drops food coloring, any color
¼ teaspoon citric acid
⅓ cup turbinado sugar

**YIELD: 30 CANDIES**

- Line an 8 x 8-inch pan snugly with aluminum foil and spray generously with nonstick spray or grease with margarine.
- In a small saucepan, over medium heat, warm the grape juice, pectin, and baking soda just until boiling. Once boiling, reduce heat to lowest setting, stirring occasionally.
- In a 2-quart saucepan, whisk together the sugar and agave and cook over medium heat, until it reaches 265°F on a candy thermometer (or Hard Ball Stage if using the Cold Water Method). Be sure to stir occasionally while this mixture is cooking, and, once the sugar dissolves, brush down the sides with a wet pastry brush to remove any crystals.
- After the sugar mixture has reached 265°F, stir in the grape juice mixture along with the desired shade of food coloring. You can easily separate these into various colors by pouring the mixture into separate bowls and coloring each a different color. Pour into the prepared pan (or pans if making multiple colors) and chill in refrigerator overnight. Remove from refrigerator and cut into shapes using a very small cookie cutters. Mix the citric acid and turbinado sugar in a small bowl and dip the cut candies to coat. Store in refrigerator in airtight container for up to 1 month.

Citric acid, which adds the sour flavor, can be located in most supermarkets next to canning goods. Of course, you could always leave the citric acid out and keep them sugary sweet instead.

## Chapter 8

# NATURE'S CANDY: REFINED SUGAR–FREE TREATS

*This chapter captures* the essence of sweet, without the need for any refined sweeteners. Instead, I've come up with a slew of recipes that utilize fruits and other refined sugar–free sweeteners such as maple syrup, agave, and stevia, and many of them use whole fruit, adding a few key nutrients in there for good measure. These desserts are especially good for little ones who may be craving something extra sweet, but don't need all the extra sugar. For recipes calling for Sweetened Whipped Coconut Cream, refer to the recipe on page 33 and use the stevia variation.

# COOKIES AND OTHER FAMILIAR FAVORITES

# NO-BAKE CASHEW CHEESECAKE  Ⓢ Ⓒ Ⓑ

The crust on this cheesecake when made by itself can be tightly packed into 1-inch balls and devoured. These are one of my favorite treats after a strenuous hike or run. For best results, let the cheesecake rest in the fridge, covered, for 1 day before serving.

## CRUST
½ cup sliced almonds
5 Medjool dates, pitted

## FILLING
3½ cups raw cashews,
    soaked for at least 1 hour
¾ cup fresh lemon juice
⅓ cup maple syrup or agave
⅓ cup coconut sugar
1 cup organic, unrefined
    coconut oil, liquefied
    (see sidebar)
½ cup water
1 vanilla bean or 2 teaspoons
    vanilla extract
½ teaspoon sea salt

**YIELD: 10 SERVINGS**

- Lightly grease a 6-inch springform pan using coconut oil.
- Blend the almonds and dates in a food processor until they are finely chopped and they ball together easily when squeezed. Press the mixture very compactly into the bottom of the springform pan. The bottom of a flat drinking glass works perfectly for this.
- Place all of the ingredients for the filling into a food processor and blend until smooth, for about 7 minutes, scraping down the sides as needed.
- Pour the filling on top of the crust and spread out using a silicone spatula until even. Rap on a flat surface a few times to remove any lurking air bubbles. Cover the top of the pan with foil and freeze overnight. Once frozen, transfer to the refrigerator. The cheesecake will be ready to serve after about 1 to 2 hours. Store in airtight container in freezer for up to 1 month, or refrigerate for up to 3 days.

### TO MELT COCONUT OIL

Measure out 1 cup of solid coconut oil into a tall drinking glass and place in shallow bowl of hot water. As it softens, stir. Replace the water in the shallow bowl with fresh hot water and repeat until all is melted, or about 4 times to make the coconut oil reach a fully liquid state.

# COCONUT CREAM TARTS

These raw treats can be made in mini muffin pans for bite-size treats or standard-size muffin tins for larger tarts. When making raw tarts, I prefer using silicone molds as it is much easier to release the treats without breaking.

**1 cup almond meal**
**4 Medjool dates**
**3 tablespoons unrefined coconut oil**
**½ teaspoon salt**
**½ teaspoon coconut extract**
**¾ cup Sweet Cashew Cream (page 32)**
**⅓ cup unsweetened flaked coconut**

**YIELD: 6 TARTS**

- Place the almond meal, dates, coconut oil, and salt into a food processor and pulse until the mixture comes together easily when squeezed. Press firmly into six cups in a standard-size muffin pan, shaping into a crust with the back of a rounded spoon or using a very small bowl.
- In a medium bowl, whisk together the coconut extract and cashew cream until fluffy. Pipe into the prepared crusts and top with flaked coconut. Freeze for 2 hours and then transfer to the refrigerator. Serve cold. Store in airtight container in refrigerator for up to 1 week.

# PUMPKIN MUFFINS

These tender morsels are studded with raw pumpkin seeds, called pepitas, to add a delightful color and texture to the muffins.

**1¼ cups brown rice flour**
**½ cup potato starch**
**¼ cup tapioca flour**
**1 teaspoon xanthan gum**
**¼ teaspoon baking soda**
**1 teaspoon baking powder**
**1 teaspoon salt**
**1 teaspoon cinnamon**
**1 cup coconut palm sugar**
**¼ cup olive or coconut oil**
**1 cup pumpkin puree**
**⅓ cup + 2 tablespoons nondairy milk**
**2 tablespoons apple cider vinegar**
**½ cup pepitas**

**YIELD: 12 MUFFINS**

- Preheat oven to 400°F and line a muffin pan with twelve liners, lightly spritz with nonstick spray, or simply grease a standard-size muffin pan.
- In a large bowl, whisk together the brown rice flour, potato starch, tapioca flour, xanthan gum, baking soda, baking powder, salt, cinnamon, and coconut palm sugar. Stir in the oil, pumpkin puree, nondairy milk, and apple cider vinegar and mix until smooth. Fold in the pepitas. Divide batter evenly among the twelve cups and bake for about 20 minutes, or until a knife inserted into the center comes out clean. Store in airtight container for up to 3 days.

# BANANA NUT MUFFINS

These muffins are just too darn delicious with the warm flavor of banana and walnuts. Be sure to grease the muffin liners on these, or use silicone muffin cups; since these muffins contain very little oil, they may have a tendency to stick.

¾ cup brown rice flour
½ cup potato starch
¼ cup tapioca flour
1 teaspoon xanthan gum
1½ teaspoons baking powder
¼ teaspoon baking soda
¼ teaspoon salt
1 teaspoon vanilla extract
3 mashed bananas, about 1⅓ cups
⅓ cup + 1 tablespoon maple syrup
2 tablespoons olive oil
2 tablespoons vinegar
½ cup chopped walnuts

YIELD: 12 MUFFINS

- Preheat oven to 350°F. Using margarine or coconut oil, grease twelve standard-size muffin cups, or spritz twelve liners with nonstick spray.
- In a medium bowl, whisk together the brown rice flour, potato starch, tapioca flour, xanthan gum, baking powder, baking soda, and salt. Make a well in the center and stir in the vanilla extract, bananas, maple syrup, olive oil, and vinegar. Stir the mixture until very well combined and then fold in the walnuts.
- Divide the batter evenly among the muffin cups and bake for 30 minutes, until golden brown on edges. Let cool completely before serving. Store in airtight container for up to 3 days.

These muffins take exceptionally well to a few cacao nibs added to the batter before baking.

# LEMON POPPYSEED SCONES

Scones have always intrigued me with their not quite biscuity, not quite cakey demeanor. I don't exactly want to eat them for breakfast (I'm more of a black coffee kinda gal myself) but they always seem perfect for a midday snacking, especially when paired with tea.

⅓ cup almond flour
⅓ cup corn flour
1 cup millet flour
½ cup brown rice flour
½ cup tapioca flour
1 teaspoon xanthan gum
2 teaspoons baking powder
1 teaspoon baking soda
½ teaspoon salt
½ cup nonhydrogenated
   vegetable shortening
½ cup maple syrup
1 tablespoon flaxseed meal
2 tablespoons water
½ cup lemon juice
2 tablespoons poppyseed
1 tablespoon lemon zest

**YIELD: 12 SCONES**

- Preheat oven to 375°F. Mix the almond flour, corn flour, millet flour, brown rice flour, and tapioca flour together in large mixing bowl. Stir in xanthan gum, baking powder, baking soda, and salt.
- Cut in the shortening using your hands, until it forms equal-size crumbles. Add in maple syrup. In a small bowl, combine the flaxseed meal and water and let rest until thickened, for about 5 minutes.
- Using a fork, combine the prepared flaxseed meal with the rest of the ingredients until the mixture becomes evenly crumbly.
- Still using a fork, mix in the lemon juice, poppyseed, and lemon zest. Once dough becomes well mixed, turn out onto a lightly floured surface (millet flour is recommended) and gently fold over about three times. Roll about ¾ inch thick and cut into squares using a sharp knife. You can also use a biscuit cutter to make circles. Place onto ungreased cookie sheet.
- Bake for about 13 minutes or until golden brown on top. Store in airtight container for up to 1 week.

Clockwise:
Pumpkin Muffins, page 272
Chaco-Cado Pudding, page 279
Chocolate-Covered Pecan Cookies, page 277
Gingerbread Squares, page 276

# GINGERBREAD SQUARES

Sweetened by banana, blackstrap molasses, and agave, this healthy gingerbread tastes just as rich and spicy as the traditional version.

**1 ripe banana, mashed**
**2 tablespoons blackstrap**
**(or regular) molasses**
**1 teaspoon freshly grated**
**ginger**
**1 teaspoon cinnamon**
**¼ teaspoon cloves**
**¼ teaspoon salt**
**2 tablespoons agave or**
**maple syrup**
**2 tablespoons ground**
**chia seed**
**1 cup almond meal**
**⅓ cup teff flour**

- In a large bowl, stir together the banana, molasses, ginger, cinnamon, cloves, salt, and agave until smooth. Fold in the chia seed, almond meal, and teff flour. Lightly grease a 4 x 8-inch loaf pan and spread the mixture into the pan. Bake for 30 minutes. Let cool completely and then slice into squares. Store in an airtight container for up to 1 week.

**YIELD: 8 SERVINGS**

# SWEET CORNCAKE COOKIES

Corn adds a sweet touch as well as a nice color to these cookies, which can be made with maple syrup or agave. Masa harina can be found in Mexican groceries or in most grocery stores along with the Mexican ingredients.

**2 tablespoons flaxseed meal**
**4 tablespoons water**
**¾ cup fine yellow cornmeal**
**½ cup maple syrup or agave**
**½ teaspoon salt**
**½ cup masa harina**
**¼ cup white rice flour**
**¼ cup tapioca flour**
**1 tablespoons olive oil**

- Preheat oven to 350°F. Line a cookie sheet with parchment or a silicone mat. In a small bowl, mix the flaxseed meal with water and allow to rest until gelled, for about 5 minutes. Mix together all the ingredients in a medium bowl in the order listed, scraping sides of bowl well while mixing.
- Drop by the tablespoonful onto the prepared cookie sheet and flatten slightly with the back of a fork. Bake for 12 to 15 minutes.
- Let cool completely before serving. Store in airtight container in refrigerator for up to 1 week.

**YIELD: 12 COOKIES**

# CHOCOLATE-COVERED PECAN PIE COOKIES

With chia seed and nuts, these delicious cookies taste sinful but are made from surprisingly wholesome ingredients. For a slightly more convenient version (and almost refined sugar–free), use nondairy chocolate chips for dipping the bottoms of the cookies instead of Raw Chocolate.

2 teaspoons ground chia seed
2 tablespoons water
1½ cups raw pecans
1 cup raw cashews
¼ cup coconut flour
½ teaspoon salt
6 dates
¾ cup Raw Chocolate, melted (page 281)

**YIELD: 20 COOKIES**

- Preheat oven to 325°F. In a small bowl, mix together the chia seed and water and let rest until gelled, for about 5 minutes.
- Place the pecans, cashews, coconut flour, and salt into a food processor and blend until crumbly, for about 1 minute. Do not overmix! Once crumbly, add the dates, two at a time, until the mixture clumps together easily. Process just until dates are well mixed. Shape into disks 1½ inches wide by ½ inch thick and place onto an ungreased cookie sheet. Bake for 15 minutes.
- Let cool and then dip bottoms of cookies into the Raw Chocolate, placing back onto a silicone mat or wax paper–covered baking sheet. Chill for about 20 minutes in refrigerator until the chocolate has set. Store in airtight container for up to 1 week.

# APRICOT COOKIES

These golden, chewy, slightly sweet cookies are just as easy to prepare as they are to eat! Packed with vitamins A and C from the apricots and protein and iron from the walnuts and coconut, these cookies are like snack-size energy bars.

3 cups dried apricots
1 cup walnut pieces
2 cups unsweetened shredded coconut, plus about ⅓ cup for rolling
¼ cup agave

**YIELD: 18 COOKIES**

- Combine all ingredients (set aside ⅓ cup coconut) in a food processor and process until very well chopped.
- Using clean hands, roll the mixture into walnut-size balls and then into the extra coconut. Flatten into cookie rounds using the bottom of a glass or measuring cup, and then gently shape with hands to create even patties.
- Store in airtight container for up to 1 week.

# CINNAMON AMARETTI

Amaretti are classic small Italian cookies that are crisp on the outside and a bit chewier in the center—and one of my favorite cookies of all. You won't miss the refined sugar in this version. For best texture, shape the cookies into small mounds, about 1 inch across, for perfect chewy-center-to-crispy-outside ratio.

**3 tablespoons flaxseed meal**
**6 tablespoons water**
**3 cups almond meal**
**1½ teaspoons cinnamon**
**1¼ cups coconut palm sugar**
**¾ teaspoon salt**
**Sliced almonds, for garnish**

**YIELD: 36 COOKIES**

- Preheat oven to 300°F. Line a large baking sheet with parchment paper.
- In a small bowl, combine the flaxseed meal with the water and let rest for 5 minutes, until gelled. Transfer to a large bowl and stir in the almond meal, cinnamon, palm sugar, and salt. Keep stirring until the mixture comes together into a stiff dough; it may not appear to be coming together, but keep stirring! This is also done effortlessly using an electric mixer.
- When the dough stiffens, pinch off 1-inch sections and form into rounds. Place onto the cookie sheet about 1 inch apart and top with a sliced almond. Bake for 30 minutes. Let cool completely. Store in airtight container for up to 1 week.

# CITRUS-KISSED MACAROONS

Lightly touched with lemon, these macaroons have only a handful of ingredients and don't need to be baked. They make a great snack post-workout or when the midday munchies arise.

**12 Medjool dates, pitted**
**1 tablespoon lemon juice**
**2 tablespoons water**
**4 cups unsweetened**
  **shredded coconut, divided**

**YIELD: 18 COOKIES**

- Combine the Medjool dates, lemon juice, and water in a food processor and blend until very smooth, scraping down the sides as necessary. Add 1 cup shredded coconut and pulse until very well combined.
- Transfer to a large bowl and by hand incorporate the additional 3 cups coconut until evenly mixed. Form the mixture into cookies and place onto cookie sheet. Refrigerate briefly to set.
- Store in an airtight container for up to 2 weeks.

# PEANUT BUTTER CHOCOLATE CHIA PUDDING

This dessert is as easy as pie (or pudding) to make, and it's healthy, filling, and delicious, too. Adjust sugar levels to your taste preferences, erring on the low side of things.

3 tablespoons whole chia seed, white or black
½ cup water
2 tablespoons nondairy milk (I recommend almond or coconut)
1 tablespoon cocoa powder
3 tablespoons creamy peanut butter
1½ tablespoons coconut date syrup or maple syrup

**YIELD: 2 SERVINGS**

- Place all ingredients into a small to medium bowl and stir vigorously with a fork until smooth. Transfer into desired serving dishes and chill in refrigerator until gelled, for about 30 minutes. Best if served cold with a dollop of whipped coconut cream. Keeps for up to 1 day if stored in airtight container in the refrigerator.

# CHOCO-CADO PUDDING

Here's another surprise ingredient from the plant world: avocado is the superstar here, making a creamy base for this insanely rich chocolate pudding.

2 ripe avocados, pitted and peeled
¼ cup Date Syrup (recipe page 29) or agave
3 tablespoons coconut sugar
¼ cup cocoa powder
½ teaspoon espresso powder
¼ teaspoon salt

**YIELD: 4 SERVINGS**

- Blend all ingredients together into a food processor until fluffy. Serve with whipped coconut cream! Store in airtight container in refrigerator for up to 3 days.

# CLASSIC-STYLE SWEETS

# RAW CHOCOLATE

This chocolate can be molded using a chocolate mold or drizzled onto desserts for a chocolaty coating. Feel free to control the sweetness to your liking without affecting the final texture too much.

½ cup melted cacao butter
⅓ cup + 2 tablespoons cocoa
    powder
⅓ cup agave or maple syrup
Pinch salt

YIELD: 12 CANDIES

- Whisk together all of the ingredients into a medium bowl. Pour the mixture into molds and rap on a solid flat surface to remove any air bubbles. Chill in the refrigerator until solid. To use as a coating, simply melt all ingredients back down and whisk well to combine. Store in airtight container in refrigerator for up to 1 week.

# COCONUTTY CANDY

This subtly sweet treat is nuts over coconut, in that it is made entirely out of coconut, save the vanilla extract and salt. To cut easily, let the solid candy thaw at room temperature for about 20 minutes before slicing and then returning to the refrigerator.

12 ounces (about 2½ cups)
    unsweetened shredded
    coconut
½ cup softened coconut oil,
    unrefined
1 teaspoon vanilla extract
½ cup coconut palm sugar
⅛ teaspoon salt

YIELD: 24 PIECES

- In a blender or food processor, blend the coconut until smooth like peanut butter. This could take anywhere from 3 to 10 minutes, depending on your appliance, the dryness of the coconut, and temperature, among other factors. Just blend until smooth, and, if it never gets smooth, add a teaspoon or two of coconut oil to move things along.
- Once the shredded coconut has blended, add the remaining ingredients and blend until smooth. Pour into an 8 x 8-inch square dish, cover loosely with plastic wrap, and freeze for 30 minutes. Cut into small squares, and transfer to the refrigerator to store for up to 2 weeks.

# ALMOND BON BONS

These are such a fun treat to snack on when a chocolate craving hits. Make a batch and store in the freezer—you can just grab one whenever you're in need of a little mood boost!

## FILLING
1 cup almond meal
2 tablespoons coconut oil, softened
2 tablespoons agave, brown rice, or maple syrup
3 tablespoons melted cacao butter
⅛ teaspoon salt

## COATING
1 recipe Raw Chocolate, melted (page 281)

**YIELD: 24 CANDIES**

- In a medium bowl, combine all the filling ingredients and let rest for about 10 minutes. Shape into balls or place into silicone chocolate molds and then chill for about 30 minutes in the refrigerator, or for 10 minutes in the freezer, until solid.
- Once the filling is cold, dip the balls into the chocolate coating until completely covered, and then place coated truffles onto a silicone mat or parchment-covered surface to harden. Dip once more in the chocolate coating and then allow the chocolate to harden completely in the refrigerator, for about 1 hour. Store in airtight container in refrigerator for up to 1 month, or in freezer bags, tightly sealed, for up to 3 months.

# RAISINETTE BONBONS

These taste so much like the popular candies, it certainly won't seem like you're eating something so good for you!

1½ cups raisins
1 cup walnuts
¼ cup cocoa powder

**YIELD: ABOUT 20 BONBONS**

- In a food processor, combine all the ingredients and blend until finely ground and clumped together, for about 1 minute. Roll into bite-size balls and place in refrigerator to chill for about 30 minutes prior to enjoying. Store in airtight container in refrigerator for up to 2 weeks.

# NOURISHING BROWNIE BITES  Ⓢ Ⓒ Ⓑ

In terms of brownies, this version is much healthier than your typical chocolaty square, but they sure don't miss a beat taste-wise. You won't feel bad about going back for seconds with these, as they are packed full of healthy stuff like dates, which contain fiber; cashews, which are high in magnesium; and cocoa, which is high in iron.

**10 Medjool dates, chilled in fridge**
**2 cups whole cashews, unroasted**
**2 tablespoons cocoa powder**
**½ teaspoon salt**
**2 teaspoons vanilla extract**

**YIELD: 12 SERVINGS**

- Remove the pits from the dates and place into a food processor along with the cashews, cocoa powder, and salt. Pulse several times to combine and then blend until very crumbly, for about 2 minutes. Once the mixture is evenly crumbly, with the consistency of a coarse sugar, drizzle in the vanilla extract and continue to blend until the mixture becomes clumpy.
- Depending on the size and moisture content of your dates, you may need to add a touch more liquid, such as water or more vanilla extract, or process for a shorter amount of time to get the right consistency. In the end, the dough should easily stick together when balled. If it is too dry, add a bit more liquid (½ teaspoon or so) and if it is too wet, add in a tablespoon more cocoa powder to dry it out.
- Place the dough into the center of a parchment paper and cover with another sheet. Roll out gently to flatten into an even shape and then cut into squares. Chill in refrigerator for at least 20 minutes before serving. Store in airtight container in refrigerator for up to 2 weeks.

# COOKIE DOUGH BITES

(S) (C) (B)

A perfect pick-me-up for after dinner, or for a quick bit of fuel on the run, these little morsels taste just like raw cookie dough.

1½ cups raw cashews
9 soft Medjool dates
2 teaspoons vanilla extract
⅓ cup almond meal
Dash salt
2 tablespoons cacao nibs

YIELD: 16 SERVINGS

• In a food processor, pulse the cashews and dates until crumbly. Add in the vanilla extract, almond meal, salt, and cacao nibs and pulse until finely ground and dough comes together easily when pinched with fingers. Shape into small balls about 1 inch in diameter. Store in airtight container for up to 2 weeks.

# PEANUTTY CHOCOLATE FUDGE BITES

(S) (C) (B)

Like the other energy bites and bars offered here, these little bits are flavor powerhouses. My husband loves these little chocolate morsels and, each time he goes for one, is always astounded that they aren't that bad for you . . . because they taste so darn good.

½ cup cacao butter
⅓ cup + 2 tablespoons
    cocoa powder
⅓ cup maple syrup
3 tablespoons creamy
    peanut butter
Pinch salt

YIELD: 20 CANDIES

• In a double boiler, melt the cacao butter until liquid. Whisk in the rest of the ingredients and pour into chocolate molds or paper liners set into a muffin tin. Place in your freezer and chill for 1 hour. Pop out of molds and place onto a flat serving dish. Keep refrigerated for firmer chocolates, or store in airtight container in cool location for up to 2 weeks.

Clockwise:
Chocolate Nanaimo Bars, page 286
Cookie Dough Bites, this page
Nourishing Brownie Bites, page 283

# CHOCOLATE NANAIMO BARS

Nanaimo bars, named after the city in British Columbia, are a popular no-bake dessert that are typically made with a LOT of butter and sugar. If you're not concerned about them being totally sugar-free, you can also use your favorite nondairy chocolate chips/buttons in place of the raw chocolate.

## CRUST
1 cup whole raw almonds
10 dates
1 tablespoon cocoa powder

## FILLING
2 cups cashews, soaked
    2 hours
1½ teaspoons vanilla extract
⅔ cup coconut oil, melted
1 teaspoon stevia powder
3 Medjool dates or ¼ cup
    Date Syrup (page 29)
2 tablespoons coconut cream
    (from the top of a chilled
    can of coconut milk)

## TOPPING
1¼ cups Raw Chocolate
    (page 281), melted

**YIELD: 16 SERVINGS**

- To make the crust, in a food processor, pulse together the almonds, five of the dates, and the cocoa powder until crumbly. Add in the remaining five dates and pulse again until evenly chopped. Press the mixture firmly into an 8 x 8-inch baking pan.
- Make the filling in a food processor by combining the cashews, vanilla, coconut oil, stevia, dates, and coconut cream until very smooth, for about 5 minutes, scraping down sides as needed. Spread the filling evenly on top of the crust by using a flat silicone spatula. Freeze for 1 hour and then cut into squares.
- Top with melted chocolate and then return to freezer. Chill in freezer overnight, or for at least 6 hours. Store in refrigerator in airtight container for up to 2 weeks.

Clockwise:
Powerhouse Bars, page 289
Chocolate Granola, page 288
Sweet, Salty, and Soft Granola Bars, page 288

# SNACK BARS AND GRANOLA

# CHOCOLATE GRANOLA

This versatile granola is perfect for all sorts of treats: Use for parfaits or to top your favorite nondairy yogurt or ice cream. Great in a bowl as breakfast cereal at home, or as a chocolaty addition to your trail mix when you're on the go.

2 cups certified gluten-free oats
⅓ cup almond meal
3 tablespoons whole chia seed
¼ teaspoon salt
⅓ cup cocoa powder
1 tablespoon coconut oil
1 teaspoon vanilla extract
⅓ cup agave or maple syrup

YIELD: 3 CUPS

• Preheat oven to 300°F. In a medium bowl, whisk together the oats, almond meal, chia seed, salt, and cocoa powder. In a smaller bowl, whisk together the coconut oil, vanilla extract, and maple syrup until very smooth. Using clean hands, or a large fork, combine all ingredients until well mixed. Spread onto a parchment-lined jelly roll pan and bake for 40 minutes. Break into bite-size pieces and let cool completely. Store in airtight container for up to 3 weeks.

# SWEET, SALTY, AND SOFT GRANOLA BARS

With its salty, sweet flavor and soft, chewy texture, this snack can satisfy multiple cravings at once! Store in an airtight container in the refrigerator for best texture.

2½ cups certified
    gluten-free oats
½ cup almond meal
1 teaspoon salt
2 tablespoons maple syrup
⅓ cup agave
¼ cup + 2 tablespoons
    softened coconut oil
¼ cup date sugar or coconut
    palm sugar
1 teaspoon vanilla extract
½ cup sliced almonds
1 tablespoon ground
    chia seed
3 tablespoons water

YIELD: 12 BARS

• Preheat oven to 350°F. Lightly grease an 8 x 8-inch pan.
• Spread the oats in an even layer onto a large baking sheet and lightly toast for 7 minutes. Remove oats from the oven and place them in a large mixing bowl. Using your hands, crumble in the almond meal, salt, maple syrup, agave, coconut oil, date sugar, vanilla extract, and sliced almonds.
• Mix the chia seed and water and let rest for 5 minutes, until gelled. Mix in with the rest of the ingredients and then using hands lightly greased with coconut oil, press the mixture tightly and firmly into the pan. Cover lightly with plastic wrap and refrigerate for 2 hours. Gently cut into bars and store chilled in airtight container for up to 2 weeks.

# POWERHOUSE BARS

With goji berries, hemp seeds, chia seed, and oats, these protein-packed bars are full of all kinds of nourishing ingredients that will keep you going strong all day long.

1 cup pecans
½ cup raw cashews
9 dates
¼ teaspoon salt
1 tablespoon coconut oil
½ cup certified gluten-free
    oats
½ cup goji berries
¼ cup hemp seeds
¼ cup chia seed

YIELD: 10 BARS

- Line an 8 x 8-inch baking pan with plastic wrap or lightly oil with coconut oil.
- Place the pecans, cashews, and five of the dates into a food processor and blend until evenly crumbly. Add the salt and the remaining dates and pulse until well combined and dates are evenly chopped. Transfer mixture into a large bowl and stir in the coconut oil to evenly coat. Fold in the oats, goji berries, hemp seeds, and chia seed. Press the mixture firmly into the prepared baking pan and refrigerate for 2 hours. Cut into bars and store in an airtight container in the refrigerator for up to 2 weeks.

# CHERRY PIE BARS

The taste is just like cherry pie but these little bars are actually pretty good for you! I recommend seeking out the highest-quality dried cherries (organic, unsulphured, with no added sugar) for these for the most authentic cherry-pie flavor.

2 cups raw cashews
1 cup dried cherries
    (not sweetened)
½ teaspoon salt
10 Medjool dates

YIELD: 8 SERVINGS

- In a food processor, combine the cashews, cherries, and salt and blend until coarsely crumbled. Add in the dates and pulse until finely crumbled and the mixture easily comes together and stays together when squeezed.
- Shape the mixture into individual bars by shaping into a tight disk, or square, and then cutting gently with knife. Wrap individually in plastic wrap or foil. Alternatively, shape into balls for bite-size snacking. Store in airtight container in refrigerator for up to 2 weeks.

# CHERRY CHOCOLATE ALMOND SNACK BARS

Like a crunchy granola bar, these chocolate bars are a great pick-me-up when your energy is down. Be sure to use only kasha (toasted buckwheat) that is brown in color, rather than greenish. Kasha is usually located next to untoasted buckwheat groats, oftentimes in the bulk or natural foods sections.

1½ cups kasha (toasted buckwheat kernels), soaked for 2 hours

⅓ cup + 2 tablespoons cocoa powder

2 tablespoons chia seed

½ cup maple syrup

3 tablespoons date sugar

⅔ cup almond flour

½ teaspoon salt

½ cup dried cherries (not sweetened)

¼ teaspoon coconut or olive oil

**YIELD: 12 SERVINGS**

- Preheat oven to 300°F. Line a baking tray with parchment paper.
- Drain the soaked kasha completely. In a large bowl, combine all of the ingredients except for the oil. Use the ¼ teaspoon coconut oil to grease clean hands and gently pat down the mixture into a rectangle, about ¼ to ½ inch thick. Bake for 30 minutes. Remove from oven, gently cut into squares using a spatula (but don't separate) and continue to bake for an additional 20 minutes. Let cool completely and then break into individual bars. Store in airtight container for up to 1 week.

If you can't locate toasted kasha, you can always toast your own at 300°F for 45 minutes, stirring often until browned.

Clockwise:
Fresh Fruitsicles, page 292
Fruit Salsa and Cinnamon Crisps, page 293
Fruit and Avocado Salad, page 294
Apple Nachos, page 295

# FRUITY TREATS

# PEANUT BUTTER BANANA ICE CREAM

This recipe couldn't get any easier with only four ingredients, and it's good for you! Eat up.

5 very ripe bananas, peeled
½ cup smooth salted
    peanut butter
½ teaspoon vanilla extract
1 cup canned full-fat
    coconut milk

YIELD: 2 CUPS

- Place all ingredients into a blender and blend until very smooth, for about 1 minute. Pour into the bowl of your ice cream maker and process according to manufacturer's instructions. Or, alternatively, freeze all ingredients in a bowl for 3 hours, and then immediately process in a food processor until smooth. Store in airtight container in freezer for up to 1 month.

# FRESH FRUITSICLES

These gorgeous pops will have you excited about eating fruit and keeping cool at the same time. I like the combo of the fruits listed below, but, along with the grapes, you could add in any chopped fruits you please. You'll need popsicle molds for these, or you can pour into silicone ice cube trays or even small paper cups.

1 cup grapes, red or green
1 kiwi, peeled and diced
⅓ cup chopped red
    raspberries
⅓ cup blueberries

YIELD: ABOUT 5

- Place the grapes into a blender and puree until smooth. Transfer to a bowl and stir in the diced fruit. Pour the mixture into popsicle molds and add wooden sticks to the center. Freeze overnight and then enjoy. Store in freezer for up to 1 month.

# FRUIT SALSA AND CINNAMON CRISPS

A fun twist on an old favorite, serve these "chips and salsa" at your next gathering for a sweet—and healthy—surprise.

## CINNAMON CHIPS
4 white corn tortillas
1 tablespoon olive oil
1 tablespoon agave
¼ teaspoon salt
¼ teaspoon cinnamon,
    or to taste

## FRUIT SALSA
1 cup berries (raspberry +
    blackberry works great)
1 cup strawberries, greens
    left on
½ cup seedless grapes, any
    variety
Juice of 1 lime
1 apple, diced with seeds
    removed
1 kiwi, peeled and diced

**YIELD: 6 SERVINGS**

- Preheat oven to 400°F. Stack the corn tortillas and cut into six even triangles. Spread the triangles in an even layer onto an ungreased cookie sheet, so that none of them are touching.
- In a small bowl, whisk together the olive oil, agave, and salt. Brush lightly onto each side of the tortilla triangle (this will get a little sticky) and sprinkle one side of the triangles with cinnamon. Bake for 7 minutes, flip, and bake for an additional 2 minutes. Let cool while you make the salsa.
- In a food processor, combine the berries, strawberries, grapes, and lime juice and pulse until the fruit has been chopped, but not pureed, for about five or six times. Combine with the diced apples and kiwi and serve with cinnamon crisps. Store in airtight container in refrigerator for up to 1 week.

# RASPBERRY CHIA JAM

Chia seed takes the wheel and adds an incredible thickness to this jam—no need for pectin! Use just as you would your favorite jam, and feel good about all the extra nutrients (like calcium and omega-3s) you're enjoying while doing so. If raspberry's not your favorite, practically any berry will work well using this method. Try it with blueberries, blackberries, or a mix!

**1½ cups red raspberries**
**2 to 3 tablespoons agave,**
    **or to taste**
**1 tablespoon chia seed**

**YIELD: 1½ CUPS**

- Place the raspberries and agave into a small saucepan and cook over medium-low heat until liquidy. Stir in chia seed and continue to cook one more minute, until thickened. Transfer to a resealable container and let cool at room temperature before transferring to the refrigerator. Store in airtight container in refrigerator for up to 2 weeks.

# FRUIT AND AVOCADO SALAD

Did you know that avocado is actually a fruit? That must be why it pairs so well with bananas, strawberries, and pineapple. Try it in this creamy fruit salad and see if you agree that these four were meant to be (along with blueberries and pomegranate seeds!).

**SAUCE**
**2 tablespoons pineapple juice**
**2 tablespoons full-fat**
    **coconut milk**
**Dash cinnamon**
**½ teaspoon vanilla extract**

**FRUIT**
**1 large banana, sliced**
**4 strawberries, sliced**
**¼ cup diced pineapple**
**¼ cup blueberries**
**¼ cup pomegranate seeds**
**1 avocado, cut into bite-size**
    **pieces**

**YIELD: 6 SERVINGS**

- In a small bowl, whisk together the sauce ingredients.
- Place the fruit into a medium bowl and toss with the sauce. Serve chilled. Keeps for up to 1 day if stored in airtight container.

# PINEAPPLE "LAYER CAKES"

These little stacks are a fun twist on the conventional version of the dessert. Handle the pineapple rings with care, if using canned, or cut a little on the thick side if using fresh. Looking for some crunch? Try adding a thin layer of crushed walnuts or pecans on top of the cashew cream! You can locate vanilla bean paste in specialty shops such as Williams Sonoma, or simply sub in the same amount of vanilla extract.

8 pineapple rings
½ cup Sweet Cashew Cream (page 32)
½ teaspoon vanilla bean paste
2 tablespoons Cherry Vanilla Compote (page 228)

YIELD: 2 PERSONAL-SIZE CAKES

- Drain the pineapple rings by placing them in a single layer on a paper towel. Let rest for 10 minutes, or until the rings are relatively dry. In a small bowl, mix together the cashew cream with the vanilla bean paste.
- On the plate you wish to serve it, create an alternating stack of pineapple, cashew cream, pineapple, etc., finishing with a dollop of the Cherry Vanilla Compote.

# APPLE NACHOS

This recipe has been one of the most popular recipes on my website, with over 5 million views, and, because of its popularity and fun factor, I had to include it in this book. There are countless variations to these, but my kids and I both adore them as listed below.

3 crispy and slightly tart apples, such as Honeycrisp or Granny Smith
1 teaspoon lemon juice
3 tablespoons creamy peanut butter
¼ cup Date Syrup (page 29)
¼ cup sliced almonds
¼ cup pecans, roughly chopped
¼ cup flaked or shredded unsweetened coconut
¼ cup cacao nibs

YIELD: 4 SERVINGS

- Remove the core from each apple and slice them very thin (about ⅛-inch thickness), using a sharp knife. Arrange on a plate so that each apple has a good amount of surface exposed. Lightly spritz with the lemon juice.
- Melt the peanut butter in a small saucepan along with the date syrup until it is very runny and drizzle it onto the apple slices. Top the apples and peanut butter with the almonds and pecans, and then drizzle with the melted date syrup. Finally, top with unsweetened flaked coconut and cacao nibs. Enjoy these with your hands, just like real nachos. Serve immediately.

### ALLERGY NOTE

To make nut-free, sub in toasted sunflower seeds for the almonds.

# STRAWBERRY BANANA FRUIT LEATHER

My kids go bananas for these wholesome snacks. I recommend using a dehydrator for best results, but you can also bake them in the oven at 200°F, spread out on a silicone mat, for several hours until dried.

**2 medium very ripe (a few brown spots is desired) bananas**
**2 heaping cups fresh small strawberries, greens on**

YIELD: 6 SERVINGS

- Blend the fruit until smooth in a high-speed blender or food processor, scraping down sides as needed. The consistency should resemble a fruit smoothie. Spread out into a fruit leather mat fitted for your dehydrator. Spread thinly and evenly and then rap the tray on a flat surface a few times to remove any air bubbles.
- Set your dehydrator to 135°F and let it roll until the fruit is no longer tacky, for about 4 to 5 hours. If using a conventional oven, simply spread thinly onto a silicone mat and set oven to lowest temperature with the door slightly ajar. Bake for 3 to 4 hours, until no longer tacky.
- Gently peel up from the tray and place onto a cutting board. Using a pizza cutter, slice into large sections and then immediately roll up onto waxed paper, so that the fruit is completely covered. Enjoy immediately or store for up to 1 month in an airtight container.

Apple Pie Milk Shake, page 299

# CARROT CAKE SMOOTHIE

Indulge at breakfast time with this delish drink! It boasts the addition of blackstrap molasses, which is chock full of good stuff like copper, iron, calcium, and potassium.

1 large carrot, stems and
    top removed
1 large banana, peeled and
    frozen
3 dates
½ cup unsweetened almond milk
¾ cup cold water
½ teaspoon cinnamon
Dash nutmeg
Dash cloves
1 teaspoon blackstrap molasses

YIELD: 2 SERVINGS

• Place the first four ingredients in a blender and process until the banana is mostly blended. Add the water, spices, and molasses and blend until creamy. Thin to taste with additional cold water, if desired. Serve immediately.

# PIÑA COLADA

This tastes so authentic you may expect to feel a bit tipsy while sipping; but, rest assured, this libation is quite good for you. It may even ward off colds with all that pineapple, which is very high in vitamin C!

1 large peeled frozen banana
⅛ cup coconut cream (from
    can of coconut milk)
4 pineapple rings (or about
    ½ cup canned pineapple)
¾ cup pineapple juice
1 teaspoon rum extract

YIELD: 2 SERVINGS

• Blend all ingredients until very smooth in a high-speed blender. Serve immediately.

# HAPPY HEALTHY HOT COCOA

This hot cocoa will leave you feeling happy and healthy after sipping as it's sweetened with date sugar and stevia, rather than the usual refined sugar mixture. I like this best made with unsweetened almond milk.

**3 tablespoons cocoa powder**
**¼ cup date sugar**
**¼ teaspoon pure liquid stevia**
**1 teaspoon vanilla or almond extract**
**1 cup unsweetened nondairy milk, plus more to thin**

**YIELD: 2 SERVINGS**

- In a blender, combine the cocoa powder, date sugar, stevia, vanilla extract, and ½ cup almond milk. Blend on high speed until very smooth, adding the additional ½ cup almond milk as it becomes more blended. You should have a very thick, creamy, chocolate syrup.
- Thin with a little more nondairy milk until desired consistency and heat over medium heat, until warm, stirring constantly. For an extra-special treat, top with Sweetened Whipped Coconut Cream, stevia version (page 33). Serve immediately.

# APPLE PIE MILK SHAKE

Easier than apple pie, and good for you, too! This "milk shake" makes a perfectly indulgent breakfast or a late afternoon snack.

**1½ bananas, chopped and frozen**
**⅔ cup apple cider (no sugar added)**
**⅓ cup pecans**
**½ teaspoon cinnamon**
**Dash nutmeg**

**YIELD: 1 SERVING**

- Combine all ingredients into a blender and mix until very smooth. Thin with a little extra apple cider or nondairy milk if desired.
- Serve immediately.

# BLUEBERRY BLIZZARD MILK SHAKE Ⓢ Ⓒ Ⓑ

Blueberries are full of antioxidants and lend a beautiful blue hue to this milk shake. And that's not the only healthy ingredient: it's sweetened with bananas.

**½ cup fresh or frozen blueberries**
**1½ peeled and frozen bananas**
**1 teaspoon vanilla extract**
**1 cup nondairy milk (almond is best)**

**YIELD: 1 SERVING**

- Place all the ingredients into a blender and blend until completely smooth. Serve immediately with a thick straw.

### ALLERGY NOTE

For a nut-free shake, use rice milk.

# METRIC CONVERSIONS

The recipes in this book have not been tested with metric measurements, so some variations might occur.

Remember that the weight of dry ingredients varies according to the volume or density factor: 1 cup of flour weighs far less than 1 cup of sugar, and 1 tablespoon doesn't necessarily hold 3 teaspoons.

~~~~~~~~~~~~~~~~~~~~~~~~~~~~~

### General Formula for Metric Conversion

| | |
|---|---|
| Ounces to grams | multiply ounces by 28.35 |
| Grams to ounces | multiply ounces by 0.035 |
| Pounds to grams | multiply pounds by 453.5 |
| Pounds to kilograms | multiply pounds by 0.45 |
| Cups to liters | multiply cups by 0.24 |
| Fahrenheit to Celsius | subtract 32 from Fahrenheit temperature, multiply by 5, divide by 9 |
| Celsius to Fahrenheit | multiply Celsius temperature by 9, divide by 5, add 32 |

### Volume (Liquid) Measurements

1 teaspoon = ⅙ fluid ounce = 5 milliliters
1 tablespoon = ½ fluid ounce = 15 milliliters
2 tablespoons = 1 fluid ounce = 30 milliliters
¼ cup = 2 fluid ounces = 60 milliliters
⅓ cup = 2⅔ fluid ounces = 79 milliliters
½ cup = 4 fluid ounces = 118 milliliters
1 cup or ½ pint = 8 fluid ounces = 250 milliliters
2 cups or 1 pint = 16 fluid ounces = 500 milliliters
4 cups or 1 quart = 32 fluid ounces = 1,000 milliliters
1 gallon = 4 liters

### Volume (Dry) Measurements

¼ teaspoon = 1 milliliter
½ teaspoon = 2 milliliters
¾ teaspoon = 4 milliliters
1 teaspoon = 5 milliliters
1 tablespoon = 15 milliliters
¼ cup = 59 milliliters
⅓ cup = 79 milliliters
½ cup = 118 milliliters
⅔ cup = 158 milliliters
¾ cup = 177 milliliters
1 cup = 225 milliliters
4 cups or 1 quart = 1 liter
½ gallon = 2 liters
1 gallon = 4 liters

### Linear Measurements

½ in = 1½ cm
1 inch = 2½ cm
6 inches = 15 cm
8 inches = 20 cm
10 inches = 25 cm
12 inches = 30 cm
20 inches = 50 cm

### Weight (Mass) Measurements

1 ounce = 30 grams
2 ounces = 55 grams
3 ounces = 85 grams
4 ounces = ¼ pound = 125 grams
8 ounces = ½ pound = 240 grams
12 ounces = ¾ pound = 375 grams
16 ounces = 1 pound = 454 gram

### Oven Temperature Equivalents, Fahrenheit (F) and Celsius (C)

| | |
|---|---|
| 100°F = 38°C | 350°F = 180°C |
| 200°F = 95°C | 400°F = 205°C |
| 250°F = 120°C | 450°F = 230°C |
| 300°F = 150°C | |

# FLOUR AND OTHER INGREDIENTS: MEASUREMENTS BY WEIGHT

| | 2 Cups | 1 Cup | ¾ Cup | ⅔ Cup | ½ Cup | ⅓ Cup | ¼ Cup | 2 Tbsp | 1 Tbsp | 1 Tsp |
|---|---|---|---|---|---|---|---|---|---|---|
| Sorghum Flour | 260 | 130 | 98 | 87 | 65 | 43 | 33 | 16 | 8 | 3 |
| Besan/Chickpea Flour | 220 | 110 | 83 | 73 | 55 | 37 | 28 | 14 | 7 | 2 |
| Buckwheat Flour | 260 | 130 | 98 | 87 | 65 | 43 | 33 | 16 | 8 | 3 |
| Cornmeal | 352 | 176 | 132 | 117 | 88 | 59 | 44 | 22 | 11 | 4 |
| Tapioca Starch | 220 | 110 | 83 | 73 | 55 | 37 | 28 | 14 | 7 | 2 |
| Potato Starch | 220 | 110 | 83 | 73 | 55 | 37 | 28 | 14 | 7 | 2 |
| Millet Flour | 340 | 170 | 128 | 113 | 85 | 57 | 43 | 21 | 11 | 4 |
| Superfine Brown Rice Flour | 340 | 170 | 128 | 113 | 85 | 57 | 43 | 21 | 11 | 4 |
| Brown Rice | 300 | 150 | 113 | 100 | 75 | 50 | 38 | 19 | 9 | 3 |
| Masa Harina | 300 | 150 | 113 | 100 | 75 | 50 | 38 | 19 | 9 | 3 |
| Sugar, Granulated | 460 | 230 | 173 | 153 | 115 | 77 | 58 | 29 | 14 | 5 |
| Sugar, Confectioner's | 240 | 120 | 90 | 80 | 60 | 40 | 30 | 15 | 8 | 3 |
| Brown Sugar, Packed | 380 | 190 | 143 | 127 | 95 | 63 | 48 | 24 | 12 | 4 |
| Cocoa Powder | 160 | 80 | 60 | 53 | 40 | 27 | 20 | 10 | 5 | 2 |
| Cornstarch | 260 | 130 | 98 | 87 | 65 | 43 | 33 | 16 | 8 | 3 |
| Sweet White Rice Flour | 310 | 155 | 116 | 103 | 78 | 52 | 39 | 19 | 10 | 3 |
| Almond Meal | 200 | 100 | 75 | 67 | 50 | 33 | 25 | 13 | 6 | 2 |
| Flaxseed Meal | 240 | 120 | 90 | 80 | 60 | 40 | 30 | 15 | 8 | 3 |
| Earth Balance | 450 | 225 | 169 | 150 | 113 | 75 | 56 | 28 | 14 | 5 |
| Coconut Cream | 500 | 250 | 188 | 167 | 125 | 83 | 63 | 31 | 16 | 5 |
| Applesauce | 490 | 245 | 184 | 163 | 123 | 82 | 61 | 31 | 15 | 5 |
| Blueberries | 296 | 148 | 111 | 99 | 74 | 49 | 37 | 19 | 9 | 3 |
| Silken Tofu | 454 | 227 | 170 | 151 | 114 | 76 | 57 | 28 | 14 | 5 |
| Olives | 360 | 180 | 135 | 120 | 90 | 60 | 45 | 23 | 11 | 4 |
| Chocolate Chips | 366 | 183 | 137 | 122 | 92 | 61 | 46 | 23 | 11 | 4 |
| Peanuts | 300 | 150 | 113 | 100 | 75 | 50 | 38 | 19 | 9 | 3 |
| Rice | 420 | 210 | 158 | 140 | 105 | 70 | 53 | 26 | 13 | 4 |
| | | | | | | | | | | |

Note: All weights in grams

# RECOMMENDATIONS

## INGREDIENTS AND TOOLS

Amazon.com: For hard-to-find nonperishable ingredients and pretty much any kitchen utensil, tool, or cake pan you could ever need.

Authentic Foods: Seek out this brand of flours at natural foods stores or online; their superfine brown rice flour really takes gluten-free pastry making to the next level. authenticfoods.com

Bob's Red Mill: My choice brand for certified gluten-free prepackaged flours, nut meals, seeds, oats, and so much more. Generally Bob gets an entire section to himself in most grocery stores, but these flours can also be found lurking amongst the gluten-free sections, too. bobsredmill.com

Earth Balance: The best store-bought nondairy butter, in my humble opinion. Every recipe in this book that calls for margarine was created using Earth Balance (soy free), and I recommend seeking this brand out if you can. Available from most US grocery and natural food stores that carry margarine. earthbalancenatural.com

Escali: My favorite inexpensive, yet reliable, scale for measuring flours and other ingredients. Comes in cute colors to boot! escali.com

Follow Your Heart: A maker of vegan and gluten-free nondairy dairy products with a "cream cheese" and mayo that surpasses the competition, in my opinion. followyourheart.com

KitchenAid: My food processor and mixer are made by KitchenAid, and I adore them both. Before I upgraded to a supersize food processor, I relied on a small KitchenAid food processor that I still keep around for sentimental reasons. KitchenAid products are great quality and long lasting. They're easy to find at most home-goods or kitchen stores. kitchenaid.com

NutriMill: A totally great flour mill for those who love to GYO (Grind Your Own). I love my NutriMill and recommend it to those wanting to start out with grinding their own flours. lequip.com

Sur La Table: The ultimate shopping experience for an exclusive and premium selection of kitchen items. Surlatable.com

Target: Offers a pretty great selection of specialty cake pans, dishes, and seasonal baking items in stores located throughout the United States. Target.com

Trader Joes: If you have a Trader Joe's near you . . . go! The prices are great, the selection is fantastic, and they have a ton of vegan-friendly foods, from nondairy cream cheese, yogurts, milks, grains, and so much more. traderjoes.com

Williams Sonoma: A specialty store with a ton of locations that will surely carry a fun Bundt cake pan or a variety of oils and spices. Williams-sonoma.com

Wilton: A trustworthy maker of cake pans and other baking supplies, such as frosting bags and tips, and fondant tools. Their products are available at department and specialty stores across the United States. wilton.com

Whole Foods: One of my favorite spots for grocery indulgence. This store has a ton of locations in cities across the United States and will most likely carry any unfamiliar or hard-to-source ingredient listed in this text; and, if not, chances are good they can order it. wholefoodsmarket.com

Vitamix: I love my Vitamix and recommend it above and beyond all other blenders I have tried. Each recipe calling for a blender was prepared using a Vitamix. vitamix.com

## INSPIRING READING

*Food in Jars*, Marisa McClellan (Running Press, 2012)

*Put 'Em Up! Fruit*, Sherri Brooks Vinton (Storey Publishing, 2013)

*The Art of Fermentation*, Sandor Elix Katz (Chelsea Green Publishing, 2012)

*The Elements of Dessert*, Fransisco Migoya (Wiley, 2012)

*Artisan Vegan Cheese*, Miyoko Shinner (Book Publishing Company, 2012)

*The Ultimate Uncheese Cookbook*, Jo Stepaniak (Book Publishing Company, 2003)

# ACKNOWLEDGMENTS

J.D., I love you so much. You're the bestest friend I could ever ask for, and a helluva support system. Thank you for believing in my dreams as much as (and sometimes more than) I do.

Landen and Olive, thank you for eating cookie after cookie and pie after pie and never once complaining, even though you had every right to. And thank you both for your honesty. I adore you two.

Sally Ekus, for being the best agent ever (ever!) and Lisa Ekus for instilling in me a ton of confidence, which certainly helped carry this book to completion. You two are a dynamic duo. And thank you to the rest of the gang at TLEG (Samantha, Corrine, Sean, Jaimee)—you all rock so hard. Thank you for making this book possible.

To Renée Sedliar, for your great edits, and, more than anything, the excitement and belief you had in this project from the get-go. Also a special thank you to Claire Ivett for all of your awesome editing skills and fabulous suggestions throughout the text. This book would only be half complete without you two!

Also, thank you to Cisca Schreefel, Martha Whitt, and rest of the gang at Da Capo for making this idea of mine a reality.

To my faithful and fabulous testers, gosh, love you all: Lisa Pitman, Jim Allen, Christine Lucas, Dianne Wenz, Lydia Grossov, Melissa Schneider, Jenni Mischel, Monika Soria Caruso, Sam Davidson, Dara Baxter, Kristina Sloggett, Katie Kleisen, John Wroan, and those of you who wish to remain unnamed. Many of you have been with me since the very beginning of my cookbookery days, and I consider you all a huge and important part of each book. Thank you so so much. So much.

Laurel VanBlarcum, thank you. Your input—as always—was incredibly helpful in every way. You have been such an inspiration in writing this big book of sweets. Thank you so much for everything you have done over the years.

My mom, Catherine Cain. Goodness gracious, I don't think I would even know how to make half of these desserts if it wasn't for all I learned from you. Thank you for teaching me to be a badass sugar wrangler. I'm following in some pretty sweet footsteps.

To all of my readers, both of this book and my website. I can't thank you enough for your support. My job wouldn't be possible without you all, and you give me reason—every single day—to be excited to work in my kitchen!

# ABOUT THE AUTHOR

Allyson Kramer is the author and photographer of two other cookbooks, *Great Gluten-Free Vegan Eats* and *Great Gluten-Free Vegan Eats from Around the World*. She has been creating in the kitchen for over twenty-five years and has over fifteen years' experience cooking vegan eats.

Her work has been featured in numerous publications including *Veg News Magazine* and *Vegetarian Times*. Kramer holds a degree in fine art and is currently pursuing her master's degree in nutrition. She resides in Philadelphia, Pennsylvania, and in her free time she makes art, makes an effort at fitness, and loves to read just about anything.

allysonkramer.com

# INDEX

Note: Page references in *italics* indicate photographs.